THE BRAIN OF ROBERT FROST

A Cognitive Approach to Literature

NORMAN N. HOLLAND

ROUTLEDGE · NEW YORK & LONDON

Copyright acknowledgment: "Once by the Pacific" and "Mending Wall" from *The Poetry of Robert Frost*, edited by Edward Connery Lathem. Reprinted by permission of Henry Holt and Company, Inc. and Jonathan Cape Ltd. Copyright 1928, 1930, 1939, 1969 by Holt, Rinehart and Winston, Inc. Copyright 1956, 1958 by Robert Frost. Copyright 1967 by Lesley Frost Ballantine.

Published in 1988 by

Routledge
an imprint of Routledge, Chapman and Hall, Inc.
29 West 35 Street
New York, NY 10001

Published in Great Britain by

Routledge
11 New Fetter Lane
London EC4P 4EE

Copyright © 1988 by Routledge, Chapman and Hall, Inc.

Printed in the United States of America

Library of Congress Cataloging-in-Publication Data

Holland, Norman Norwood, 1927–
  The brain of Robert Frost.

  Bibliography: p.
  1. Frost, Robert, 1874–1963—Criticism and
interpretation. 2. Psychoanalysis and literature.
3. Brain—Case studies. I. Title.
PS3511.R94Z745 1988 811'.52   88-18464
ISBN 0-415-90023-9
ISBN 0-415-90083-2 (pbk.)

British Library Cataloguing in Publication Data

Holland, Norman N. (Norman Norwood), 1927–
  The brain of Robert Frost.
  1. Literature, to 1980—Psychological
aspects
  I. Title
  801'.92

  ISBN 0-415-90023-9
  ISBN 0-415-90083-2 Pbk

Contents

To Jane,

again.

Acknowledgments

Obviously, I owe my first and weightiest thanks to Robert Frost himself. Although he had no choice in the matter, he has lent himself most graciously to this book in spite of its having an unflattering title and not being about him at all. He has played the perfect gentleman throughout, obligingly demonstrating again and again the wisdom and truth of the assertions I have made about him and his brain. I trust that wherever he is, he grins his wonderful grin as he contemplates our interplay.

This book is not an evaluation of Frost and therefore has nothing to do with the controversy that in recent years has clouded Frost's personality and posthumous reputation. His biographer, Lawrance Thompson, portrayed Frost as often egotistical, spiteful, and petty. Some have proclaimed that Thompson rightly revealed a monster, while others have countered with testimonials of friendship and devotion. Any man could be proud of having evoked such eloquent defenders as William Pritchard, Stanley Burnshaw, or R. W. Flint. This book has nothing to do with the controversy, however. Knowing him only through his writings, I can contribute nothing either to praise or censure Frost the man. My way of looking at Frost's personality, moreover, yields an X ray, not a portrait.

Nevertheless, in arriving at Frost's identity, I derived much information from both the detractors and the defenders. I remember with a special pleasure, though, Randall Jarrell, Lionel Trilling, Reuben Brower, and Richard Poirier. These gifted critics revealed to me a complexity in Frost's poetry and through that complexity a beauty far beyond anything possible for the merely bucolic poet he was once thought to be. I am happy to be able to thank them for the understanding of Frost they and the many other Frost critics acknowledged in my notes have made possible.

This is not a book about Robert Frost, though. This is, I believe, the first book to bring to bear on literary criticism and theory the revolutionary discoveries of cognitive science and recent research into the brain. Frost serves as my springboard into those grey waters. As you will see, I am drawing a great deal from the startling new understanding of our human-ness provided by researchers in "cognitive science," brain physiology, and artificial intelligence. Without their work, this book could not exist.

I am combining the achievement of these contemporaries with Freud's. Teaching a seminar on Freud this year, I have gained a new respect for his intellectual boldness and courage. Truly he was a conquistador, to be followed in the new territory by many brilliant analysts. I am grateful to them and to my teachers at the Boston Psychoanalytic Institute. I hope this book justifies their confidence in me a quarter of a century ago. What they taught me then has proved a firm foundation on which I and my students have built, now, for decades.

In that sense, I also owe myself a thank-you, for I am drawing extensively on my own previous book, *The I* (Yale UP, 1985). That book synthesizes psychoanalysis and cognitive science as a psychology. This offers in a more literary form and context what *The I* said right out in psychological terms. It would be exactly the right response to *The Brain of Robert Frost* to follow it up with a reading of the earlier book.

If I owe much to psychologists, I owe much, too, to my colleagues in literary criticism for their concern to establish a theoretical understanding of the way we write and read literature. Without this new emphasis, I could not gain a hearing. At the same time, in focusing cognitive science on today's literary theory I intend a challenge to that theory. It seems to me that some modern thought about literature—whatever in it rests on the idea of "signifying"—runs contrary to both old and new psychology. As you read this book, I hope you will feel an impulse to rethink some of the conventional wisdom about literature. Follow that impulse, and again, you will do well by *The Brain of Robert Frost*. I designed it as a guide to that rethinking.

This brings me to the many people who have helped me make this book. For their adroit drawings, I am indebted to Marjorie Summers and Gabe Martinez. I want to express my appreciation to the State of Florida, the University of Florida, and the late Richard J. Milbauer for providing me an Eminent Scholar's chair and, with it, unstinting support and warm encouragement. Among the many students who have over the years assisted my research, I give special thanks to those who have focused their efforts on Frost and this book: Patrick Hogan, Sam Kimball, Louise Magavern, Laura Keyes Perry, Linda Lane Reinfeld, and most recently and most intensely, Craig Saper. Stuart Krichevsky of Sterling Lord Literistics expertly placed the book, and William Germano of Routledge,

Chapman, and Hall wittily guided its author, while Cecilia A. Cancellaro, Diane Gibbons, and Michael Esposito were skillfully producing it.

I have for a long time been using Robert Frost to think about literature. As a result I have published some of these ideas in articles as early as 1970. Although I have rewritten them quite extensively, I want to thank the editors both for permission to use the earlier materials and, most of all, for the original publication which provided me a chance to test my thinking:

"The 'Unconscious' of Literature: The Psychoanalytic Approach." *Contemporary Criticism*. Stratford-Upon-Avon Studies 12. London: Edward Arnold (1970): 130–153.

"A Touching of Literary and Psychiatric Education." *Seminars in Psychiatry* 5 (1973): 287–299.

"Unity Identity Text Self." *PMLA* 90 (1975): 813–822.

"Driving in Gainesville, Florida: The Shared and the Individual in Literary Response." *Hartford Studies in Literature* 16 (1984): 1–15.

"The Brain of Robert Frost." *New Literary History* 15 (1984): 365–385.

"The Miller's Wife and the Professors." *New Literary History* 17 (1986): 423–447.

Thanks then to Malcolm Bradbury and David Palmer, Paul Myerson, William D. Schaefer, Charles S. Ross and Catherine B. Stevenson, and especially to Ralph Cohen for his many years of encouragement to me and his spirited devotion to the discipline we both enjoy.

I have also tried these ideas out in a wide variety of forums:

Australian Association of Teachers of English

Australian Reading Association

British Psychological Society (Welsh Branch)

European-American Conference on Literature and Psychology (First Annual Meeting in Pécs, Hungary)

Group for the Application of Psychology (Florida)

Midwest Modern Language Association

Nederlandse Verenigung voor Algemene Literatuurwetenschap

New York Hospital (Grand Rounds, Department of Psychiatry)

Université Paris VII (Institut d'Anglais)

University of Chicago

University of Colorado (Reynolds Lecture)

University of Florida (Grand Rounds, Department of Psychiatry)

University of Hawaii
University of Iowa (Ida Beam Professorship)
University of Melbourne (Psychosocial Group)
University of Michigan

Among my many hosts, I want to thank particularly Charles Proudfit, for starting it all, Douwe Fokkema, Audrey Grant, Elrud Ibsch, Graham Little, Rien Segers, and Robert Silhol for their kindness in foreign parts.

In the course of all this lecturing and articling, I have learned much from friends and colleagues who have given me the benefit of their thoughts. I have thereby incurred many an intellectual debt—to Robert de Beaugrande, Richard Brantley, Gerald Graff, Molly Harrower, Kathryn Gibbs Harris, Ihab Hassan, Wolfgang Iser, Edward Jayne, Manfred Kets de Vries, Eugene Kintgen, Joseph Masling, Bernard Paris, Hilary Putnam, Robert Rogers, David Willbern, and others whose names I will never know. Some just contributed a particularly astute comment after a lecture. Some wrote articles. Some, like Joseph Masling, read whole chapters and commented on them in detail. Howard Gardner and Murray Schwartz read and commented on the whole manuscript. Anne G. Jones reminded me at a crucial moment that this was a book about the *brain* of Robert Frost. All these commentators have given, all have improved the book, and none is responsible for whatever deficiencies remain. Thank you, all. I am happy to give especial thanks to my students at the University of Paris VII (Charles V) who were willing to try out with their eccentric American professor a reader-response approach to "The Mill" quite outside of current French thinking about literature.

Thinking of Paris, I want to record again my deepest gratitude. I have already indicated it by my dedication to Jane Holland who, while I was writing up these ideas, cheerfully marched up six flights to an apartment on the Cours de Vincennes that took us right back to graduate student living. I am indebted to her for more than I can say in public, and daily my debt grows and has grown, these thirty-four years.

1

Thoughts about Brains

Wags will say *The Brain of Robert Frost* is so short a book because its subject is so small. No. The brain of Robert Frost is my starting-line, not my subject. I want to use Frost to find a way to think about any brain, not just Robert Frost's, as it engages literature and language.

The title of this book, I know, sounds more than a little wacky, indeed like the mad scientist Lew Ayres played in that grand old science fiction film, *Donovan's Brain*. Donovan, a ruthless and powerful tycoon, dies in an airplane crash near the scientist's desert lab. The over-eager scientist, seeking like all good movie scientists the secrets of life itself, recovers Donovan's brain. At first, it is the same as any human brain, a three-pound chunk of some stuff that looks and feels like a soft avocado and has a shape about like your two fists (with the thumbs tucked in) pressed knuckle to knuckle together. The scientist keeps Donovan's brain in a fishtank with electrodes and wires and chemicals. He feeds it mysterious nutrients, and it grows and grows. Before long, the brain has developed a weird glow and telepathic powers. It starts throbbing and going "Glub glub glub" in the best sci-fi manner. He feeds it still more and the brain gets more and more telepathic power until it begins to take over the scientist and use him to carry out the ambitions and revenges Donovan had been planning in real life.

I trust Robert Frost will not take me over, except as I am rapt in his poetry. Nevertheless, I find it enticing, even compelling, to imagine the very me-ness of me being preserved after death to carry on the loves and ambitions of my lifetime.[1] I find it attractive just to think of the me-ness of me or the Frost-ness of Frost engraved in the texture of a brain, finite though that brain's life is. I was surprised to learn that this inscribing of one's essential self in the architecture of one's brain may, in fact, happen.

Douglas Hofstadter makes a startling observation about earthworms and humans in his well-known book, *Gödel, Escher, Bach*. Because the earthworm has only a few thousand brain cells, every earthworm brain is like every other earthworm brain. If you point to a particular brain cell in one earthworm, you can point to an exactly corresponding cell in another earthworm. Hence, Hofstadter writes, "There is only one earthworm." That is to say, there are no "personal" differences among the Lumbricidae, no earthworm Robert Frosts or Norman Hollands.

That is not true of humans, or even of mammals, like the Hollands' cat Rachel. Once brains have evolved into millions of neurons, the cells of one brain no longer correspond one to one with the cells of another brain, even though each of these brains may have the same suborgans (like the cerebellum or hippocampus). Birds and mammals are alike in the suborgans of the brain, and some levels down from there, but not down at the single neuron level or some levels above it. For example, the number of columns in which the visual neurons are arranged differ between different humans and between different birds and mammals of the same species. Because of variations like these, Hofstadter concludes, "There is not just one human."[2]

As any visitor to the Hollands' house knows, Rachel has a "personality." (She is masterfully manipulative.) It seems to me to follow from what the brain physiologists are telling us that she owes that personality to variations in the growth and structure of her brain cells. If you can observe a distinct personality, as you can with Rachel or Robert Frost, you must also be observing a slightly different, slightly special brain in action. There is not just one human—or one cat—in the sense that there is only one earthworm.

The brain physiologists are finding that in the course of development, any advanced mammal establishes connections among its brain cells that some other members of the same species do not. I find that a rather astonishing idea. Your toes and mine, your heart and mine, your pancreas and mine are, give or take a little, the same. But our brains, our most essentially human organs, differ. How can we think about that difference? Is this difference a cultural thing? Is a French brain different from an American? (Does that explain Jacques Lacan?) Or do our brains differ purely as individuals?

Brain researchers work within a tradition that stems from the phrenologists of the nineteenth century who poked at people's skulls looking for an honesty bump or an amorousness dent.[3] That is, they were trying to localize psychological functions in particular sites on the brain, and they thought they could find the sites by high and low spots on the skull. Immeasurably more sophisticated today, researchers still proceed by trying to connect particular mental actions, memory, say, to a particular wrinkle in the cortex. In this tradition, neuroscientists regard the brain as an aggregate of separate organs.

Another tradition, however, collided with the simplicities of the early locationists. The antilocationists, after some decades of unsuccessful locationist searches, insisted at first that the whole was greater than the sum of the parts and that "mind" would never be reduced to "brain." Mental activity, they asserted, is a single, indivisible phenomenon, a function of the whole brain working as a single entity. Then came successes in localization that led to a retreat from this extreme view. Brain researchers arrived at the important concept of the "vertical organization of functions." Neuroscientists began to consider the hierarchical relationships of the different levels of the nervous system.

Central in the subsequent period of research, from 1950 to the present, is the magisterial work of Aleksandr Luria. He carried on dialogues and experiments with brain-damaged patients. By a battery of simple but ingenious tests, Luria was able to localize small functions that were used in a variety of "higher" processes. He would carefully study brain-damaged patients' malfunctions, and so he would learn what subsystem was failing. He could thereby localize the subsystem to the area of that patient's injury. By a sufficiently ingenious experiment, Luria might, for example, be able to see that patient X, suffering from a lesion on a certain area in the visual cortex, was unable to perceive edges, and thus Luria would isolate the perception of edges as a process and find its location in the visual cortex.[4] He succeeded in doing this with a great variety of small subsystems, and he was even in some cases able to infer how the subsystems come together to carry on a larger function. Thus he developed a position that synthesized (in the best Marxian tradition) localizationists and antilocalizationists: "that the material basis of the higher nervous processes is the brain as a whole *but that* the brain is a highly differentiated system whose parts are responsible for different aspects of the unified whole." For example, visual analysis of edges will play a part both in throwing a frisbee or reading a text. Some of these functions have to do with literary processes or, to use Luria's more general term, "speech," which he divides into receptive speech (including reading) and expressive speech (including writing).

In an altogether different direction, three intrepid theorists (at least three) have attempted to relate classic psychoanalytic concepts to particular brain features: Jonathan Winson of Rockefeller University; Morton F. Reiser of Yale; and Jay E. Harris of New York Medical College.

Winson reasons from what is surely one of world's odder creatures, the echidna or spiny anteater, to link Freud's ideas about dreaming and the unconscious to the functioning of the hippocampus and the neocortex. It is in the prefrontal cortex that mammals formulate plans for future behavior. This primitive mammal, the echidna, has a relatively huge neocortex. If we humans had a cortex that size, we would need a wheelbarrow to carry it around. The echidna also does not have REM (rapid eye movement) sleep or "theta rhythm" in the hippocampus. Theta rhythm indicates the synchronizing of complex behaviors toward species-specific goals, like a rat's sniffing or a cat's stalking. REM sleep is an indicator of dreaming. Winson hypothesizes that the echidna has such a huge cortex because it does not have these brain functions. Hence higher mammals must have evolved these brain functions so as to carry out the functions of the big cortex in the echidna. Dreaming must combine with hippocampal processing to process plans "off-line," when the higher mammal is not physically acting in its environment. This is Freud's unconscious: dreaming divorced from action in the real world.

Why are dreams so distorted then? Because the plans and goals we try out in dreams were inscribed on the cortex in the "critical period," that is, during the growing and ungrowing of the brain—childhood. All the simplistic or distorted perceptions of childhood continue into dreaming and the adults' unconscious processes. In this way Winson arrives at functions in the brain for two of the central concepts of psychoanalysis: unconscious thinking and the persistence of childhood in unconscious goals.[5]

Morton Reiser notes that neurophysiologists have shown definitively that object constancy—our ability to imagine a person or thing even when it is not present—occurs in the prefrontal cortex. From this known point, Reiser suggests how a person's memories in a psychoanalytic session might be organized physiologically. Reporting on his psychoanalytic patient Carol, Reiser draws for her an associative memory network. Her free associations connected a certain subway ride with her grandmother and an early experience of suffocation. Then, drawing on research that traces how monkeys' brains process the input from the senses, Reiser suggests a physiological route by which those two percepts, widely separated in space and time, might acquire a shared "meaning" for Carol.

Studies on monkeys show that the brain first registers sensory percepts in primary cortical projection areas and then processes those percepts along a complex series of cortical association pathways. Their transmittal depends on the amount of the neurotransmitter dopamine that is present, which in turn depends on the amount and kind of emotion involved.

If enough dopamine is present, a sensory input will be connected to "affect systems through bidirectional cortico-limbic pathways." If so, the new sensory input will be retained for recall in contexts associated with the much earlier memory, and we have a physiological basis for Carol's associating the early fear with the later subway ride and developing a subway phobia.[6]

Dr. Reiser proceeds cautiously, step by step. By contrast Dr. Jay Harris boldly proposes to connect the whole of psychoanalytic theory with the new neuroscience. For example, "The dopamine, norepinephrine, and serotonin systems correspond particularly to the libidinal, aggressive, and neutralizing drives of Freudian psychology."[7] I cannot possibly in this brief layman's account do justice to the force and complexity of Dr. Harris's arguments (although I shall return to them as they bear on literary processes specifically). Harris draws not only on the work of Luria and the other neurophysiologists but also on recent drug research tying specific drugs to specific brain functions. Let me simply give a sample of his method as he deals with anxiety.

Today's psychoanalysts think of anxiety as a signal of danger that rapidly, automatically, and unconsciously triggers characteristic defenses. Harris makes this far more precise. Harris connects anxiety in this sense to two inhibitory systems "among the widespread inhibitory gamma amino butyric acid systems (GABA-gabaminergic)." "Once the switchboard system [of the prefrontal cortex] has been turned on, two inhibitory systems—one for each hemisphere—must form an alliance with the dopamine and norepinephrine systems in determining whether cortical programs will go on to completion." The gabaminergic systems can shut chloride channels and thereby reduce the potential activation of neurons, thereby inhibiting those neurons. Hence, "The bilateral GABA inhibitory systems comprise the mechanism through which anxiety deactivates programs which are going awry."

> In psychological terms, the dual anxiety systems are made up of *error-anxiety* in the dominant hemisphere and *novelty-anxiety* in the nondominant hemisphere. This is clear from an inspection of the mechanism of the two major anxiety systems. One inhibits wrong actions and is therefore related to dominant hemisphere functioning. The other inhibits further input of perception into consciousness of reality when novelty is encountered. It is therefore a nondominant hemisphere-related anxiety system.[8]

He rests this hypothesis on recent research on the brain. This recent work changes earlier thinking, that the two hemispheres amounted to two separate personalities, to a newer view, that the two hemispheres work together, each inhibiting and controlling the other to form a unified system of consciousness.[9] In this instance, Dr. Harris combines brain physiology, psychoanalytic theory, biochemistry, and logic to locate the analyst's signal anxiety on two fairly specific brain sites and, incidentally, to sharpen the psychoanalytic concept. His book proceeds in this way through all of psychoanalytic theory and the major diagnostic categories, a truly remarkable achievement—if further research and thinking bear him out.

Whether or not Harris or Reiser or Winson is correct, however, is not the point. They may very well be overruled by research we cannot yet imagine. The point is that we are beginning to know enough about the brain to think we can connect behaviors that we describe at a psychological level to physical structures in the brain. We can localize low-level brain functions to particular sites (frontal lobes, lateral nondominant hemisphere, and so on), just as the functions of the liver or the pancreas would occupy particular sites. We can tie brain functions to particular biochemical transactions. Our new knowledge of the brain is beginning to make a more powerful psychology.

In the "traditional" view, that is, the view that has emerged in the last few decades, the brain is inherited (like any other organ), and the sites and features of that organ come from our genes. In just the past few years, however, that picture has received a remarkable challenge. It is to that challenge that Hofstadter refers when he contrasts mammals (Robert Frost or Rachel) who have all kinds of personalities to the unitary, monotonous earthworm. It is to that challenge that Winson refers when he speaks of a "critical period" during which our unconscious mind is formed.

Research in the last few years has evolved the picture of a changing brain that first grows and then ungrows.[10] In one researcher's image, nature is like a sculptor of the brain. First, to an armature provided by genetics, nature applies plaster, more than is needed but in roughly the shape that is desired. Then nature chips the excess away until the adult brain appears.[11] The bigger the animal and the longer it takes to develop from infant to adult, the greater this growth and ungrowth relative to the rest of the brain. All of the higher mammals that have been studied show this brain growth and ungrowth, and it is unlikely that humans vary the rule.[12]

Indeed, there is mounting evidence that we do not. The child's brain develops virtually all its potentially useful neural interconnections by the age of two, and then goes on to develop a lot more. The brains of children from three to eleven use twice as much energy as adults' brains. Specifically, in the first year of life, the metabolic rate of the baby's brain (established by PET scan) is about two-thirds that of an adult brain. By the age of two, the rate equals the adult's. During those two years, the neurons have been branching and interconnecting. Indeed, during the first year of life, "dendritic and synaptic elaboration" increases by a factor of 20. Then, by three or four, the metabolic rate becomes twice that of an adult's. By the age of six or seven, a child's brain equals in weight and volume an adult's, but it uses twice as much energy, and it has twice the number of synaptic connections. The brain stays "supercharged" until early adolescence. Then, from eleven to fourteen, the metabolic rate begins to fall until it subsides to the adult level. Similarly, there are twice as many synaptic connections in the cortex of a child's brain as in an adult's. Then that number falls by half in early adolescence. Young children experience twice as much deep sleep as adults, and then from eleven to fourteen years of age, children move into adult sleep patterns.

Further, as is well known, a child's style of thinking differs from an adolescent's or an adult's. Young children can often propose brilliant concepts, but they cannot take them further. They cannot concentrate for long. They daydream, perhaps (these researchers suggest) because too many neural connections interfere with sustained logical thought. Possibly the adolescent changes in the brain explain why well-adjusted children can become schizophrenic in adolescence, or why children between four and ten can learn languages or musical instruments more easily than adults, but (as Jean Piaget found) it is only in adolescence that we can learn to solve complex, abstract problems at all. A brain-injured child of three or four can recover speech pathways, but a similarly brain-damaged adolescent cannot.[13]

In effect, nature first grows and then prunes away vast numbers of neurons, axons, and synapses in the course of bringing a mammal from infancy to adulthood. Moreover, this growth and ungrowth results from activity—from early experience. It is well known that a lack of activity in animals deprived of sensory input leads to a lack of development of connections in the brain. Conversely, "Well-used neurons and synaptic connections seemed to release nerve growth factors, substances that help insure their survival." When a baby cat's motor activity is blocked, its eye cells develop differently. In the same way, activity by the heart or by hormones can change the kind of chemical transmitter a given neuron is programmed to emit. Muscular activity promotes the growth of neurons in the spine.[14] In general, neural circuits that get lots of use generate substances that help them to survive. Neural circuits that get little or no use are sacrificed, probably in the interests of stabilizing the brain itself and reducing the energy consumption that the supercharged childhood brain had required.[15] In effect, to survive, nerves compete for a limited supply of such things as NGF (nerve growth factor), and since those nerve cells and brain cells that survive are those we use the most, we grow nerves and brains suited to the environment in which the whole human being has to survive. In this mechanism lies the extraordinary ability of the human animal to thrive in environments as different as the ice floe and the jungle, New York and the Australian outback.[16]

Hence, in the nature-nurture, heredity-environment controversy, these researches establish a *physiological* role for nurture alongside nature's. In the older view, the genes set the physical layout of the brain and the routes of synaptic contact. In fact, the human brain has one hundred million million synapses. There are not enough genes in the human complement to account for this much complexity. Genes determine over-all aspects of brain architecture and wiring patterns, but factors outside the genome must change the details in the basic organization. Evidently, then, *childhood experience is the outside factor that shapes the final architecture of the individual brain.* Experience strengthens the neural circuits that are used in childhood and then, in adolescence, further development eliminates the unused ones, perhaps through the influence of those well-known changing hormones of the "awkward age."

As this layman sees the matter, the new view does not contradict the old, but it radically complicates it. We need to think of three elements in any given action (such as the making and appreciating of literature): heredity, environment, and personal activity. Brains are a genetic "given," but they change because of life experiences, which in turn depend upon how the individual chooses among the various activities his or her environment offers and demands. Brain functions do occupy sites, but the sites and the architecture of each brain may differ. To write, then, of the brain of Robert Frost as a special, individual thing may not be so silly a thing to do. *If* that is what I am going to do.

I am a psychological literary critic. That is, I use psychology to explore basic literary questions like, How and why do we humans write poems and stories?, and particularly, How and why do we respond to them as we do? I have undertaken this book to respond to a radical change in psychology as we have known it. The last two decades have seen remarkable discoveries about the architecture and chemistry of the brain. These decades have also brought us artificial intelligence, computer technology, psycholinguistics after Noam Chomsky, and a variety of other disciplines that make up "cognitive science."

All this has led to what one team of psychologists describes as "a ferment in psychology." "The whole point of view about what constitutes the proper goal of psychology has changed." Until quite recently, psychologists saw their task as establishing lawful relationships between observable stimuli and observable responses, with the accent on "observable." "Assumptions about what goes on under the skin were to be made cautiously, if at all. Now human experimental psychology takes as its proper goal modeling what the mind knows and how it knows."[17] In other words, psychologists today are ready to try to look inside the skin, skull, and brain.

In the first half of the twentieth century, psychologists advanced beyond their nineteenth century colleagues by a change in method. "Scientific" experimentation replaced the systematic observation of one's own mind at work. Perhaps in reaction to the nineteenth century tradition of introspection, the inside of the self or brain became taboo. The "mind" was to be "black boxed" or gotten round somehow in favor of "objective," "empirical" observations of visible external behaviors, an experimentation strongly colored by behaviorism. This approach had the great virtue of turning psychology toward the same rigor as the "successful" sciences of physics and biology.

From the point of view of today's "cognitive science," however, Howard Gardner writes, "It is difficult to think of this phase as other than primarily negative and regressive."[18] Psychologist Richard C. Anderson comments, "A large number of American social scientists fairly recently have become convinced that the presuppositions of their traditional world view were fundamentally wrong." Traditionally, twentieth century psychologists have thought of the human being as "driven" by inputs through eyes, ears, and the other senses. Traditionally, these stimuli "evoke" responses or even "control" them. Then the overall hope of psychology was to chain these simple stimulus-response units (or, more strictly, correlations of independent and dependent variables) into higher-order structures, processes, and patterns of behavior.

If there is one person who knocked this framework apart, it was Noam Chomsky. His *Syntactic Structures* (1957) showed that it "is logically impossible to account for language proficiency in terms of stimulus-response chains."[19] The premier behaviorist, B. F. Skinner attempted to do just that in *Verbal Behavior* (also published in 1957), and Chomsky focused his attack on behaviorism and proved its inadequacy for language in a slashing review of Skinner's book.[20]

In today's psychology, language has become a benchmark. If a psychology cannot account for human speech or reading, it cannot be much of a psychology. Nevertheless, one leading authority in modern "human information processing," David Rumelhart, notes that for all of today's ferment, we have only the most rudimentary idea of the specifics of the immensely complex process of understanding language. By putting specifics aside, however, Rumelhart has been able to point to "agreement on the broad outline." To be sure, different writers use different terms, and that creates the appearance of disagreement. Artificial intelligence theorists who follow Marvin Minsky use the term "frame." Some cognitive psychologists use the term "schema," while others use "definition." Schank and Abelson, in their well-known computer simulations of the "restaurant-script" use as their operative term "script," and, for higher levels, "plan." Rumelhart uses "schema" to refer to their "script." All these different words, however, refer to just one thing: the hypothesis a human being tests against some physical or linguistic reality "out there." This is, of course, an idea that may ultimately go back to Immanuel Kant's 1787 *Critique of Pure Reason*.[21]

We can imagine the human along two axes: top-down and inside-outside. That is, the sensory inputs so basic to both the old and the new psychology occur at the body's outer boundaries: toes, fingertips, eardrum, or cornea. The stimuli move from outside in. We also usually think of the mind or brain as having "higher" and "lower" functions. The raw sensations of eye and ear, like an edge, a color, a pitch, or a tone, are "low-level" processes. When we combine those low-level sensations to experience a Rembrandt portrait or a Beethoven sonata, we speak of "high-level" processes.

The consensus about language, according to Rumelhart, is that a verbal stimulus does not simply act from outside in and bottom up to cause a response.

> Fundamental . . . is the idea that language is not a simple *bottom-up* process in which we somehow construct the meaning of input sentences out of the stimuli impinging on our eyes or ears. Rather, language understanding is an active process involving the interaction of sensory information with our general knowledge of the world. . . . The details of how these systems work together is not known, but *that* they work together is clear.[22]

To understand language, we have to bring to bear not only knowledge about language, but about other people, the world of objects, and ourselves. We test hypotheses, and not just hypotheses about words. We reach actively into a book from inside out and from top down, creating and shaping the text even as it acts on us from outside in and from bottom up.[23]

This complex outside-in, inside-out, bottom-up, top-down processing applies not only to language but to any perception. Consider vision. Probably, according to the brilliant work of David Marr, our eyes see objects by means of a series of linked modules that work together to compute a representation of an object within the constraints of the physical world and the processes of the brain.[24] We can imagine, for example, the modules for seeing a flying frisbee: a processor for converting the sequence of electrical pulses from the retina into a two-dimensional shape; a processor for converting a succession of these two-dimensional shapes into a visualization of the three-dimensional frisbee; a system for calculating its distance; a system for converting distance calculations into speed and direction, and so on. Vision proceeds somewhat as a desk calculator does, blinking out a representation of what is punched into it, and that representation is determined both by that input and by the way the calculator is wired. We see according to what the world offers us to look at, and we see as these modules in our internal physiology let us see. Yet the numbers the calculator blinks out do not simply equal either the input or the wiring. Similarly, vision works by a computation on the input signals from the eye to yield a mental representation that does not correspond to "reality" as such but abides by constraints from both the physical stimulus and the brain's modules. In effect, those modules try out schemata on the world, just as the keys of the calculator, in effect, wait to see what you will punch in.

It may be that different styles in the visual arts systematically play with one or another of these computational processes—this is a theory advanced some years ago by Morse Peckham.[25] That is, cubism may test our module for perspective, pointillism may test our module for converting bits of color to wholes, sculpture our module for representing three-dimensional objects, and so on. Poetry may test our systems for parsing sentences or assigning stress to syllables. It may be, Peckham suggested, that the function of all the arts is systematically to exercise our various modes—or modules—of perception.

At any rate, it seems likely that other, similar modular hypotheses operate on sounds, language, thought, and perhaps emotion and that these modules also work, in broad outline at least, by the well-known mechanism of feedback. That is, we have inside our brains various standards, for example, for temperature. What temperature feels "right" to me? My skin constantly tests the temperature of my study to see if it matches my internal standards for comfort. In the jargon, my senses try to match representations of temperature from inside the brain or body against representations of the physical stimulus outside. If the room feels too warm or too cold, I act to make it right. I may act on the environment, for example, by turning down the thermostat. Or I may act on my own body by raising goose pimples or shivering. Then I test again. If the temperature feels right, I subside. If it doesn't, I act again. My standard is an individual one—I am always turning the air conditioning temperature up, because my wife turns it too far down for me, and native Southerners who visit us two displaced Yankees tell us our house is too cold anyway.

Feedback is essential to the new psychology. It is also an assumption we can safely embody in literary thinking, because it is unlikely to be upset by future researches. For example, it is a "hot topic" in artificial intelligence in 1988 whether the modules in people's brains work in series or in parallel. However the AI researchers decide, though, their model is most unlikely to deviate from the overarching principle of feedback:

> A person's ability to perform a given task, reasoned Hillis [W. Daniel Hillis, an expert in artificial intelligence], is dependent upon his receiving a continual flow of sensory information relating to the task and by continually calculating and adjusting for that information.
>
> "If you look at how we pick up a glass of water without spilling it, you see that it doesn't have anything to do with how precisely we position our hand or how precisely we apply a force" both of which can be programmed easily into a machine, explains Hillis. "It has to do with our getting very good feedback from our fingers. We can do this even with our eyes closed, by just feeling how well it's working out. And if it's not working out, we adjust our grip."
>
> Hillis calls this rapid-fire feedback mechanism a "controlled hallucination." A person has a hypothesis, or hallucination, about the real world—for example, the position of the water glass. Sensory feedback from the fingers causes the person to adjust the hypothesis; the fingers then provide additional feedback about the validity of the adjusted hypothesis; and so on, until the individual succeeds in picking up the glass.[26]

Feedback is a general principle that describes many kinds of biological information processing. We reach actively into the world from inside out and from top down, creating and shaping the stimulus even as it acts on us from outside in and from bottom up. "We now find," writes John Z. Young,[27] "that every organism contains systems that literally embody set points or reference standards. The control mechanisms operate to ensure that action is directed to maintaining these standards."

These control modules operate on the external world, using low-level internal standards. They also cooperate, answering to some overarching, high-level standard (serially perhaps, but more likely in parallel). "The brain has many distinct parts but there is increasing evidence that they are interrelated to make one functioning whole, which gives a unique and characteristic direction to the pattern of life of that one individual."

In such a pattern, Young is pointing to what I would call human identity, but more of that later.

I am, as I say, a literary critic, and for me the important reality detected by our brains' feedbacks is poems, stories, plays, and movies. I am, however, not about to step forward with neurophysico-psychological explanations of how people write poems or read stories. The brain physiologists, cognitive scientists, and psycholinguists themselves are far from having such knowledge, and I am far from their expertise. I cannot write intelligently about cholecystokinin, 6-hydroxy dopamine, or the hippocampus. I can, however, propose a minimal assumption about the human being engaged in literature that accords with what we know today of the systems of the brain and is not likely to be altered by what we learn of those systems tomorrow.

In offering this minimalist psychology, I will not pretend that I am providing anything like a full description of the brain or mind as it engages poems and stories. What I am trying to offer is a picture to carry about in our minds with which to think about what is going on in our brains as we create and respond to literature. I am proposing a guiding metaphor or the beginnings of a model to counterbalance the one we already have.

It is impossible to make any cogent statement about the human as a literary, aesthetic, political, or social being without making some assumptions about the human as a psychological animal. Those of us who write critically and theoretically about literature, then, already have such a model, but not, usually, one that reflects these new trends in psychology. That is unfortunate, I think. We ought to rest our criticism on the best psychology we have. Literary people, however, turn more readily to philosophical or imaginative texts for their models than to the leaden prose of most psychological writing. Then, too, writers, critics, and philosophers characteristically endow language with great, even magical power. Frost, for example, does so. Most writers hope (for obvious reasons) the poems, scripts, or stories they create will somehow enforce a certain literary response, presumably favorable. When literature "works," it is the language that did it.

At root, then, most thinkers about literature imagine a stimulus-response model of the mind as it engages literature, a model from early twentieth-century psychology. Most writers, critics, and theorists posit what is, in the language of today's cognitive science, a model that is only bottom-up, outside-in, not both outside-in and inside-out, top-down and bottom-up. By contrast, psychologists of reading understand that, in order to read, we have to bring to bear our concept of the meaning as a whole, our ideas about texts, our knowledge of the world, in short, a whole complex of top-down and inside-out strategies. We read by testing these strategies against texts. Hence, in the psychology of reading, models based on feedback are commonplace.[28]

In this book, I shall urge a minimal model of the brain's engaging literature. It is a manageable model for those of us who are not cognitive scientists or neurophysiologists, slightly more complicated than the stimulus-response picture, but not unduly so. It is consistent with what the cognitive scientists and the neurophysiologists are telling us now, and it is unlikely to be defeated by what they discover in the future.

Why Frost? Mostly because everybody knows something about Robert Frost. I can count on your recollection of half a dozen poems as well as a general sense of the kind of writer Frost was and the kind of public personality he projected. Further, Frost himself sometimes commented on his own processes of creation in quite telling ways.

It is odd, I know, to think of Robert Frost, the craggy-faced impersonator of New Hampshire virtues as a brain, as the gray, cheesy, convoluted object you might see in a laboratory jar full of formaldehyde. Yet evidently, me-ness resides in that organ, there creating and recording its being. It is there that Frost wrote poems and read them. It is there that we must read him, and we cannot read him except through our own brains, with all the circularity that implies.

The gray organ in a lab jar ought to look more or less the same for all of us, Robert Frost or you or me, and it does. It reaches out through nerve and sinew to test the world, and nerve and sinew look much the same in all of us. But the tests it brings to bear look very different. They combine somehow the heredity that defines this particular biological and physical human, the culture in which we different humans grow, and the individuality we have become. Apparently those differences are all engraved upon one little three-pound organ. Inside, in its architecture, its biochemistry, its very texture, Robert Frost's brain is as different from mine as Robert Frost, New Hampshireman, writer of georgic allegories, is from Norman Holland, psychological critic. How can we think about that? How can we have thoughts "about" a brain? What is the relation between one's essential self, the me I know and love, and the organ that we could look at in a jar of formaldehyde?

It is a brain that poses that question and a brain that must answer it, and that is a second reason it is hard to think of Robert Frost as a brain: because I will have to use my own brain to do it. To look at the "behaviors" of Robert Frost, I have to commit a "behavior" myself. Writing about his personality is a function of *my* personality as well as his. Looking at a three-pound lump of what looks like soft cheese may not invoke much of the essential Norman Holland, but formulating Frost's personality does. Talking about the brain of Robert Frost involves therefore the brain of Norman Holland.

Nevertheless, even within that paradox, I can offer some thinking about (and by that preposition I intend both "in reference to" or "all around") the brain of Robert Frost. I can offer some thinking about his brain, about my brain, and about "the" brain. I can ask some essential questions about the brain and literature. What is the relation between Frost's highly individual, personal style and the things you and I share with him: the shape of our fingers, the movements of our eyes, our sinewy American English and the printed pages that (we sometimes say) "contain" the spirit of Robert Frost?

2

Reading Frost

We can explore the workings of Frost's brain—or mind—through one of his better-known poems, "Once by the Pacific." I think this poem had at the core of its creation a widespread and well-known childhood fear. I find it of particular interest therefore, because it allows us to see how Frost defended himself against fears we may well have experienced ourselves.

Once by the Pacific

The shattered water made a misty din.
Great waves looked over others coming in,
And thought of doing something to the shore
That water never did to land before.
The clouds were low and hairy in the skies,
Like locks blown forward in the gleam of eyes.
You could not tell, and yet it looked as if
The shore was lucky in being backed by cliff,
The cliff in being backed by continent;
It looked as if a night of dark intent
Was coming, and not only a night, an age.
Someone had better be prepared for rage.
There would be more than ocean-water broken
Before God's last *Put out the Light* was spoken.[1]

As I put the poem together for myself, I respond most immediately to its violence, to words like "rage," "din," or the menacing phrase, "dark intent." The first substantial word I hear is "shattered" and the final rhyme is "broken," although, to be sure, it is only "water" that is shattered and broken, a water that is (ironically) "Pacific"—peaceful.

This night is unique: the waves "thought of doing something to the shore / That water never did to land before." And immense. I imagine huge dimensions from phrases like "great waves," "ocean-water," or words like "land," "continent," or (in time) "an age." I find these sizes made still bigger by a pattern of buttressing, doubling, and increasing. The shore is backed by cliff, and the cliff is backed by continent. "There would be *more* than ocean-water broken." Waves looked over *other* waves. This was not just a night, but an age. And finally, the poem, having begun with the storm, ends with God and the Last Judgment, a final doubling, a bigness bigger than even waves and continent, an immensity of words called forth by words. In reciting this poem, one of the critics recalls, Frost would drop into a deep voice for God's words at the end.[2]

I hear about a "misty din," and waves think of "doing something." "Someone had better be prepared." I get a feeling of indefiniteness from these phrases. "You could not tell" exactly, but you surmise a "dark intent." "More than ocean-water" would be broken—but what? "Something," Stanley Burnshaw points out, is "the most significant single word in the poems." It occurs 137 times in the Frost canon, "someone" 77 times, and "somehow" 8 times. They are all part of what Frost called in an essay of his, "Extravagance," the going beyond domestic boundaries to find something wild and, here, ominous.[3]

"Someone" is going to be a victim, and in "some*one*," I find yet another tendency, one that works along with the vagueness, namely, personification. Frost gives the whole scene human attributes. The sea "looked" and "thought." The night has an "intent," and the land is "lucky" because it is backed by other land. One critic, Judith P. Saunders, is "amused to see waves and clouds endowed with the motives and appearance of stock villains in a Grade B movie." Most see it as beginning ominously and becoming still more ominous.

One would think that personification would counter the sense of indefiniteness, but somehow, in my mind, at any rate, it makes it still more ominous: the people are huge and vague and therefore all the more menacing. Intimations of warring personalities reach a height for me in lines 6 and 7, when the poem pivots from "the gleam of eyes" associated with the skies to a direct "you." It is as if the interpersonal conflict comes about precisely because *you looked.* Finally, at the end of the poem, there is God who seems to be both the instigator of violence and the one who puts an end to it. Possibly, C. Hines Edwards suggests, Blake's picture of God inspired Frost's imagining here.

It also part of my critical style to seek some centering idea with which I can unify all these pairs and subthemes that articulate my feelings about "Once by the Pacific": peace and violence; vast size; indefiniteness; things becoming persons; doubling contrasted to the unique. It is also part of my critical style to try to put such a "center" into words. (Otherwise, how can I know and perhaps improve my experience of the poem?) Such a phrasing might be: a vision of nature as vast, vague, half-human forces in conflict. Sometimes these forces seem two, sometimes one. Their conflict is controlled by a still vaster half-human force. I might call it a poem about bigness as violence in which a still bigger bigness limits that violence, and limits it specifically by words.

You see, it seems to me that Frost is as much concerned here with controlling the violence as evoking it. For example, it is only water that is shattered or broken, and I begin to think of the visual shapes of waves rather than an actual act of shattering something solid. Frost sets the poem in the past tense. Further, in the last line of the poem I meet an intellectual puzzle that distracts me from feeling the darkness and violence: What is meant by the "last *Put out the Light*"? Indeed, that final line ends with "spoken" as the verbal answer to the "broken" that closes the violent first thirteen lines.

Consider what we might think of as normal poetic diction for a storm, these lines from *Julius Caesar*:

> I have seen tempests when the scolding winds
> Have rived the knotty oaks, and I have seen
> Th'ambitious ocean swell and rage and foam,
> To be exalted with the threat'ning clouds
>
> (1.3.5–8).

Or these from Byron's *Childe Harold's Pilgrimage*:

> Most glorious night!
> Thou wert not sent for slumber! let me be
> A sharer in thy fierce and far delight—
> A portion of the tempest and of thee!
> How the lit lake shines, a phosphoric sea,
> And the big rain comes dancing to the earth!
> And now again 'tis black—and now, the glee
> Of the loud hills shakes with its mountain mirth . . .
>
> (III,93)

Compared to that large language, Frost's poem seems colloquial and simple. He brackets the storm in wry phrases like "it looked as if," "being backed," "was lucky." "Someone had better be prepared." The rhetorical term for this would be meiosis (or ironic understatement), but the category does not get at my feelings precisely. What I sense specifically is a decisive contrast between a vast, cosmic, even godly, violence and such chatty, trivializing expressions. Again, language limits.

Perhaps, then, a better statement of my center for this poem would be: huge, malevolent, half-human forces, evoked, doubled, and magnified by some phrases, but by other phrases, brought down, limited, and made manageable. I experience this as a poem about bigness as violence and the power of words both to call up that bigness and to tame it.

Why did bigness need to be tamed? We could infer a core of fantasy from the poem itself, but, as it happens, Robert Frost's associations to this poem exist in at least three versions, each of different reliability and emphasis. In the first that I shall quote, the poet was well into his seventies, reminiscing to his friend Louis Mertins at the very place described in the poem:

It was a very long time ago that it happened. It was before Coney Island [honky-tonk] had come in to spoil the beach here at the Cliff House. I was very small and very impressionable—a child full of imagination and phobias. I watched the big waves coming in, blown by the wind. I recall that I was playing on the sand with a long black seaweed, using it for a whip. The sky must have clouded up, and night begun to come on. The sea seemed to rise up and threaten me. I got scared, imagining that my mother and father, who were somewhere about, had gone away and left me by myself in danger of my life. I was all alone with the ocean water rising higher and higher. I was fascinated and terrorized watching the sea; for it came to me that we were all doomed to be engulfed and swept away. Long years after I remembered the occasion vividly, the feeling which overwhelmed me, and wrote my poem "Once by the Pacific."[4]

The old poet emphasizes the theme of power, the sea's power but also the child's imaginings and prophecies (and, finally, the poem) in response to the feeling of being overwhelmed by the mighty ocean. Specifically, he identifies the gigantic characters represented by the storm as his absent mother and father who seemed to the five- or six-year old boy to have abandoned him.

In Frost's associations to this poem, the reference to Coney Island emphasizes the emptiness of the place then as opposed to the disreputable, noisy honky-tonk Frost and his friend saw at the time of Frost's reminiscence. That honky-tonk, I recognize as a familiar "Freudian symbol," especially if I also hear the whip the child was playing with as something sadistic. Perhaps the boy felt guilty about his private fantasying by the seashore and that was the reason for the frightening, punishing fantasy. Most literally, it was a fantasy of being abandoned. Possibly it had another, doubled sense in this setting. My mother and father are

involved with each other—Frost's father was celebrating some professional *coup*. They are indifferent to me, and I am "fascinated and terrorized watching . . ." Then, in an earlier, more global form, one almost
universal among children: I have to depend on them, but they—she—
could abandon me. I—and my whole world—would be overwhelmed
with my own helpless needs. "It came to me that we were all doomed
to be engulfed and swept away." Then, Frost reassures himself against
that fear: his parents were "somewhere about."

I have another reason for believing the huge, half-human characters
in the storm represent a feeling about parents. It think it likely that
Frost's poem, in its imagery of big, noisy, violent goings-on (not prosaic
honky-tonk) in a night of dark intent, represented for him a fantasy that
many children have and that can, by association, turn other, lesser fears
(like—perhaps—the boy Robbie's fright at the lowering storm) into utter
terror. I think the poet might have created this half-human imagery for
a storm from an actual or imagined look at "great" people of an "age,"
one of them "continent," one "low and hairy," "doing something to the
shore / That water never did to land before," both finally shattered and
broken. I think the boy Frost may have been frightened by seeing or
imagining his parents in the sexual act. Reuben Brower, for example,
called this poem a "parody of Genesis."[5]

As we have learned in recent years, such experiences, even in 1880,
were by no means rare. In Western cultures, children typically misin-
terpret the physical act of love, so different from adults' other behavior,
different, too, from anything the child does, as violence. The child reads
passion as rage, embraces as sadistic hurting, and penetration as assault
or castration—breaking. Some children fantasy all this from no more
than seeing animals mate or hearing sounds that go bump in the night.
Even today, when children commonly view R-rated movies, the mis-
interpretation of sex as violence is usual.[6]

This poem, with its three repetitions of "looked," with the "gleam of
eyes" in the assaulter, sounds to me as though the man and child who
wrote it might have been dealing with a frightening actual sight. I think
the adult Frost used (and used as a child on the Cliff House beach) a
frightening image of his parents in the sexual act to make the storm
more frightening in exchange for making his parents more distant and
more like impersonal natural forces. Maybe. Maybe the natural storm
substituted for the still more frightening and unnatural memory of his
parents. In any case, the poet submerged the whole scene in "God's last
Put out the Light."

I hear this key phrase as linking the poem's awesome storm to the
processes of creation (sexual creation?) and "Genesis," which began with
an immense first, "Let there be light." It ends with a "last *Put out the*

Light," exactly what a mother would say to a child before putting him
to bed, leaving him alone in the dark. (Frost uses the phrase that way
in "Too Anxious for Rivers,"[7] to quiet children who ask too many questions.) Or what a pair of parents might say to a child who unexpectedly
turned on the lights while they were having sex. Indeed, in "Paul's
Wife,"[8] his Paul Bunyan poem, Frost uses almost the same phrase in a
gigantic sexual encounter. A group of ruffians interrupt the huge lum-
berjack on the night of his wedding to a supernaturally glowing tree-
bride. "The shout reached the girl and put her light out" (perhaps because
Bunyan covered her by putting his body between her and the watchers).
In "The Thatch,"[9] a poem only two pages away from "Once by the
Pacific" in *West-Running Brook,* Frost associates the putting out of a light
with a quarrel between two people whom I take to be husband and wife.
The male speaker cannot come in until the light goes out.

The most explicitly sexual meaning I (and the other critics) derive from
Shakespeare. Frost's words echo Othello's speech, "Put out the light,
and then put out the light," just before he smothers Desdemona in their
wedding sheets. The phrase could also suggest the repression that usually overtakes a "primal scene" experience, replacing the frightening
memory with one more tolerable (the storm screening the adults alone
together). Above all, however, the line says to me that *special words can
limit the terror.* And perhaps it said the same to the boy Robbie whose
associations speak of "a child full of imagination and phobias."

Frost's remarks when he was in his early fifties suggest more directly
the sexual fear that I believe gave rise to the poem:

> They [friends] run away with someone else's wife and then avoid me as if
> it was my umbrella they had stolen. Now what do you suppose is the
> psychology of that? And some of them get into such tragic messes that I
> feel as if it was my proverbs failing me and not just my friends. And still
> I can't say that I didn't always know it was coming. My prophetic soul told
> me I was in for it forty-five years ago come yesterday on the cliff house
> beach [sic] at San Francisco. Is it not written in a poem of mine. The one
> thing I boast I can't be, is disillusioned.

And the poem referred, he went on to say, to a mighty storm he had
witnessed at the Cliff House at the age of five or six.[10]

His associations here are sexual, specifically to sexual betrayal, with
a hint that Frost felt that the friendships that nurtured him were being
disrupted by sexuality (as in the associations to Mertins he imagined his
parents going off by themselves, abandoning him). His phrasing here
is odd, but I think it fits the other associations. He writes as if "someone
else's wife" was being stolen from *him.* Again his associations run to
abandonment, the friends who "avoid me" and are "failing me." He tells

us he always knew "it" was coming. What? "We were all doomed to be engulfed"? Betrayed? "I can't *say* that I didn't always know . . . " Frost is quite explicit about his own saying as a response to the failure of other protections, friends, proverbs, or that startling simile, the umbrella.

It is surprisingly reminiscent of one of the examples in Freud's treatise on jokes: "A wife is like an umbrella. Sooner or later one takes a cab."[11] In an old-fashioned psychoanalytic way, one might call an umbrella a phallic symbol or one might take it as a symbol for a woman—either way Frost seems to be saying *he* feels deprived, not the someone else. *He* has had a protection stolen.

Frost took pride in writing every sentence so that you would know how to read it aloud simply from seeing it. But this sentence? How should we accent "umbrella"? "As if it was *my* umbrella they had stolen"—instead of someone else's umbrella (=wife). "As if it was *my umbrella* they had stolen"—as though a wife were no more than an umbrella. Or "As if it was *my umbrella* they had stolen"—as if to steal someone's wife is about equal in importance with taking Frost's umbrella. The whole idea may have been more charged for Frost than he was letting on.

He limits whatever anxiety might appear, however, by such minimizing, homely touches as the umbrella or his reference to his proverbs. At the same time, he has a "prophetic soul" so that he always knew it was coming (whatever "it" is). Again words have magic power, both to evoke and to allay anxiety. By means of words, he can anticipate and manage events. He can't be "disillusioned," as if to say he had had an illusion and already lost it (a vision of his parents, perhaps) or as though he has no illusions (has imagined nothing), hence cannot lose them.

A third phrasing of these associations comes from Lawrance Thompson, Frost's meticulous biographer. Thompson adds several details to the others when he paraphrases Frost's remarks about "Once by the Pacific," and I suppose he got the amplifications from Frost himself.

Whenever his father chose to celebrate a minor stroke of luck in gambling, in politics, or in the stock market, the impetuous man splurged by taking his family to dinner at one of his favorite restaurants. For the children, the best of these was the Cliff House, with its lofty view out over the Pacific. After one particularly cheerful dinner there, the entire Frost family descended the long flight of board steps to the beach for a walk along the shore in the dusk. Robbie, soon absorbed in a solitary game of lashing stone targets with a seaweed whip, unintentionally dropped so far behind the others that they passed out of sight beyond outcroppings of rock and ledge. When at last the boy turned to look for them and realized that he was alone under the cliff, he was frightened. The roar of the waves seemed hostile. The towering wall of rock leaned out and threatened. Dark clouds reached down with crooked hands. Overwhelmed with terror, he ran and kept running until he overtook his parents. Years later, in the poem "Once by the Pacific," he tried to capture the mood of that moment: he endowed with prophecy the menacing images of waves, clouds, and cliff.[12]

Again, I detect the solitary sadistic fantasy in "lashing stone targets," possibly the basis for the punishing waves and rocks. Thompson describes a paranoid moment in which the boy is "under" the cliff, the waves are hostile, the rocks threaten, and the clouds reach down. I am about to be assaulted—again, an idea all too consistent with what a child might fear at coming upon his father seemingly assaulting his mother. (Also, fears often disguise wishes.) Frightening as Frost's picture of the storm may be, the paranoid fear says, I am not alone. They care. It thus defends against a still deeper fear, of being utterly abandoned. As Thompson or Frost reads the poem, Frost "endowed with prophecy the menacing images"—again, Frost substitutes a magical power from words for a physical menace.

I have written at such length about this short poem, because Frost himself tells us it was his effort to cope with a frightening experience. We can interpret his memories both of the poem and the associated childhood fear as showing his characteristic strategies of defense and adaptation. We are seeing Frost use words in a magical, evocative way precisely to manage a childhood fright, and this presumably has much to do with Frost's thought in general, if you will, his brain.

Here, he imagined the world (at that moment) as focused *on him,* full of menace and punishment. Yet even that frightening view of things was preferable to his still deeper fear—of abandonment, specifically his parents' abandoning him because they were absorbed in each other. To avoid that darkest prospect, he used words two ways. He used words to conjure up the image of a world animate and threateningly focused on himself, and then he used words to control and manage and finally to end that frightening prospect.

In another well-known poem, Frost reassures us, or himself, against a familiar fantasy.

Mending Wall

Something there is that doesn't love a wall,
That sends the frozen-ground-swell under it

And spills the upper boulders in the sun,
And makes gaps even two can pass abreast.
The work of hunters is another thing:
I have come after them and made repair
Where they have left not one stone on a stone,
But they would have the rabbit out of hiding,
To please the yelping dogs. The gaps I mean,
No one has seen them made or heard them made,
But at spring mending-time we find them there.
I let my neighbor know beyond the hill;
And on a day we meet to walk the line
And set the wall between us once again.
We keep the wall between us as we go.
To each the boulders that have fallen to each.
And some are loaves and some so nearly balls
We have to use a spell to make them balance:
'Stay where you are until our backs are turned!'
We wear our fingers rough with handling them.
Oh, just another kind of outdoor game,
One on a side. It comes to little more:
There where it is we do not need the wall:
He is all pine and I am apple orchard.
My apple trees will never get across
And eat the cones under his pines, I tell him.
He only says, 'Good fences make good neighbors.'
Spring is the mischief in me, and I wonder
If I could put a notion in his head:
'Why do they make good neighbors? Isn't it
Where there are cows? But here there are no cows.
Before I built a wall I'd ask to know
What I was walling in or walling out,
And to whom I was like to give offense.
Something there is that doesn't love a wall,
That wants it down.' I could say 'Elves' to him,
But it's not elves exactly, and I'd rather
He said it for himself. I see him there,
Bringing a stone grasped firmly by the top
In each hand, like an old-stone savage armed.
He moves in darkness as it seems to me,
Not of woods only and the shade of trees.
He will not go behind his father's saying,
And he likes having thought of it so well
He says again, 'Good fences make good neighbors.'[13]

This is one of Frost's most often anthologized and analyzed poems,[14] justifiably so. I sense from it deep and widely shared psychological issues like those of "Once by the Pacific," but first, I want to concentrate on reading toward a conscious theme.

Several phrases refer to the seasons, particularly in a repetitive, cyclic way: "spring mending-time," "frozen ground-swell," "once again," "spring is the mischief in me." One of the major themes I see, then, is the cycle of the seasons. Associated with it, critic George Monteiro points out, is an ancient ritual antedating the Romans, the *Terminalia*, an annual reaffirming of boundaries, surely not unknown to Robert Frost, student of the classics.

Another theme I would use to bring together a number of particular lines and images is parallelism or the lack of it. Sometimes this parallelism takes a physical form, associated with the wall, as we imagine the two men walking parallel paths: "We meet to walk the line." "We keep the wall between us as we go." "One on a side." It is a mental wall, though, as well as a physical one, and I read the gaps as making possible a meeting of minds and attitudes as well as of lands and bodies. Closing the gaps in the wall means closing off points where the two men might meet physically or mentally. As the poet says, "If I could put a notion in his head," but he can't. The two men, the two minds, will remain parallel, on opposite sides of a wall.

I find parallelism in the language as well as in the central image of the two men walking along a wall. I find it in phrasings like "To each the boulders that have fallen to each." "And some are loaves and some so nearly balls." "Walling in or walling out." I find it most centrally in "Good fences make good neighbors," whose neat parallelism contrasts in my mind with the redundancy, the tangled, circling syntax of "Something there is that doesn't love a wall."

The parallelisms in phrasing lead me to think of speech and language themselves as themes. I find many phrases like, "I tell him," "He only says," "I'd rather he said it," "his father's saying," "He says again." The neighbor speaks "his father's saying" twice. The poet also speaks twice, and both their repetitions represent a hardening of position, a re-building of the wall. Speech can seem almost ominous, when I hear about those yelping dogs or when the poet spells out the magic he uses to balance rocks. Richard Poirier points out that the poem is not only about the making of fences but the making of speech between men and, even more tellingly, the way the making of fences leads to the making of speech— poetry, really, against "the claustrophobias of mechanical forms." "Walls have a power of confinement which creates a counter-movement of 'mischief.'" Richard Poirier points out a significant fact: the mischievous poet "who voices his opposition to wall-building is also the man who

each year informs his taciturn neighbor that it is time to build them."
"Voice and nature are thus potentially allied."[15]

The cycles of nature and the seasons; parallelism; speech and poetry;
the contrast between the physical and mental—I state such themes explicitly so that I can try to make each item of the poem relevant to every
other through one or more of the themes. For example, what significance
can I find in, "We wear our fingers rough with handling them"? The
skin, it says, is another boundary being firmed up, and I can fit this line
"under" the theme of walls and parallelism. Frost's psyche has nothing
to do with this way of reading. Thematizing, as today's critical jargon
has it, or simply "theming" is essential to my own sense of coherence
in the poem and hence to my experience of it, although the themes
themselves do not describe that experience, which remains finally emotional and private.

The last step in such a theming or cohering is to phrase one central
theme or meaning for my four themes or subthemes. Then I can play
the details of the poem against that central theme. What idea would
unite seasons, parallelism, physical and mental, speech? I can borrow
from Northrop Frye's reading of this poem and speak of the center of
the poem as two human attitudes toward a wall, one wintry, one spring-
like. Frank Lentricchia describes the two men in the poem this way:
"One moves in a world of freedom because, aware of the resources of
the mind, he nurtures the latent imaginative power within himself and
makes it a factor in every-day living, while the other, unaware of the
value of imagination, must live his unliberated life without it." I need
not assume that Frost favors the walls-down, spring-like attitude over
the walls-up, colder one, only that he is playing with the contrast between
them. In fact Frost said, "Maybe I was both fellows in the poem."[16] "I've
got a man there; he's both of those people but he's man—both of them,
he's a wall builder and a wall toppler. He makes boundaries and he
breaks boundaries. That's man."[17] Indeed that there are two such types
and that one person can be both—those very facts make up one of the
human walls that the poem, for me, is about.

Having arrived at some such centering theme, I can make parts of the
poem relevant that otherwise would not make sense to me. "Some are
loaves and some so nearly balls . . . " Why does Frost trouble to say
that? I can read it as a dualism right inside the wall itself, a wall within
a wall, a division within a division. (But is that enough? See the last
pages of this book.) Why "elves"? I can fit them in as nature-spirits, as
having to do with the "something" that takes the wall down—hence
they fit under the theme of the seasons. Why cows? And what is the
sense of Frost's saying his apple trees will never eat the cones under

his neighbor's pines? I daresay I could rationalize these images (St. Armand, for example, notes that Frost knew pine cones could seed a nearby orchard). My task, however, is not to cohere the poem so much as to read the mind of Robert Frost.

When I look at "Mending Wall" psychologically, I see Frost dealing with an issue fundamental to human relations, the establishment of a clear sense of self. The wall stands, on the one hand, for separateness and identity, on the other, for one's relatedness to other humans. The poem speaks about precisely this, as I read it. This is a central issue in Frost's mind, as it must be in any human mind, for the emergence of the self is the key event of early infancy.

Daniel Stern's recent account of this momentous event draws on new evidence about babies. Newborns can see and hear more and think and know better than psychologists and psychoanalysts had previously thought.[18] Stern theorizes that the infant's self emerges in four stages. At first, the baby demonstrates a core sense of self, in its most basic terms, the self as that invariant that accompanies all other experiences and actions. Then the child becomes aware of "self-with-another," the other, usually a mother or "primary caregiver," who shares some experiences with the infant. Third, corresponding to the "self-object differentiation" in psychoanalysis' more traditional account, the baby becomes an intersubjective baby, understanding that another person might share a similar state of mind. Fourth, the baby becomes able to represent all this in language. Through language, the baby can split the lived experience of self and other from the represented experience. It is these last two issues that "Mending Wall" treats. The neighbors share their parallel states of mind: the distancing established by one neighbor's language, and the undistancing attempted by the poet's.

"Mending Wall" also images, however, a more traditional psychoanalytic account of human development, one we would find in the writings, say, of Sigmund Freud, Erik Erikson, D. W. Winnicott, or Margaret Mahler.[19] This version rests more on an infancy inferred from the free associations of adults but to some extent also, like Stern's account, on laboratory observation of mothers and babies. According to this earlier picture, the first, most basic concern of our lives was taking in through mouth, eyes, touch, or ears, and in the course of this taking in, we achieved certain fundamental tasks of maturation. In this first, "oral" stage, we became individuated. We learned there is a self and a not-self, an inside and an outside. We achieved separateness and a personal identity, and the ability to put them aside to fuse with another person or an idea or an experience—precisely the theme of "Mending Wall."

In the regular psychoanalytic account, a baby during the first weeks of life is preoccupied with his—to avoid a clumsy "his or her" I will, reluctantly, say "his"—insides. He draws no real distinction between inner and outer, only between well-being and dissatisfaction.

Feeding plays the crucial role in developing the infant beyond this phase. At first, the newborn does not sense himself as separate from the world around him, particularly his primary caregiver. As she—again reluctantly, but for clarity, I will call the primary caregiver, "she"—as she gratifies his hunger, he feels as though he and she were one. He does not think of the two of them as "in a relationship." He feels merged or fused with her.

Her gratification of his needs can never be perfect, for they are not in fact one. Sometimes he has to wait. Sometimes he has to be frustrated. Sometimes he gets into a rage. As he feels the discrepancy between his inner needs and their satisfaction from his mother, from outside, he thereby learns that they are not one.

This learning is not a gentle thing—the baby can feel rage and terror at having to wait—but some frustration is necessary. Were there no delay, were the baby's wishes gratified before he could ever feel them not being gratified, he would lose an experience essential to development: the body experience of an outside being who feeds him, on whom he is dependent, and who is separate from himself. As he learns that he must wait, expect, endure delay from that Other and, finally, trust that she will come, he realizes that she is, in fact, a separate being, not a part of his own will. Only through frustration can the baby make that absent Other (in Erikson's phrase) "an inner certainty as well as an outer predictability."[20] Once he knows she is reliably Other, he necessarily knows that he is himself separate, a not-Other, a self. In other words, according to this psychoanalytic theory, his—our—whole sense of our individual, separate identity is predicated upon our being able to imagine that a nurturing, caring other exists and that she *will* come.

Both Daniel Stern's and the more traditional psychoanalytic account agree that the basic task of our first year of life is to establish a sense of self, whether that involves separating from a mother-and-child matrix or simply developing a sense of "I." As I read it, "Mending Wall" is about just this issue: setting up and breaking down boundaries, especially boundaries between people. Shall we have separate identities or shall we get rid of the boundaries between ourselves and the world outside? Frye and Lentricchia have stated the attitudes on either side of the wall in adult terms. In terms of child development, our first "wall"— our sense of a boundary between self and not-self—came about by means of the mouth. If so, I can imagine why Frost's poem about a wall has so many images of speaking and eating: "the yelping dogs," stones which are "loaves," the speaking of a spell, the neighbor's twice saying "his father's saying," phrases like "I tell him," "He only says," and so on.

I can also imagine why, although both Frost and his neighbor are grown men, the poet should offer his pixyish explanations through "elves." The poem itself offers something of a clue: "Spring is the mischief in me," and elves are tiny and child-like as well as imaginative and playful. Frost as a poet allies himself with that elfin playfulness but also with an impulse to lose the boundary between self and other and so return to earliest childhood, when one is an elf, living in a world where spells work.

In this way Frost projects onto nature his own playfulness: "Something there is that doesn't love a wall, / That wants it down." The verb "love," by calling for an animate subject, makes the something that doesn't love more than some *thing*. Besides, the "frozen-ground-swell" is really frost, and that concealed pun again mixes up self and outer world as does "Spring is the mischief in me." The reference to cows, which I find somewhat puzzling, introduces other infantile themes, milk and motherhood most obviously, a note of femininity, but I also think of the cow as an eat-and-be-eaten animal. Hence I hear in Frost's "But here there are no cows" a denial of rivalry and eat-and-be-eaten anger—we don't need a wall.

It seems to me Frost is working with an infantile fantasy about breaking down the wall which marks self so as to return to a state of closeness to an Other. To lose the boundary between self and Other is to perceive one's own impulses as part of the outer world and to feel the actions of the outer world as one's own. Keats called this the essential ability for a poet: negative capability, being able to put one's own identity aside and imagine oneself into the things and persons of the world outside the self. Such a return to a child's at-oneness, however, is not without risk. One gives oneself over to "projection" and "introjection" which, Erikson remarks, "remain some of our deepest and most dangerous defense mechanisms."[21] They may be good for poets, but they are dangerous for, say, politicians and generals or for a child frightened by the waves at the Cliff House beach. I am thinking of paranoid projections.

In the section of the poem where Frost entertains the possibility of just letting the wall fall down, I sense a faintly paranoid loss of boundary between himself and his neighbor: "I wonder / If I could put a notion in his head." "I'd rather / He said it for himself." There is a link, widely recognized in psychiatry, between a paranoid view of the world (It is all directed at me) and the projection of homosexual impulses (I don't love him—he loves me). In this context, the poem's fantasy of merger may not be directed at a woman ("no cows") but another man, and (in psychoanalytic terms) I can hear other levels of merger, in those hard boulders the two men carry: as weapons, as "balls," "handling them," and so on. In this vein, I am hearing wishes and fears about being close to another man, particularly a strong, primitive one, a "savage." I am hearing wishes about excrement, testicles, assault, or penetration of one man by another.

I hear, too, the primitive rage of the so-called "oral stage," in "the work of hunters," a rage that can carry over into all later hungers and desires.

> they have left not one stone on a stone,
> But they would have the rabbit out of hiding,
> To please the yelping dogs.

Still more ominous is the picture of the neighbor holding a stone in each hand, "like an old-stone savage armed." The palaeolithic reference images in yet another way regression to a violent, primitive state of mind.

Knowing something about the sources of this rage helps me make sense out of what seem to me the oddest lines of the poem:

> He is all pine and I am apple orchard.
> My apple trees will never get across
> And eat the cones under his pines, I tell him.

Using language to cope, Frost is *telling* the neighbor that he is being unrealistic. In a manifest way, Frost is simply being sarcastic: you only need a wall if you think immovable trees will cross over and eat inedible seeds. In the poem, however, as necessarily in Frost's and my minds, boundary and eating and identity and the ability to deal with reality all go together. A failure to keep one's boundaries marks the most severe mental disorders. It could indicate either a regression to the earliest stage of infancy or a failure to develop out of that oral stage. Thus, when the speaker imagines that wall down, he says, "He is all pine and I am apple orchard." If the wall comes down, individual identity will be destroyed. Unconscious anger is masked as gentle sarcasm, but the chaos comes through unchanged. I hear the neighbor (and the poem) saying, If there is no wall, craziness will break through.

That, it seems to me, is the core of fantasy that corresponds to the imagining and controlling of a sexual scene in "Once by the Pacific." When 'something' takes the walls down between self and other, a chaotic, violent, irrational, primitive attack appears. As in the shorter poem, Frost uses language to imagine that aggression (the Stone Age image of

the neighbor, for example). He then uses language to limit it: "He says
again, 'Good fences make good neighbors.'" "Put out the light."

At the conscious level (if we adopt Northrop Frye's centering theme)
the poem plays off two human attitudes, one wintry, one spring-like.
The warm spring-like (but dangerous) walls-down feeling corresponds
to a poet's wish for a cozy but risky return to some original one-ness.
The neighbor's wintry, New England standoffishness, his walls-up sense
of privacy and separateness, corresponds to the cold, hard, more grown-
up reality of individuation. In a theme Richard Poirier develops, the
walls-down feeling corresponds to the poet's wayward imaginings, the
walls-up to the control of that imagination.

In this context, consider what Frost thought he was doing when he
wrote his famous poem, "The Death of the Hired Man." In the poem
an old man comes back dying to the farm where he had worked and
been fired. He meets the farmer's resentment and the wife's pity. This
is what Frost said in reaction to several critics' reading of the poem:

> They think I'm no New Dealer. But really and truly I'm not, you know, all
> that clear on it. In *The Death of the Hired Man* that I wrote long, long ago,
> long before the New Deal, I put it two ways about home. One would be
> the manly way: "Home is the place where, when you have to go there, /
> They have to take you in." That's the man's feeling about it. And then the
> wife says, "I should have called it / Something you somehow hadn't to
> deserve." That's the New Deal, the mother's love. You have to deserve
> your father's. He's more particular. One's a Republican, one's a Democrat.
> The father is always a Republican toward his son, and his mother's always
> a Democrat. Very few have noticed that second thing [in the poem? in me?];
> they've always noticed the sarcasm, the hardness of the male one.[22]

What interests me is that Frost conceives his poem, his thought, really,
in twos. He pairs man and wife, father and mother, Republican and
Democrat, hardness and nurturing, obligation and lack of obligation. To
be hard that way is to be male, or, said the other way round, to lose
that hardness is to lose one's very masculinity. The punning, elfin mischief that would take walls down may be playful, but it may be felt as
a terror.

Those same verbal games, however, can distance us from a dangerous
experience. By deflecting us toward language, Frost lets us manage and
tone down the fear we might feel at that union with another. The psychological crux of "Mending Wall"—the risking and re-establishing of
some ultimate boundary of self—becomes translated into wordplay like
the pun in "Before I built a wall I'd ask to know . . . / To whom I was
like to give offense." The sequence of parts also tones down the possible
dangers. For example, after the noisy, violent hunger of the yelping dogs

come stealthy and mysterious gaps, which "No one has seen . . . made." As with "Once by the Pacific," Frost uses a final phrase to clamp down and seal off the dangers he has conjured up.

Here, it seems to me, we are coming very close to the nature of Frost's creativity as a poet, perhaps the creativity of all poets. Language occupies a special, pivotal place in Frost's psychic economy. He can use words two ways: to call up the kind of thing he most fears (being overpowered, unmanned, unselved, fused into another) and to manage that same fantasy. He can use words both to evoke a fantasy that feels particularly dangerous to him and to limit that same fantasy. To the extent we can re-create in our own terms our equivalent for that fearful fantasy and manage it using *his* words (because we share Frost's language), we say his poem succeeds. We award its author the accolade of "creativity."

In effect, language serves Frost as an agent both of fantasy and of mastery. In "Once by the Pacific," he uses a poetic form that resembles a familiar defense mechanism: projection. He starts with a storm, but it turns out to be more than a storm. In this poem, he starts with a wall but it turns out not to be "just a wall." In both instances, his language enables him and us to build a process of projection: "something" doesn't like the wall; its gaps have a mysterious quality ("No one has seen them made or heard them made"); it seems to be engaged in a struggle between human beings (as the high waves by the Pacific were). In effect, Frost's language projects (in a paranoid way that probably accounts for the faint *frisson* I feel at this poem) human attributes onto the inanimate world. His words put the dangerous wishes and fears within himself out into the world around him. Then his poem explores those mental states in the guise of physically dealing with the actualities of a New England farm or the San Francisco coast.

With that uncanny self-knowledge of the artist, Frost seems almost to have recognized this tendency in himself to project, as when he wrote in his favorite preface, "The Figure a Poem Makes" (1939), "Like giants we are always hurling experience ahead of us to pave the future with."[23] Or, in the poem "For Once, Then, Something,"

> Others taunt me with having knelt at well-curbs
> Always wrong to the light, so never seeing
> Deeper down in the well than where the water
> Gives me back in a shining surface picture
> Me myself in the summer heaven, godlike, . . .[24]

The poem ends, explaining its title, by describing how once he *did* see a vague "whiteness." "Truth? A pebble of quartz? For once, then, something."

Often Frost's poems leave his projections still in the air that way, and those are the poems that leave me in strangeness, awe, and dread, at their headiest, a kind of paranoia. Ultimately he has not provided, as much as he might, language to limit the fantasy. Other Frost poems, like "Mending Wall" or "Once by the Pacific," make the whiteness solid. The words let us frame a more or less reassuring solidity instead of a paranoid projection. "He says again, 'Good fences make good neighbors.'" "God's last *Put out the Light* is spoken." They let us (and Frost?) seal off the danger.

In many ways I have been saying in clinical language what has often been said more gently. Much of what we admire in Frost is his way of transforming the colloquial language of everyday human concerns into poetry about the largest themes of life. Yet this is not simply Frost's manner as a poet, but a pattern one can trace in many different aspects of his life. It constitutes not only a literary but a personal style. Indeed, it is the way Frost himself thought of style: "The style is the man. Rather say the style is the way the man takes himself; and to be at all charming or even bearable, the way is almost rigidly prescribed. If it is with outer seriousness, it must be with inner humor. If it is with outer humor, it must be with inner seriousness. Neither one alone without the other under it will do."[25] There has to be a balance.

Frost is a wonderfully wry, ironic writer, yet, as he describes his humor it is not good-natured:

> I own any form of humor shows fear and inferiority. Irony is simply a kind of guardedness. So is a twinkle. It keeps the reader from criticism. . . . At bottom the world isn't a joke. We only joke about it to avoid an issue with someone, to let someone know that we know he's there with his questions: to disarm him by seeming to have heard and done justice to his side of the standing argument. Humor is the most engaging cowardice. With it myself I have been able to hold some of my enemy in play far out of gunshot.[26]

Frost's irony, by his account, served him to achieve a fearful, guarded stand-off against the kind of parallel but hostile person represented by the man on the other side of the wall to be mended. Frost treated his own feelings in the same balancing way he treated readers and other adversaries, developing an almost uncanny ability to balance seriousness with humor. As he wrote to his daughter after his wife's death, "No matter how humorous I am, I am sad. I am a jester about sorrow."[27]

Frost acted out such balances in his personal manners. He was known to his close friends for his anger and rages—he himself called them "my Indian vindictiveness"—but he was known to the public for his folksiness and his gentle, proverbial humor and irony. All his life he needed to make himself into a legend this way, often falsifying the actual facts to do so. "Don't trust me too far . . . . don't trust me on my life," was his often repeated caution to scholars and would-be biographers. It was as though he needed to put on myth like a mask to help him, not just with his public image, but with his deeper need to cope with an important polarity in himself. The small, cozy mannerisms may have served to deal with anger. Perhaps.

On other occasions, Frost denied that adversary relation with the world (or parts of it), but his very denial took the form of defining adversaries.

> I may say I've never got on by setting poetry in opposition to science or big business or academic scholarship, although some poets seem to live on that contrast . . . Science cannot be scientific about poetry, but poetry can be poetical about science. It's bigger, more inclusive.[28]

Frost said that on his eighty-fifth birthday, but he had used much the same strategy thirty years before to cope with the threat from science that some literary people perceived in the 1930s. He had poetry gobble up science by treating it as metaphor. "Isn't science just an extended metaphor: its aim to describe the unknown in terms of the known? Isn't it a kind of poetry, to be treated as plausible material, not as cold fact?"[29] He took the same tack with Albert Einstein's theory, another headliner in the thirties: "Wonderful, yes, wonderful, but no better as a metaphor than you or I might make for ourselves before five o'clock."[30] The folksiness lets his hearers minimize and limit Einstein's stunning innovation and bring it within the scope of Frost's Georgian poetry.

In the same way, he addressed a lively philosophical question of the thirties, materialism, as a form of poetry—indeed as a poetry close to his own practice:

> Greatest of all attempts to say one thing in terms of another is the philosophical attempt to say matter in terms of spirit, or spirit in terms of matter, to make the final unity. That is the greatest attempt that ever failed. We stop just short there. But it is the height of poetry, the height of all thinking, the height of all poetic thinking, that attempt to say matter in terms of spirit and spirit in terms of matter. It is wrong to call anybody a materialist simply because he tries to say spirit in terms of matter, as if that were a sin. . . . The only materialist—be he poet, teacher, scientist, politician, or statesman—is the man who gets lost in his material without a gathering metaphor to throw it into shape and order. He is the lost soul.[31]

Obviously Frost himself was a poet who expressed spirit in terms of matter and a champion at finding a "gathering metaphor." He saw science, too, as such an attempt to achieve a gathering metaphor but, given his attitude toward superior forces, he was not about to allow that science was superior or opposed to poetry as a way of managing the big unknowns.

He adopted an idea of Emerson's that "the world is a temple whose walls are covered with emblems, pictures and commandments of the Deity . . . there is no fact in nature which does not carry the whole sense of nature . . ."[32] "I am a mystic," he told a reporter. "I believe in symbols. I believe in change and in changing symbols."[33] In the same vein, "I believe in what the Greeks called synecdoche," he said, "the philosophy of the part for the whole; skirting the hem of the goddess. All that an artist needs is samples."[34] Synecdoche being the figure of speech in which a part stands for the whole (like sail for ship, hand for sailor), Frost even claimed, "I started calling myself a Synecdochist when others called themselves Imagists or Vorticists. Always, always a larger significance. A little thing touches a larger thing."[35] George Bagby has said how important this trope is for Frost, how part-for-whole "is altogether characteristic of the way [his] mind works." "It reflects a whole way of perceiving reality: fundamental epistemological assumptions, perceptual habits, linguistic assumptions, and structural preferences." "Again and again, the poems move naturally from description of an object or scene or event to a commentary or meditation on its significance."[36]

One can also see, in just my few quotations from Frost, how he sets up the world as paired opposites: matter and spirit, humor and sorrow, little thing and larger thing, part and whole, the goddess and the hem of her dress. In the booming if inequitable economy of 1926, for instance, he wrote of the strain of "trying to decide between God and the Devil, between the rich and the poor (the greed of one and the greed of the other), between keeping still about our troubles and enlarging on them to the doctor and—between endless other things in pairs ordained to everlasting opposition."[37] This is an unpublished couplet he said was inspired by Emerson:

> It is from having stood contrasted
> That good and bad so long have lasted.[38]

Responding to Lionel Trilling's disturbing speech at his eighty-fifth birthday dinner, Frost said, "No sweeter music can come to my ears than the clash of arms over my dead body when I am down."[39]

In accepting John F. Kennedy's invitation to read at his inaugural, Frost wired: "If you can bear at your age the honor of being made

President of the United States, I ought to be able at my age to bear the honor of taking some part in your inauguration."[40] More opposites and balancings, as in his remarks about people's red-baiting. "They get all worried about 'reds' in the country . . . And all the time they forget that there are limitations to all things; that there always is a balance to everything. . . ."[41] Early in his career he said, "All a man's art is a bursting unity of opposites."[42] Always a balance, as in this poem he never published and never completed:

> But tendencies seem to be paired
> And there seems to be provision
> The pairs shall be in collision
> And many collisions shall lace
> Entangle and mass in space
> To make a bristling sun.[43]

And if we hear that "sun" as "son," we can hear a hint of the sexual fantasy of "Once by the Pacific." The pairing or collision that makes a son pervades the whole solar system. Possibly that early fear colored his entire world-view, creating his need for balanced pairs. We shall never know, of course.

Sometimes Frost's need to see balances led him to equate things others might not, as in this section from a letter he wrote in 1942 about World War II:

> I should regard it as too bad if we hoped the war would leave us without a foe in the world. Everything has its opposite to furnish it with opposition. There are those in favor of democracy like you and me and there must always be the contrary minded. With us the emphasis is on the answerability of the ruler to those he rules; with our opponents the emphasis is on the answerability of the ruler to the highest in himself and to God. The conflict is a matter of emphasis. Each side has something of both principles in it.[44]

For Frost as much as for Marx, opposition—answerability—is a principle to be found everywhere, but I hear something else in that passage. It is surely surprising, not to say shocking, to see an intelligent and moral man in the middle of World War II describing Hitler as simply a ruler who is answering to God or to the highest in himself.

In that euphemizing, I see another pattern besides just the posing of opposites. In all these pairs, Frost makes one item smaller than the other or more known or more safe or more finite than the other, like the hem and the goddess. "A little thing touches a larger thing." Hitler answers to something beyond himself and is thereby minimized. "I've been to

Niagara Falls, and what did I see there? I saw a lot of water falling, just what I've seen falling out of the faucet many, many times."[45]

Frost pairs things: metaphor and theory, known and unknown, limited and limitless. His pairings not only contrast the two items but place one (synecdochically) inside the other, so that the lesser somehow manages or limits or endures the bigger, more threatening term. A metaphor that anybody can make stands up to Einstein's large, obscure theory. The limited matches the limitless. Hitler is answerable. The part stands for the whole. The known balances the unknown. He described his own art: "Like a piece of ice on a hot stove, the poem must ride on its own melting."[46] Again: "Every poem is an epitome of the great predicament; a figure of the will braving alien entanglements."[47] "When in doubt there is always form for us to go on with. Anyone who has achieved the least form to be sure of it, is lost to the larger excruciations."[48]

All are in their way "samples." Which is bigger, which includes the other, is the test of survival. "Science cannot be scientific about poetry, but poetry can be poetical about science. It's bigger, more inclusive."

You could call this way of using one small object to test a larger one Frost's "style." I call it his "identity" in a special sense of the word. Erikson taught us the term as a way of describing the way we achieve two continuities, one an inner sense of personal continuity, the other a sense of continuity and mutuality between one's self and one's community. I would like to enclose Erikson's usage in a larger, earlier sense of this word, whose root is the Latin word for "the same," *idem*. Identity refers to the sameness I read in a self in time and in different activities as I see a similarity between Frost the writer of poems and Frost the holder of opinions and, in Erikson's sense, in his sense of himself and his sense of himself in relation to his community.

Furthermore, the brain scientists provide a biological basis for such a sameness. Until relatively recently, it was thought the right and left halves of the brain constituted separate activities, perhaps even separate personalities. Now we know that the two hemispheres mutually inhibit each other so as "to form a unified system of consciousness."[49] This unified system of consciousness formulates plans and creates complex programs of behavior. Located in the frontal lobes, it apparently uses interior speech to do so, for damage to the speech centers also damages the ability to move one's arms or legs in a planned way. This verbal consciousness monitors these programs and checks actions against the original plans so as to provide "a system of feedback on the basis of which complex forms of behavior are regulated."[50]

Someone like Robert Frost has a continuing style, perhaps rooted in his frontal lobes, which he brings to ever-new contents. We can perceive such a style only by singling it out from change, just as we can see change only against a background of sameness. To see the constancy in one another, we need to see it against newness, and to see newness as newness we need to be aware of constancy. We humans perceive one another, in my view, through a dialectic of sameness and difference.

To explore that dialectic of style and content, sameness and difference, the best way I have found is through an idea of the psychoanalyst Heinz Lichtenstein:[51] that we think of identity as a theme and variations the way we read as theme and variations a piece of music or poetry. I can think of sameness or style as a theme, and I can think of the constantly changing contents in which I see that style as variations played on that identity theme. Thus I can think of Robert Frost's identity at any given moment as an identity theme plus the variations he is then living on it. I can think of his total identity as the history of his identity theme plus the history of all the variations he has lived on it. In this definition, identity includes both a personal style and the history of that style. Hence, in thinking about Robert Frost's identity, I—his historian for the moment—want to phrase a theme that will join together all the elements I see in Frost's characteristic style.

Poetry, a known quantity, minimizes a great unknown, science. Frost's formulas make the Nazis a manageable concept. Irony means familiar humor balancing the great unknown sorrow. Frost's fondness for symbols means making a part represent the whole. "Every poem is . . . a figure of the will braving alien entanglements."

I can understand my various quotations from Frost as each a different variation on a theme that I might phrase, *to manage great unmanageable unknowns by means of small knowns*. Again, I insist on phrasing the theme, reductive though that may seem, so as to see what I have got and to be able to test and, if need be, change it. Ultimately, though, I think I could cohere Robert Frost's whole, rich poetic achievement by means of that phrasing. He used the language and materials of small New England farms to grasp the largest issues human beings can face. That is, he used colloquial language to talk about big themes, small knowns to manage big unknowns.

So far, we have talked about the way Frost wrote and thought. He also perceived in this style, however. He saw things through the lens of his personal mode, as indeed this definition of identity would suggest. "The most exciting movement in nature," he said, "is not progress, advance, but expansion and contraction, the opening and shutting of the eye, the hand, the heart, the mind. We throw our arms wide with a gesture of religion to the universe; we close them around a person. We explore and adventure for a while and then we draw in to consolidate our gains."[52] Again, Frost has perceived in twos, expansion and contraction, opening and shutting, outward or inward. Beauty will be continuous with other functions of Frost's identity, like his views on life in general or his perceptions of other people. Beauty is in the I of the beholder.

Here is the way he imagines a politician and a hypothetical religious man:

Take the President in the White House. A study of the success of his intention might have to go clear back to when as a young politician, youthfully step-careless, he made the choice between the two parties of our system. He may have stood for a moment wishing he knew of a third party nearer the ideal; but only for a moment, since he was practical. And in fact he may have been so little impressed with the importance of his choice that he left his first commitment to be made for him by his friends and relatives. It was only a small commitment anyway, like a kiss . . . And behold him now, a statesman so multifariously closed in on with obligations and answerabilities that sometimes he loses his august temper. He might as well have got himself into a sestina royal.

Or he may be a religious nature who lightly gets committed to a nameable church through an older friend in plays and games at the Y.M.C.A. The next he knows he is in a theological school and next in the pulpit of a Sunday wrestling with the angel for a blessing on his self-defensive interpretation of the Creed. What of his original intention now?[53]

Frost minimizes them by language, Harry Truman involved in a sestina royal, the preacher with his "self-defensive interpretation." Frost imagines the president or this religious man in the language and dimensions of his own character, the small facing the large entanglement, a kiss that becomes a wrestle. As the young man goes on, that first commitment becomes, in Frost's image, "like the almost microscopic filament of cotton that goes before the blunt thread-end and must be picked up first by the eye of the needle."[54] Again, Frost phrases human experiences, committing oneself, in terms of his own identity, as something small entering something large which he hopes will accept and not threaten it.

Both coping with the world and perceiving it are functions of Frost's identity (at least as I interpret that identity). One phrases Frost's identity theme by abstracting patterns of repetition and contrast from the individual's choices, here, his choice of words. He is constantly writing and reading new poems, thinking and doing new things, yet in all that creativity one can trace characteristic patterns, a personal style, a

Frost-ness in everything Frost does. By phrasing that sameness as an identity theme and the changes and growth as variations on that identity theme, I can develop continuities through both his life and his writing.

I can phrase, for example, a relation between Frost's adult style of life and his efforts as a child to cope with his parents. His father was a drunken, unpredictable newspaperman. His mother was a devout Swedenborgian who saw symbols in everything in the world. I can see how, with parents like that, he might have taken as his life's work, his "project" in Jean-Paul Sartre's word,[55] the managing of mysterious forces through the symbolic power of smallness. I can see a continuity between that childhood and his efforts late in his life, on a tour of Russia, to treat Chairman Nikita Krushchev as just another farmer like himself.

One can trace an identity theme through the long spaces and times of a life. One can also trace it to the extremes of a life. Suffering from unrequited love, Robert Frost tried to commit suicide at the age of twenty. His method was to travel all the way from Boston to North Carolina and try (rather halfheartedly, I'm glad to say) to drown himself in the Great Dismal Swamp. Surely this is a devious way to kill oneself. It is remarkably characteristic of Frost, though, if one thinks of him as submitting himself to a big, mysterious entity.

When I consider such extreme evidence as Frost's attempted suicide, I can believe that there is an identity theme *in* a person. Identity seems "there," a mental structure that is established in infancy and that governs or determines conduct. I know that sometimes people find the idea of an identity theme built into the self threatening. It seems deterministic and controlling. Such a structure suggests a limit to one's ability to change oneself. It defines a self by what is ultimately other, not-self, that is, parents and society.

Yet there is paradox here. If control there be, it is a control one can never feel as a control. The influence of heredity and earliest infancy on us cannot *feel* "other," because it is no longer "other." It cannot feel like a control from outside because it is a part of the outer world that has become inner world. To feel this part of self as "other," one would have to step outside of oneself and become another self. Or, to the extent that that "other" is unconscious, truly unconscious in the psychoanalytic sense, then one would have to translate conflict between conscious desire and unconscious into a radical separation of the two, whereas, in fact, conscious desire expresses unconscious desire as well.

Possibly, beneath this fear is a wish. "They" have made me something

I do not want to be. They can't do that to me. I won't take it! Perhaps under the fear of domination is a wish to be someone different from the person I am, perhaps even a purely intellectual mind exempted from unconscious wishes. If my guess is right, if this be the psychology of the fear of an inner identity, then the answer to the fear is to become more comfortable in one's own skin. That is not an easy task, but it is better than chasing the illusion that one can reconstruct or deconstruct oneself at will.

All of this, however, both the fear and the reassurance, may be speculation, since no one knows for sure if a personal identity has been written into our brains or not. In chapter 1, we have considered Douglas Hofstadter's speculation plus strong evidence from the brain scientists about the growing and ungrowing brain. A brain which changes from infancy to adolescence has room for an identity to be inscribed in it, but the chips (no pun intended!) are by no means all in.

Certainly, we do not have to assume that an identity theme is somehow inscribed on our brains. Although I believe I can trace a theme through Robert Frost's writings and biography, I need not go so far as to say it is "in" Frost. I need say no more than that I *can* phrase such a theme. I *can* find words like "big" or "unmanageable" which will trace continuities in Robert Frost's choices. I *can* invent a continuous dialectic of sameness and difference for his life in time and for his mutuality with his environment. I *can* connect his style of perception to his style of creation.

I *can* phrase such a theme. That does *not* (repeat *not*) imply there is such a theme inscribed somewhere in Robert Frost's brain decreeing that what Robert Frost does will emerge with a certain Robert Frost-ness. That second, deterministic idea simply does not follow from the first.

On the other hand, if we can phrase a certain Frost-ness, doesn't that suggest—not prove, to be sure, but suggest in some more loose way—that our analysis has arrived at something (some thing) that is somehow *in* Frost? Something that fits the growing and ungrowing of the brain reported by the neuroscientists. Their research into the "supercharged" brain of the child suggests that identity might indeed be inscribed by heredity and early infancy in the dendrites and axons of Frost's grey matter. Even if Frost's identity were so inscribed, though, when I read Frost's identity, my own brain and identity make the comparison and thereby become involved in the comparison. There is no way of knowing an identity except through another identity. But more of this in chapter 8.

Here, the only claim that I can finally make, the hypothesis that I am testing (and testing successfully, I think) is that I *can* read Robert Frost as a theme and variations. I *can* phrase a theme against which I can interpret his poems and his opinions as variations. I claim, then, no more than this: I, you, one can usefully consider Robert Frost holistically, as Paul Diesing defines that term.[56] That is, we can usefully think of Frost as an "individual in its individuality," a system of rules, goals, values, techniques, defense mechanisms, methods for maintaining or crossing boundaries, and procedures for exchanging, socializing, and deciding: Robert Frost as organism, as village, or as theater. Robert Frost as brain.

There may be other ways to imagine a human being holistically, but the one I have found best is to read Frost by means of a series of small themes that pervade various behaviors and converge those themes toward a single "identity theme." We can try out themes against Frost's actions, the words he wrote, the opinions he expressed, or the suicide he attempted. Whatever identity theme we settle for may or may not be "in" Robert Frost, but it certainly is "in" my reading of him, and thus we move from Frost and writing to the whole matter of reading and interpretation.

3

Frost Reading

The scene: London, 1913. The characters: Robert Frost and Ezra Pound. They are both living in London, and it is the first time the rural Frost has ever sat down to talk about poetry with another poet. Frost was fresh from America, and fresh from having read Edwin Arlington Robinson's 1910 volume, *The Town down the River*. Pound and Frost chuckle over the (now) well-known poem, "Miniver Cheevy."

The poem muses about a man who scorned the modern and lived the days of old Thebes and Camelot and Troy. Recalling his response three decades later, Frost wrote:

> I remember the pleasure with which Pound and I laughed over the fourth "thought" in [this stanza:]
>
> > [Miniver scorned the gold he sought,
> >   But sore annoyed was he without it:]
> > Miniver thought, and thought, and thought,
> >   And thought about it.
>
> Three "thoughts" would have been "adequate" as the critical praise-word then was. There would have been nothing to complain of, if it had been left at three. The fourth made the intolerable touch of poetry. With the fourth, the fun began . . .
>
> There is more to it than the number of "thoughts." There is the way the last one turns up by surprise round the corner, the way the shape of the stanza is played with, the easy way the obstacle of verse is turned to advantage. The mischief is in it.[1]

In reading Robinson's stanza, Frost literally *hears* it in terms of his characteristic big-little, manageable-unmanageable dualism: he *hears* the poet struggling against his poetic form. As Frost said of meter generally, the poet "must learn to get cadences by skillfully breaking the sounds of sense with all their irregularity of accent across the regular beat of the metre"—or, here, the fourth "thought" across the shape of the stanza. Frost perceives Robinson's extra "thought" as an opposition, either to the regularity of the stanza or the three "thoughts" that would have been "adequate." Four "thoughts," by the way, make a two times two, a double dualism. A fourth "thought" provides a detail that invokes the larger "fun" or "mischief" that Frost calls "the intolerable touch of poetry." Notice too how Frost balances off the big word "intolerable" with the little word "touch," how he converts his own complicated thought to mere childish "mischief," as in "Mending Wall" he makes his spring-like reaching out to his neighbor into "mischief" and elves.

Although we could never have predicted it, Frost's reading of the fourth "thought" should come as no surprise. Frost uses small knowns to call forth and manage big unknowns. That is his identity (or, at least, that is my effort to phrase Frost's style). If one can trace this style in everything he does, I would expect to see it in his reading as well as in his writings and his opinions, and I do.

You can almost tell ahead of time what Frost would single out from the next passage. Here Robinson describes the drunken, superannuated Mr. Eben Flood offering himself a swig of whisky on a hilltop:

> 'Only a very little, Mr. Flood—
> 'For auld lang syne. No more, sir: that will do.'
> So, for the time, apparently it did,
> And Eben evidently thought so too;
> For soon amid the silver loneliness
> Of night he lifted up his voice and sang,
> Secure, with only two moons listening,
> Until the whole harmonious landscape rang—
> 'For auld lang syne.' The weary throat gave out . . .

This is what Frost picked out:

The guarded pathos of "Mr. Flood's Party" is what makes it merciless. We are to bear in mind the number of moons listening. Two, as on the planet Mars. No less. No more . . . One moon . . . would have laid grief too bare. More than two would have dissipated grief entirely and would have amounted to dissipation. The emotion had to be held at a point.

> He set the jug down slowly at his feet
> With trembling care, knowing that most things break;
> And only when assured that on firm earth

It stood, as the uncertain lives of men
Assuredly did not . . .

There twice it gleams.[2]

Frost again picks out the two-ness of things, and he finds beauty in a
precise balance between that duality and something larger (like "Mars")
or stronger (like "grief"). Frost finds it beautiful when something small
succeeds in holding something larger to a point of balance. Once, he
put it especially simply. "Most things break."

Here, for example, is the way Frost perceives a single line from another
Robinson poem, this one a surrealistic study of suicide. Frost quotes
from the poem:

The miller's wife had waited long,
    The tea was cold, the fire was dead;
And there might yet be nothing wrong
    In how he went and what he said:
"There are no millers any more,"
    Was all that she had heard him say.

Frost comments:

> "There are no millers any more." It might be an edict of some power against
> industrialism. But no, it is of wider application. It is a sinister jest at the
> expense of all investors of life or capital. The market shifts and leaves them
> with a car-barn full of dead trolley cars. At twenty I commit myself to a life
> of religion. Now, if religion should go out of fashion in twenty-five years,
> there would I be, forty-five years old, unfitted for anything else and too
> old to learn anything else.[3]

Frost translates that fifth line into the against-ness he likes to perceive.
First he finds some power big enough to take on "industrialism." Next
he reads the line as a jest against "all investors of life or capital." Another
big issue. Then in his characteristic rhythm of expansion and contraction,
his mind seems to run from "investors" to the failure of the street-railway
companies. (He was writing in 1936, when the automobile companies
were buying up and closing down street railways, and you really could
find a "car-barn full of dead trolley cars.") Next he moves on to himself,
"I," and a "life of religion," and then religion is eclipsed by "fashion,"
a much lesser thing. All this from "There are no millers any more." He
hears that small known phrase bearing on several big unknowns.

His mind moves in a constant rhythm of small to large to small to
large, the small somehow managing to stave off or cope with or survive
within the large. It is this characteristic of his *own* mind that he discovers

and admires in Robinson's poetry and in other things he likes. Among his favorite reading, he included the *Odyssey* but not the *Iliad*, the escape from Troy and the homecoming rather than the deadlock and entanglement and mortality of the grander *Iliad* (or so I understand his preference). He singled out Poe and Emerson as favorites. Both deal with efforts to master supernatural forces by natural ones. Strangest of all, he liked such romances as *The Last of the Mohicans*, *The Prisoner of Zenda*, or *The Jungle Book*. They act out Frost's own exaggerated need for courage as a reaction against the unmanageable in himself. He would set up heroes and worship them (as he did with John F. Kennedy), and he tried to build himself up into the sturdy stoicism he admired. He was especially fond of Kipling; and, he said, "*Robinson Crusoe* is never quite out of my mind. I never tire of being shown how the limited can make snug in the limitless. *Walden* has something of the same fascination. Crusoe was cast away; Thoreau was self-cast away. Both found themselves sufficient."[4] Indeed this was the way he thought about all literature. "There are no two things as important to us in life and art," he said, "as being threatened and being saved."[5]

Understanding what Frost prizes is what a modern theory of personal identity adds to the old maxim, Beauty is in the eye of the beholder. Beauty is in the *I* of the beholder. When he looked at a Robinson stanza, Frost singled out the pairings and the balancings. He even created balancings where you or I might see none. For example, he found the fourth "thought" something that plays with the shape of the stanza and turned the obstacle of verse to advantage. He turned the phrase "no millers" into a general pattern of against-ness and the failure of commitment. He went so far as to imagine the double gleam of the double moon on Mr. Flood's jug, although Robinson's poem does not mention it.

It was from these appreciations of beauty in others' poems that Frost formed his own credo. Good practice is what yields poetry he finds beautiful. Hence, Frost *defines* poetry and metaphor as a stand-off: "There are many other things I have found myself saying about poetry, but the chiefest of these is that it is metaphor, saying one thing and meaning another, saying one thing in terms of another, the pleasure of ulteriority."[6]

This sense of balancing also comes across in his many comments on the tension between meaning and meter. "If one is to be a poet he must learn to get cadences by skillfully breaking the sounds of sense with all their irregularity of accent across the regular beat of the metre."[7] "I am never more pleased than when I can get these [metrical scheme and natural speech rhythm] into strained relation. I like to drag and break the intonation across the meter as waves first comb and then break stumbling on the shingle."[8] As he explained rhythm and meter to fellow-poet Robert Penn Warren, "The one's holding the thing back and the other's pushing it forward—and so on, back and forward."[9] "I want something there—the other thing—something to hold and something for me to put a strain on."[10]

As a psychological critic, I find it interesting that Frost had a psychological theory of reader response behind his poetics:

> We begin in infancy by establishing correspondence of eyes with eyes. We recognized that they were the same feature and we could do the same things with them. We went on to the visible motion of the lips—smile answered smile; then cautiously, by trial and error, to compare the invisible muscles of the mouth and throat. They were the same and could make the same sounds. We were still together. So far, so good. From here on the wonder grows. It has been said that recognition in art is all. Better say correspondence is all. Mind must convince mind that it can uncurl and wave the same filaments of subtlety, soul convince soul that it can give off the same shimmers of eternity.[11]

It is the most important balancing for him. Writer and reader mirror each other.

They do so even when poetry fails: "No tears in the writer, no tears in the reader. No surprise for the writer, no surprise for the reader."[12] And of course they resonate when poetry succeeds: "For me the initial delight is in the surprise of remembering something I didn't know I knew. I am in a place, in a situation, as if I had materialized from cloud or risen out of the ground. There is a glad recognition of the long lost and the rest follows."[13] Hence, whether Frost is functioning as author or as reader, success takes one and the same form:

> In literature it is our business to give people the thing that will make them say, "Oh yes I know what you mean." It is never to tell them something they don't know, but something they know and hadn't thought of saying. It must be something they recognize.[14]

The unfamiliar poem was something we knew all along. The unknown turns out to be the known.

Once mind has matched mind and soul has mirrored soul and recognition has been established, "At no point would anyone but a brute fool want to break off this correspondence. It is all there is to satisfaction; and it is salutary to live in the fear of its being broken off."[15] The possibility of alikeness being broken off and replaced by difference is essential to the fullness of experience. "How does a man come on his difference, and how does he feel about it when he first finds it out?"[16] "The object in writing poetry is to make all poems sound as different as possible from each other."[17] And finally that difference, that shock of recognition, leads into the unmanageable largeness at which Frost aims: "My poems . . . are all set to trip the reader head foremost into the boundless."[18]

Frost praises for all of poetry and art the special combination of the contained familiar and the boundless surprise that marks his own poetic themes and style. I hear in these quotations the two attitudes of "Mending Wall." They recur in his personal poetic theory, and they constitute the beauty he finds in the writing of others. "Every poem is an epitome of the great predicament; a figure of the will braving alien entanglements."[19] Poems run from delight, an originality or surprise, to wisdom, "a momentary stay against confusion."[20] "The figure is the same as for love. Like a piece of ice on a hot stove the poem must ride on its own melting."[21]

Frost sees more than poetry as balancing. He thinks, as we have seen, of religious men and politicians as well as poets this way. He sees politics and science as balancings and, he says, love. He fantasies in this synecdochic way. In short I will be able to trace that same combination of small known confronting and managing big unknown in other functions of Frost's identity, like his social opinions, his views on life in general, or his perceptions of other people. As the definition of identity would suggest, he sees *everything* in the same style or, more exactly, *I* can see Frost as seeing everything in the same style.

This concept of identity holds for you and me. We perceive, as Frost does, in a certain style, as a function of identity or an identity theme. We see things in terms of the expectations we hold, and those expectations in turn combine cultural and personal patterns. Hence, when I look at Robert Frost, I see him differently from the way you do. When I phrase his identity theme, I will arrive at a different formulation from yours. When I write, "I will be able to find that same combination in other functions of Frost's identity," what I am finding is at best partly "there." It is "in here," too.

What then is the status of identity? Is it merely some "subjective" maundering? An elaborate way of saying what is merely my "subjective" impression of Frost?

What is the status of perception itself? If what Frost perceives when he looks at Robinson's text is a function of his identity, then what I perceive when I look at the text of Frost's response to Robinson is a function of mine— How can that be? Surely the outer world controls my perceptions to some extent, at least. It is impossible, surely, to see this black and white " A " in front of me as a " Z " or to claim that "zebra" or "zombie" begin with A. The world is not just "subjective." Not every response is possible for a given stimulus, and there must be such a thing as a predictable response for us to be able to communicate with one another.

Robinson's poem is about a miller, m-i-l-l-e-r. It is not about a miler, m-i-l-e-r, or a milker, m-i-l-k-e-r, and no amount of identity-mongering will make it so. The print on the page rules out certain perceptions.

"Miller" means a grinder of grain. Or does it? My desk dictionary offers milling machines and moths as meanings 2 and 3 for "miller." Nevertheless, it is simply not possible for Frost to say that Robinson's stanza is about miller moths or machinists (without being mistaken, crazy, drunk, or doped). Then, of course, finding a miller, being creative and being committed to pairs and balances, Robert Frost may arrive at a *significance* for "miller" and its fixed meaning as grinder of grain which is richer than you or I might be able to create or at least different, his idea that the miller represents "all investors of life or capital." That is a distinction literary theorist E. D. Hirsch, Jr. would draw,[22] between a fixed meaning, established by the author's intention, binding on us all, and a personal significance, different for everyone.

Surely he is right, isn't he? There is no way for "miller" to be other than a grinder of grain. Or is there? No, of course there is not—except for people who are mistaken or who don't read English or are psychotically fixated on milling machines or moths. Even so, if we are formulating a psychology of literature, wouldn't we like our theory to take these unusual people into account, too? Stanley Fish has put it the other way round, lumping together "Normal Circumstances, Literal Language, Direct Speech Acts, the Ordinary, the Everyday, the Obvious, What Goes without Saying, and Other Special Cases."[23] Quite properly, it seems to me.

Such niceties aside, we should not unnecessarily limit our inquiry. We should not put the question as, Does the printed word "miller" control Robert Frost's mind, or does Robert Frost control "miller"? That would put stimulus and perceiver into an either-or. Either the stimulus dictates the response, or else the perceiver does and then it's all "subjective." That way of thinking about "subjective" and "objective" falsifies the process by forcing us into unreal extremes. We would have ruled out from the start the bottom-up *and* top-down, the outside-in *and* inside-out processes we have learned about from the psychologists, who tell us this more complex model of mind applies especially to reading.

Traditional psychology offers us the terms "exogenic" and "endogenic": responses that are caused from outside ourselves and responses that come from inside. If we start from the position that "subjective" and "objective" are inevitably mixed, that responses are necessarily *both* exogenic and endogenic, some interaction of inner personality and outer stimulus, then we can rephrase the central question of this book. What is the relation between Robert Frost's highly personal and individual commitment to small knowns balancing large unknowns and our uniform recognition (all of us who are neither psychotic nor mistaken, that is) that that stanza by E. A. Robinson talks about grinders of grain and not milling machines or moths? How does Frost's individual experience of the poem, his highly "creative" response, come from the text of a poem which is the same for all of us (who are not psychotic or mistaken)? To explore that question, I suggest we look at some other reactions to Robinson's poem, reactions less poetic, perhaps, than those of Robert Frost, but no less idiosyncratic.

4
The Miller's Wife and
the Six Professors

The scene: spring at a large midwestern university. 10:15 a.m. A seminar room. Around the long table and in outer rows of seats are gathered a score or so of professorial-looking types from the English department, some senior, some junior. About a quarter are women, some of them, it turns out, faculty wives. They have assembled for a "Working Teachshop" by the Visiting Fireman.

It is the morning after the lecture and party the night before. People are gearing up for the day or, having taught 9:00s, gearing down. Those seated at the table are holding photocopies of a poem. As they banter, they seem to be approaching the morning's exercise in a spirit of curiosity. Let's play the Visiting Fireman's game and see what happens.

The Visiting Fireman himself, neatly dressed if slightly hung over, sits in the middle of one long side. He speaks in a friendly but hesitant voice, feeling his way with this group, new to him. He begins by reading the poem aloud:

The Mill

The miller's wife had waited long,
  The tea was cold, the fire was dead;
And there might yet be nothing wrong
  In how he went and what he said:
"There are no millers any more,"
  Was all that she had heard him say;
And he had lingered at the door
  So long that it seemed yesterday.

Sick with fear that had no form
  She knew that she was there at last;

And in the mill there was a warm
   And mealy fragrance of the past.
What else there was would only seem
   To say again what he had meant;
And what was hanging from a beam
   Would not have heeded where she went.

And if she thought it followed her,
   She may have reasoned in the dark
That one way of the few there were
   Would hide her and would leave no mark:
Black water, smooth above the weir
   Like starry velvet in the night,
Though ruffled once, would soon appear
   The same as ever to the sight.

"The Mill," he announces, is by Edwin Arlington Robinson, 1920. This morning's consensus is, Not a great poem, but good. One senior man in American literature gravely opines that Robinson is "much underrated."

The Visiting Fireman remarks that he picked this particular poem because part of his lecture the night before dealt with Robert Frost's comments on it. He therefore thought the assembled company might find this poem a useful starting point. This morning, as advertised, he would like to apply some of the psychology of reading developed in the lecture the night before. Last night we looked at Robert Frost's reading of this poem as a function of his identity and at his identity as a theme and variations. Now, for something more practical, how can we apply all that to the teaching of literature? How can we use the personal quality of reading, as demonstrated by Frost, to deepen our students' reading? How can we use the theme-and-variations concept of identity to understand what we are doing when we teach?

Hence this workshop. How can the things we professors of literature teach enter into an otherwise personal response? The Visiting Fireman suggests they begin by comparing their own readings of "The Mill" to Robert Frost's. Would the assembled company be so kind as to fill in answers to the five questions on the questionnaire now being handed out?

Actually, of course, the Visiting Fireman has a hidden agenda, questions of his own, like those with which he—I—ended the last chapter.

If reading is a function of identity, as Frost's seems to be, does that make all readings and interpretations "subjective"?

How, if at all, does a text like this poem, "The Mill," control or dictate or
limit readers' readings?

Can we divide a reader's reading into a part controlled by the text and a
part which is personal to Robert Frost or indeed to these professors?

To elicit these questions, to test and discuss them, and perhaps even
to lay them to rest, the Visiting Fireman has put together some materials
for a workshop for professors of literature. If I coalesce several occasions
on which, as Visiting Fireman, I got groups of professors to work on
these materials, I come up with the scene with which this chapter began.
All told, I have collected forty-four questionnaires in America, on which
I am drawing in this chapter, and a number of others (similar but not
reported here) in Adelaide and Paris.

Meanwhile, back in that seminar room, the Visiting Fireman, ever
hopeful, distributes questionnaires. Sensing a tension in his audience,
he promises to hand out his own answers in exchange for their candor,
but that is not enough to ease the atmosphere. The professors assembled
round the seminar table are a little shy, a little reluctant, a little put on
their professional mettle.

1. To what does the clause "what was hanging from a beam" refer?
2. To what does the clause "What else there was" refer?
3. What is the most important single word in the poem? Why?
4. What does the miller's wife look like (features, build, clothing, etc.)?
5. Whom does she remind you of, and why?

The Visiting Fireman's questions artfully span a gamut from the most
"objective" to the most "subjective." You could also say they illustrate
different ideas of the way we read (or perceive). They range across three
models of the reading process. One is a "text-active" model of perception,
in which the poem is active, the respondent passive. In a "text-active"
model the poem dictates the response. In the second, a "bi-active" model,
the poem sets limits for the response, but within those limits the reader
is free to arrive at his or her own response. Both the poem and the
reader are active within their spheres, and each is passive in relation to
the other. Third is a "transactive" model in which the reader controls
the response. The reader is active, and the poem reactive.

Question 1 asks a grammatical question which I think most skilled
readers would agree has one definitely "right" and various "wrong"
answers. In that sense, it presupposes a "text-active" model of reading:
if poems dictate the responses of properly trained readers, "The Mill"
should dictate the right answer to a grammatical question asked of a
group of English teachers.

In form, Question 2 looks like 1, but there may well be no definitely right answer. A number of words and phrases would be acceptable, in that sense, "right." Still, most people would call some answers clearly wrong. Suppose you answered "the miller"?

I also had in mind in Questions 1 and 2 the concept of an "interpretive community." This is an idea developed by my fellow-theorist Stanley Fish. By it he accounts for the similarities in readings in academic situations (classrooms, for example, or learned papers) or in professional settings where interpretation matters, like courts of law or clinical conferences. Although interpretations can vary greatly as academic or psychiatric or jurisprudential fashions change, readings tend to be similar among any given group of readers so long as those readers share similar beliefs about the proper ways to read a poem, story, statute, judicial opinion, or patient's case history. When we ask a grammatical question of "The Mill," we apply the procedures and conventions of the community of university litterateurs, today's professors and students, to answer it. We use "interpretive strategies" that we learned from that "interpretive community." These, says Fish, "enable," "constitute," "make available" such ideas as a clause's referring to something.[1]

If Fish is correct, the professors' answers to Question 1 should show a clustering around the "right" answer and perhaps a scattering of wrong answers. The answers to 2, however, should show no particular clustering, since the "interpretive community," professors and students in American universities today, does not dictate any one answer to the question. Would the professors' answers demonstrate Fish's claim?

Question 3 asks for a more freely imaginative response. There are no "wrong" answers to "What is the most important word?" except (I suppose) words that do not occur at all in "The Mill." Could you dismiss "the" or "had" as wrong? I wonder. Suppose my answer began, "The most important word never appears in the poem itself. It is 'economics.'" Would I have committed myself to a wrong reading? Would you give me an F? (It comes close to Frost's reading, though.)

At any rate, I took the question from a book by David Bleich on "subjective" techniques of teaching. Bleich says an answer to this question "begins in complete subjectivity and is then transformed into judgments that appear to be objective."[2] The question implies that readers are wholly in control, but attribute their feelings to the activity of the poem. Would the professors' answers fit such a model?

Question 4 asks for even more projection, since the poem does not describe the wife at all. I wrote this question hoping to get answers that reflect today's most popular model for the reading process, articulated with particular lucidity and learning by the leading German theorist of reading, Wolfgang Iser. Iser's model is bi-active: the poem sets limits within which the reader is free to respond imaginatively as the reader sees fit. More precisely, Iser says the poem leaves gaps (here, the wife's appearance) which the reader feels impelled to fill, but the reader is free to fill them as he or she wishes.[3] If I am reading Iser's bi-active model correctly, and if he is right, then the professors should feel some compulsion to provide an image of the wife but they should all come up with quite different pictures.

Question 5 admits a wholly personal response. That is, anyone would understand a description answering 4 (thin, gaunt, even "like an Eskimo"). No one in the room except the answerer, however, could understand some of the answers possible for 5: my mother-in-law; a former girlfriend; a woman I saw once. Question 5 asks, in effect, what will responses to the poem look like if we encourage readers to be totally free and idiosyncratic? You could say 5 calls for a "very subjective" and 1 for a "very objective" answer. The responses certainly came out that way.

Incidentally, in designing my questions, I was meeting some objections to my studies of actual student readers raised by another theorist at an English Institute panel on reading.[4] He objected to my studying reading through the free associations of undergraduate readers on several grounds. They were not "competent." The search for free associations will hide the agreement of "ninety-three out of a hundred" readers. The questions led away from the text. And so on. Here, the readers are professors, committed to professional techniques in reading. The occasion was public, not a private interview. The questions pointed to the text rather than seeking long chains of associations away from the text. I believe the experience with the forty-four professors (or graduate students or faculty wives) who answered this questionnaire shows that the extraordinary variety I found in my *5 Readers Reading*[5] holds in this situation, as well as for undergraduate free associations.

The professors' answers seemed consistent, at any rate, with *5 Readers Reading*. About two-thirds of them gave the "right" answer to the grammatical Question 1 (thereby, I suppose, demonstrating that at least two-thirds of the professors were "competent" in my critic's sense):

The miller

the miller's body

The miller's corpse

the miller

THE DEAD MILLER

refers to a new subj. serving as gr. subj. of verb "could not have heeded."
 serves as antecedent of "it"—applies to hanged miller.

Inevitably, some arrived at special results:

fear or the fear of what the future holds

I have no idea.

Seems something dead, fearful, underscoring her fright.

Question 2, allowing more leeway, elicited more varied answers and
more varied wordings of the same answers. A majority, however, gave
the same answer as for Question 1.

THE DEAD MILLER

Again it is referentially the hanged body of No. 1.

This also refers to the hanging body of the miller.

Various possibilities: Hanged miller—smell of hanged miller (bowels loosening, etc.—in contrast to pleasant "fragrance"), what was "there" beside
 the fear, finally given form—the scene & situation—

Maybe those who said in answer to Question 2 the miller's body (in-
correct, in my reading) had some sort of carryover from Question 1.
They tended to use more words in 2, possibly expressing some uncertainty about their answers.

Some people wrote for 2 what seems to me, at least, the "right" answer,
namely, other things that embody the miller's outmoded craft:

The other reminders in the mill of the dead occupation.

Everything in the mill that reminds the wife of the Miller's life & that Millers
 are now unnecessary.

Still others suggested vague fears or futures or failures:

"what else there was" to "what he had meant" and "what was hanging
 from the beam." The referents are nonspecific and what floats around is
 the phantom of fear, or doubt or distrust—something that has no form.

It refers to that "something" that pervades the room, fills it with suspense.
 Not knowing what that something is half the reason for its powerful
 effect.

It refers to the *non*-reassuring aspects of the mill—what speaks to her fears (of the future), not to her knowledge of the past. Fear directs itself toward the future.

Questions 1 and 2 should evoke the effects of Stanley Fish's interpretive communities, and they do. The professors clearly were drawing on shared principles of reading and a common store of syntactic knowledge. On the other hand, there was no great unanimity. In particular, there was almost as much agreement in answer to Question 2 (where neither the poem nor our interpretive community assigns one "right" answer) as to Question 1 (where either the poem or the community does say one answer is right and the rest wrong). To explain these responses, interpretive communities may be necessary—I think they are—but they are not sufficient.

Question 3 asked what was the most important word in the poem and had no "wrong" answers within the poem. 3 elicited (as I had expected) a wide variety of answers.

dead.   is right at beginning of poem & puts weight on everything that follows

"dead."   It suggests what happens.

fear.   Because of her first phrase "There are no millers anymore" which is, it appears, the point of her fear of economic downfall. Such things as yesterday, past, linger

Fear.   It colors all responses to her encounters in the mill

hanging.   Because he's hanging (the miller) in a society that no longer needs him.

hanging.   everything in the poem seems to hang, be suspended, the wife waiting, the miller, no need, the dead miller, hope etc.

Some said there was *no* most important word. They left the question blank or fussed with it. (They demonstrated in this backhanded way that texts—in this instance, the text of the questionnaire—do not *force* responses.)

There isn't one.   To answer, though: dead
   so much death, everywhere—no more millers (other words seem to say again what it had meant).

I'm uncomfortable choosing—each word seems to be dependent on the others. "There" is used many times in different ways — as a place, as a non-place—The poem draws attention to *place* (The Mill) as determining action.

Others showed remarkable ingenuity:

> same.   The irony that there are no millers anymore—and yet no change, no mark, everything still appears the same.
>
> what.   brings reader in
>
> "No"   that which *is* disappears; connects to "nothing," "no millers," "no form," would not, "no mark."
>
> MIL.   The assonant found in "meal" & "miller"—it ties the entire poem together—especially in "mealy fragrance"
>
> mealy?   pleasant, warm ground-down grain, devastated people, "mealy-mouthedness" of the probably-uncomplaining wife to the miller, & miller to anyone who might have heard or understood
>
> yet.   she does not know—yet—and so the poem hangs in the moment before knowing, when she suspects, doesn't know, doesn't want to believe

There was a joker, naturally. The most important word? " 'Hangs.' It jars you."

One could say with Bleich that these answers begin in subjectivity and end in seeming objectivity, but does that statement do more than describe what is taking place? You could, of course, call these answers "subjective," but they make specific "objective" appeals to the poem. The answers draw on parts of the poem that are "objectively" present or, in a term Iser prefers, "given." There must be more helpful metaphors than "begins" and "ends" for developing the relation between the text, common to us all, and the unique feeling that this or that word is the most important. There is, for example, Iser's model in which the poem rules some answers out, but within those limits the reader can freely imagine meanings and pictures.

This is a freedom, though, some of our professors declined. Asked in Question 4 to project visually, some of the professors hesitated, agreed to make an image, but insisted they did not know for sure.

> I remember nothing of her appearance. She seems an image—abstract—of domesticity.
>
> She is not described at all, of course, and the poem seems to convey a sense of formlessness. There is a sense of evasion, of dimly making out the forms and outlines of things. Yet I see her as a heavy set woman, with a pale face, broad features, a woman who has worked hard all her life.
>
> No clue in poem—probably small, plain, calico & gingham—anything but velvet

They were, I take it, tacitly following one of the rules in our interpretive community of today's professors and students: Do not go beyond or outside the words on the page. Others, following the same rule, tried to reason an image into being from clues undeniably in the text:

> ? young?
>
> She is *probably* short, as she must look up at the beam where he is hanging
>
> Apron (tea). White face in fear, Hands red with hard work. Slightly overweight = the diet of poor people who eat a lot of starch.

Some simply went ahead and described her:

> Older woman, motherly, has known hard times
>
> apron, thin, long hands & fingers, gaunt cheeks
>
> Slightly over-weight, plain, middle-aged woman—wearing work clothes (housedress)
>
> like a fat Russian peasant-woman in late middle-age

Others resorted to more far-fetched pictures and analogies:

> Not described—we are free to create our own image—I see a Breughel.
>
> Like a weaker version of the woman in Grant Wood's "American Gothic"
>
> Several possibilities: the mother in the Katzenjammer Kids strip (older, obese/sturdy/hard-farm working immigrant with apron)—in this case suicide results of economy, *or* Nastasia Kinsky (grey peasant dress unbuttoned at the top showing inner breast & chest wall, hair seductively falling over left eye, pushed back, falls again—then suicide due to jealousy, etc.

The variability in these pictures raises, for me, a number of doubts about a bi-active model like Iser's in which the reader freely imagines within limits fixed by the poem. For one thing, Iser writes as though the bulk of the response were controlled by the poem and the reader simply fills in some inessential gaps. The poems these people describe, however, are *so* different (Grant Wood, Breughel, thin wife, fat wife, Katzenjammer Kids and Nastasia Kinsky) that the balance seems rather the other way. Also, the answers to Questions 1 and 2 suggest that, even in simple grammatical matters, readers are not constrained or limited. Finally, it is not clear to me that readers are "impelled," as Iser seems to say, to fill in gaps. Several of these professors simply refused. Perhaps they are showing that the wife's appearance is not a "gap" in Iser's sense.

To the last and most projective question of the five, there were the predictable blanks and responses like—

no one

I can't think of anyone right now

Can't think of a literary character just now

As in that last response, most of these professors of literature assumed, more or less automatically, that what was called for was a literary association, and most provided one, although my question made no such stipulation. I take it they were following another—I will not call it a "rule," but a bias of our profession: Only literature is relevant to literature.

Some of their literary associations were fairly predictable, others quite ingenious:

Chaucer—connotations of famous Miller?

The Wife in "Death of a Salesman"

Tristan, Romeo

Woman in the Death of the Hired Man, Hedda Gabler

The old peasant woman whose shoes Heidegger writes about in "The Origin of Art"—because she seems to have been totally and unreflectively absorbed in her work (or her husband's) until the event which precipitates the poem occurs. Then, she is incapable of going on.

Others did what, for the purposes of my demonstration, I had hoped for. They came up with associations personal to them, unsharable by the rest of us:

An old woman I saw once.

My grandmother—because she was old world & full of care & overworked

My Aunt Betty, who discovered her husband dead on his workshop floor

A former girlfriend, a timorous and dependent person, who gave meaning to her own life by identification with others — an identification with me I couldn't tolerate in the end.

They recalled figures entirely personal to themselves, people no one else in the room would know—except for—

She does not remind me of anyone I know. In her fear that something may have happened to hurt a loved one, she reminds me of me.

Others turned to works of art or places, personal recollections that were not entirely personal but partly cultural:

Woman figure in Dorothea Lange's depression photo. Sense of being lost, bereft, nowhere, empty.

Any Iowa farmer's wife, perhaps from a photo in the depression, black & white

I saw many working women in England who had that stoical air about them; they were worn by life, not very "well cared for" but still cheery and tough. She's probably like that only without much fight left in her. Her ending seems so quiet and undramatic—just a bowing to the inevitable.

Finally, others *imagined* a person to be reminded of:

She reminds me of someone who someone wants taking a less active role—content to let things happen "They also serve who stand & wait" She is unaffected by what's happening & partly paying no attention

And, of course, there was a joker. "Whom does she remind you of?" "The miller."

So far, we have been looking at answers by many different people to one question. Although these are skilled professional readers, although they are part of an interpretive community—American university teachers of literature—although most are drawing on an essentially similar "New Critical" training in close analysis of the words on the page, their answers vary all over the place. Question 1 has "right" and "wrong" answers, but after that, responses go every which way.

When we look at many answers to single questions, we can trace some rather vague patterns, but the whole picture is a jumble. We can get much more coherence, if, instead of comparing many persons' answers to one of the five questions, we look at one person's answers to all five questions, paying the close attention to choice of words that a psychoanalyst would. For example,

1. body hanging there
2. the only thing that was left was his found body—
3. fear   gives feeling of dread
4. no idea—housewife—heavy set; placid
   air of waiting—doesn't pay much attention
   Keeps on with her

5.   She reminds me of someone who someone wants taking a less active role—content to let things happen "They also serve who stand & wait" She is unaffected by what's happening & partly paying no attention

In these five answers by someone I'll call Professor One, I can read back from the last to the first. Answer 5 seems to have a slip of the pen: the repeated "someone," as if the final clause could stand alone, "Someone wants taking a less active role," as if that "someone" could apply to One herself as well as to the miller's wife. (Evidently she felt rushed—see 4.) To 5, the most projective of the questions, the one that allows most room for individual feelings and associations, she speaks of someone "less active," who only stands and waits, who is partly paying no attention.

I see the same theme in her 4: placid, waiting, not paying attention. Again, as though what Professor One was saying applied equally to the miller's wife and to herself, she does not finish her last clause in 4. Perhaps she as well as the miller's wife is not paying attention. Perhaps she has identified herself with the wife.

In 3, she names "fear" as the most important word because it "gives feeling of dread." The word does something to One. It "gives feeling." The phrasing is passive and vague, and the verbs in 2 are exaggeratedly passive: "The only thing that was left was his found body." Finally, in 1, "body hanging there," we get a "correct" answer to this "objective" question, but stated so as to emphasize the theme of passivity ("hanging") and vagueness ("there") that I find more obvious in her longer, more projective responses.

Sometimes it is difficult to formulate a theme for such laconic materials. Possibly the thread I see in Professor One's reading will appear more clearly if we contrast Professor Two's set of five responses:

1.   refers to a new subj. serving as
gr. subj. of verb "could not have heeded." serves as antecedent of "it"—
applies to hanged miller.

2.   2d attribution of something in the mill—1st thing being "fragrance"

3.

4.   Unspecified—yet implied she follows, by drowning, her husband's departure by hanging.

5.   Tristan, Romeo

Two is reluctant to project at all: he leaves 3 blank and insists in 4 that the wife's looks are "Unspecified." He makes up the lack by a process of inference which he attributes to the poem: the poem "implied" she drowned. Similarly, in 5, he explained to me afterwards, Tristan and Romeo fit in a sort of logical way. Each is a literary figure in a double suicide or mutual love-death who commits suicide on seeing his beloved dead. Two's appeal to logic and observable behavior (as in 4) outweighed the woman's sex: few respondents to 5 were reminded of men by the miller's *wife*.

The wife reminded him of literary figures, Tristan and Romeo, and he showed in 1 and 2 a similar turning away from the physical world toward language or literature. In 1, he spelled out a grammatical answer to a grammatical question exactly, almost fussily. In 2 he provided a grammatical answer—two grammatical answers—to a question that most people answered by an appeal to the events. In 4 he phrased the distressing facts of the poem in tangled euphemisms, "departure" for death or suicide, "follows" for the second death. From just these brief responses, I can phrase a pair of themes that will unify Two's responses for me: displacement to logic, language, or surface behavior; conversely, a reluctance to imagine what is not directly observable.

Young Professor Three was unusual in trying to be witty:

1. The husband (miller) who has hanged himself. Poem draws attention to, depicts the transformation of person → object ("it" followed her); woman submerged beneath water, which then heals itself.

2. Various possibilities: Hanged miller—smell of hanged miller (bowels loosening, etc.—in contrast to pleasant "fragrance"), what was "there" beside the fear, finally given form—the scene & situation—

3. I'm uncomfortable choosing—each word seems to be dependent on the others. "There" is used many times in different ways—as a place, as a non-place—The poem draws attention to *place* (The Mill) as determining action.

4. We don't know; the poem doesn't tell us. Wet.

5. The miller.

She, too, is reluctant to project in 4 and 5. Her jokes in 4 and 5 serve as an amusing evasion of the imagining the questionnaire asked her to do. Her jokes take us, like Professor Two's focus on language, somewhat stubbornly back to what is demonstrable and obvious. Other themes: smells (2), body wastes (2), being "wet" (2, 4), autonomy and dependency both for herself and for the words (3), persons as inanimate objects (1) and vice versa (1), delivering a precise and "professional" reading of the poem even if not called for (1). A psychoanalytic critic might well call this cluster of themes of self-rule and rule by others, obsessional, or, in a bodily terminology, "anal" themes. That is, to make a unity of this reading, I draw (from *my* interpretive community) psychoanalytic accounts of the kind of conflict parents and children have over who is autonomous and who is dependent. Whose rules will be followed, particularly about delivering from one's body something that may or may not be a living part of oneself? Possibly Professor Three applied that question to her own feelings about this questionnaire: Will I let this Visiting Fireman get something out of me?

I will call the next reader Professor Four, although I am not sure whether this woman was a professor or a graduate student.

1. fear   or the fear of what the future holds
2. millers who are no more.
3. fear: Because of her first phrase "There are no millers anymore" which is, it appears, the point of her fear of economic downfall. Such things as yesterday, past, linger
4. Older woman, motherly, has known hard times
5. poverty or a woman on the brink of it.

The themes that come across to me are fear—the word occurs four times—, loss, and deprivation or poverty, specifically in an economic sense (2, 3, 4, 5). In her metaphors, the future is a container that holds something to fear (1). Poverty is a pit one can fall into (5). She gives graphic versions of psychosocial deprivation from a "primary caretaker." I would call the container and pit symbols for what Four calls "motherly." One ultimate fear (in psychoanalytic theory) is annihilation at the hands of such a failing caretaker. Four repeats the threat of annihilation twice (2, 3), and she attributes the phrase to the wife instead of the husband. Four's defense against this fear seems to be simply to face the danger, as the analysts might say, counterphobically: to fear the future, to know hard times, to be on the brink. If the choice is fight or flight, Four says fight: accept the fear and live with it.

The dominant motif I see in Professor Five's responses is also fear, but with a somewhat different tone:

1. The miller's wife's fears of her husband's suicide: she sees him *as if* hung
2. It refers to the *non*-reassuring aspects of the mill—what speaks to her fears (of the future), not to her knowledge of the past. Fear directs itself toward the future.
3. "Dead"

The "dead" fire suggests the failures—and fears—which haunt the poem.

4. I remember nothing of her appearance. She seems an image—abstract— of domesticity.

5. She does not remind me of anyone I know. In her fear that something may have happened to hurt a loved one, she reminds me of me.

Five's last, startlingly candid answer may be saying how his whole set of responses reflects some anxiety of his own, leading to his error in the "objective" question, 1. The other answers suggest he may have a characteristic way of speaking about that fear: saying it applies to the unknown rather than the known, a kind of denial. The miller is only "as if" hung (1). Something "may have happened" (5). Fears apply to the necessarily unreadable future (2) and to abstractions, the "non-reassuring aspects" of a mill (2), or the "nothing" of an abstract image of domesticity (4). Five moves from relatively concrete images, "mill," "fire," to abstractions: fear, failure, domesticity, future. The hanged man is only "as if" hung. He thus wards off literal fear: "She does not remind me of anyone I know." But he does make a mistake in 1.

Professor Six's responses somewhat resemble Five's:

1. The miller

2. His absence

3. "No"   That which *is* disappears; connects to "nothing," "no millers," "no form," would not, "no mark."

4. apron, thin, long hands & fingers, gaunt cheeks

5. Woman figure in Dorothea Lange's depression photo. Sense of being lost, bereft, nowhere, empty.

If Five was defending against anxiety, Six was dealing with a sense of absence, emptiness, or depression, as she (like Five) frankly says in her last response. She chooses "no" for the most important word, coupling it with phrasings of absence. In 2 she speaks of absence directly, and in 4 she imagines thinness and gauntness and, first of all, an apron obscuring the woman's body. In 1, perhaps one can find a significance in her speaking of "the miller" who is absent instead of "the miller's body" which is present.

In short, if I look question by question at all the forty-four sets of answers, I can find no coherence, even for the question with a "right" answer. If, however, I look at the sets of answers person by person, I can formulate a theme or themes that permeate each of these six sets of five answers:

One: being passive and vague
Two: displacement to language
Three: "anal" themes
Four: loss from a mother
Five: fear of loss, displacement to the unknown
Six: depression at absence; painful acceptance

Permeates? Does Two's displacement to language or Three's anality enter into a statement of grammar as much as an imagining of the wife's appearance? Evidently they do, to judge from the small differences in phrasing even the "correct" answer, such details as "body" instead of "corpse" or "miller" instead of "husband."

"Identical" answers can evidently come from very different underlying concerns. That is to say, in the professors' readings, we are dealing with a two-level process. The lower level consists of simple readings of letters, words, sentences, and syntax that are, more or less, the same for all. The higher level consists of a governance that is highly individual. Psychologists studying learning and memory notice, "In strategy-free tasks, such as simple recognition and judgments of recency or frequency, there is little evidence of person-to-person variation." "Individual differences are likely to appear if the tasks involved some degree of cognitive complexity." "What could be the underlying reason for these individual differences?," they ask, and answer: "the executive processes of the modal information-processing model."[6]

That is, in using questionnaires to study cognitive performances, we are dealing with a feedback system governed by what they call "executive routines" that plan, coordinate, sequence, monitor, and check the outcomes of various sub-performances. If you are testing only the sub-performances, a questionnaire will show only quantitative differences, like speed, accuracy, or percentage of correct answers. If you look at complex performances, like our professors' interpretations, performances that require more planning, checking, and coordinating, then personal, qualitative differences appear, because you are drawing on these more sophisticated executive processes.

It is important, obviously, for researchers to recognize that *all* cognitive tasks involve both the higher-level executive and the lower-level sub-processes. It is particularly important for basing psychological or literary research on questionnaires.[7] The same answer on a questionnaire may not express the same high-level executive process at all. If one is simply counting deodorant users or Democrats that may not matter. If one is studying reading, it will matter very much.

The answers to Questions 1 and 2 look more or less alike for most of the people who filled out the questionnaire. If we were to judge by those answers alone, we might conclude that most of the professors were reading the same text in more or less the same way. We might decide that the poem was constraining or limiting their responses. We might infer they were applying the canons of an interpretive community. We might say they were constrained another way, by my questionnaire or by the workshop in which we were all engaged.

Having the answers to Questions 3–5 as well, though, we can see that the professors were reading the same text in very different ways. Some were concerned with realism, some with logic, some with language, some with literary form. Some were concerned with fear, others with loss, and others with deprivation. When we interpret their responses thematically, moreover, it looks as though they brought these concerns into play in answering even the "objective" questions.

Question 1 asked a question with "right" and "wrong" answers. The "right" answers say the same thing, but phrase it slightly differently (as in these, a sample from the whole group of forty-four):

The miller

the miller's body

The miller's corpse

the miller

THE DEAD MILLER

By contrast, since Question 5 asked each person to imagine or remember in a very personal way, people's answers to Question 5 both look different and say very different things: a woman paying no attention, a woman in a Dorothea Lange photograph, poverty, Tristan or Romeo, the miller, the professor himself.

We can, however, phrase for any one set of five answer similarities that run through all five, just as we can trace similarities or Frost-themes in Robert Frost's poems, his opinions, or his readings. To be sure, it may be easier to trace Frost's consistencies in his poems than in his opinions, but one *can* trace them in both. So here. We *can* trace the same concerns in both the "objective" Answer 1 and the "subjective" Answers 3, 4, or 5.

We may find it easier to see identity in the answers to Question 5 (or 4 or 3). We may find it difficult to see identity if we look only at the answers to Question 1. (Or we will see it only as capitals or lower case or such slight differences in phrasing as "the miller," "the miller's body," or "his found body.") Nevertheless, if we put the slight differences in the answers to 1 and 2 alongside the considerable differences in the answers to 3, 4, and 5, we can, to my satisfaction anyway, trace a consistency through all the answers by one person.

If so, if we can trace such a similarity, then both the "objective" answers and the "subjective," the similar answers to 1 and the very different answers to 5, must come from one and the same process. In that process themes of interest or concern to the answering professors shaped the way they worked with a text which was the same for all of them and these concerns also shaped the way they used the "New Critical" and other skills they all shared. *Both "objective" and "subjective" responses emerge from a single process in which "subjectivity" shapes "objectivity."* In fact, the very words, "subjective" and "objective" turn out not to be making any useful distinction.

Robert Frost is not the only one to read creatively, then. To judge from our six professors (or the collection of forty-four sets of answers which represents them), we all read as functions of our identities. The professors read "The Mill" as a function of their identities, and I interpret the professors' questionnaires in terms of mine. The same idiosyncrasy must go on in teaching—this was the Visiting Fireman's conclusion that spring morning on a midwestern campus. The professors teach "objectively" but in the manner of their personal identities. Students learn "objective" things that they can deliver on examinations and term papers, but they learn and believe them in personal terms—but more of that in chapter 7.

As a general principle, our six professors' readings of the miller's wife show that any reader is reading both individually and typically. Frost and the professors may have very different experiences of Robinson's "The Mill," but they all do experience a poem in which Edwin Arlington Robinson says something about a miller and his wife. They all do talk about the obsolescence of mills, the miller's suicide, and the wife's subsequently drowning herself. Since collecting these, however, I have had one reader, in Adelaide, and then several others, justify their readings that the wife did *not* kill herself, by pointing out that the poem only says she *thought about* drowning herself. Even so, no one maintained that this was a poem about a millworker or a milling machine or a miller moth. Indeed, each of us is *necessarily* arriving at a reading which *all* the other readers shared in at least some ways.

With the professors, with Robert Frost, with you, and with me, two seemingly inconsistent things are going on. We all share the same text. Moreover, each of us uses skills for interpreting words and sentences which are exactly the same for most people. But we each arrive at a highly individual reading. How can we visualize the interaction of these different, individual responses with a shared text and techniques?

5

"We Are Round"

Frost's experience of "The Mill" differed from any of the forty-four professors' experiences. To judge from the six we looked at closely, the forty-four professors seem to have had forty-four different experiences, to say nothing of the teacher from Adelaide. Frost and the professors all "got" Robinson's poem, however, and in that sense they have all read the same poem. The poem was different for all of them—but the same.

These various readings of "The Mill" seem to me to pose two large questions. First, if everyone responds to the poem in a different and individual way, how can we explain or articulate that fact? Second, given that everyone responds individually, then how can we explain or make sense of the equally obvious fact that we also respond somewhat the same?

This mix of sameness with difference also seems to me to raise the philosophical question of other minds. That is, we each feel the poem differently from any other reader (we think!), but we also feel it somewhat the same. (Evidently, since we can compare our reactions.) We live in private, internal worlds, but we *do* communicate. How?

The mix of sameness and difference in the literary process also seems to me akin to the classical philosophical problem of mind-body or mind-brain. (That is the reason this book has the odd title it does.) We have a brain which is an organ like a lung or a pancreas, shaped about the same for everybody. We have a mind, an experiencing self, which is unique for each one of us, and that mind is, we all believe, in our brains somehow. The mind of Robert Frost is uniquely his own, but the brain of Robert Frost is, give or take a little, like your brain or mine. How can we imagine one organ giving rise to two thousand million different versions of the human?

The brain physiologists tell us of a growing and ungrowing brain. If they are right, Robert Frost's use as a child of his heredity and his early experiences inscribed his individual, uniquely gifted mind on the pulpy neurons, dendrites, and axons of his physical brain. But if they are right, we all did the same thing. How can we put that process into words that will speak of Robert Frost in particular?

For literary critics, the problem becomes particularly pointed. For any reader of English an   A   is an A, a   B   is a B, and so on. Similarly the printed letters m-i-l-l-e-r are "miller" for everybody. The physical poem we read or write is, obviously, the same for everyone, and everyone processes it physically more or less the same way, but the meaning each of us derives from those a's and b's or that "miller" differs for each of us. (Frost, for example, interpreted it as "all investors of life or capital.") The experience of the poem differs even more. How, again, can we reconcile two such differing processes? More specifically, how can we put together reading as an individual act (as Frost and our forty-four professors demonstrate it) and reading as an activity shared by an "interpretive community"?

I am neither philosopher, cognitive scientist, nor physiologist of the brain. I do not expect to lay the mind-brain problem to rest. I cannot give you a cell-by-cell account of the way our brains engage literature. I do hope, however, I can give you a way of thinking about the literary process that will in turn yield a way of thinking about the self. Not a full-fledged explanation, but a guiding idea, a metaphor, a picture. Enough so that one can articulate that curious combination of individuality and shared humanity which is the human experience of literature, of life, of anything, really.

Writing literature involves complicated questions about individual style and inspiration. As for reading, however, we are asking two specific questions. How can we articulate everyone's responding differently? How can we articulate everyone's responding—partly—the same?

The first I have already tried to answer by a concept of identity. In the opening chapters I was able to formulate a certain Frost-ness in the way the poet wrote and read and lived. In chapter 4, I was able, on much less evidence, to arrive at a certain One-ness for Professor One, Two-ness for Two, and so on up to Six. An "identity theme" phrases the sameness, consistency, or style of a person. There will be sameness but also difference, since each new moment of reality asks of us a new response. By thinking of identity as, first, an identity theme, and second, variations, we can put into words the dialectic of sameness and difference that is a whole human life. Identity says no more than that we *can* find some such personal style for each of us or, more exactly, that we can phrase such personal styles for one another. One *can* propose a certain Frost-ness or Professor Three-ness. One *can* trace a personal style in the many different things Frost or Three does.

Reading, writing, listening to the words of others—these are simply acts among other acts we carry on. They too allow one to infer a sameness or continuity. This concept of identity gives us a way of talking about the uniqueness of a person's reading or writing (as I have said in earlier books),[1] and to that extent answers our first question.

The second question this book asks, however—If we all respond to language differently, then how can we communicate?—requires that we refine that theme and variations concept of human identity. If you say, The miller hanged himself, but I interpret language as a function of my personal identity, what, if anything, prevents me from hearing you as saying, The miller made a mistake (hung himself up)? Or, The miller was a picture? How can we arrive at right and wrong interpretations? After all, we do.

I find help in an idea from nineteenth-century science, namely, feedback. James Clerk Maxwell, the mathematical physicist renowned for the electromagnetic theory of light, published in 1868 the classic paper on feedback in the governors of steam engines.[2] It was not until World War II, however, that scientists, confronted with the problem of anticipating the maneuvers of gunners, first applied the mathematics of feedback to living organisms. It is sometimes said that the first paper to make this transfer of an engineering concept, the governing of energy through feedback, to the biological idea of processing information was the classic "Behaviour, Purpose, and Teleology" by Arturo Rosenblueth, Julian Bigelow, and Norbert Wiener.[3]

Historically, feedback as a biological concept descends from Walter B. Cannon's medical idea of homeostasis, the idea that the body's systems of chemicals and hormones self-correct so as to maintain various balances. Incidentally, this was an idea basic to Freud's thinking. He believed that every organism tends to seek a constant, low or zero level of excitation. Freud thought this the deepest level of human motivation, governing even the pleasure principle. He called it variously the "Nirvana principle" or the "principle of constancy" or the death instinct "beyond the pleasure principle." Ernest Jones goes so far as to claim that in this idea (which he got from G. T. Fechner) Freud anticipated Cannon's homeostasis and the whole science of cybernetics.[4] I am not so ambitious on Freud's behalf. I want to claim only that feedback is deeply consistent with psychoanalytic psychology.

In 1940 the application of feedback theory to biological creatures set off one of the most astonishing confluences of scientific thought in our own or perhaps any century. Norbert Wiener tells the story in the introduction to his mathematical text, *Cybernetics* (1948), and Howard Gardner in his history of cognitive science.[5] Mathematicians like Wiener, John von Neumann, and Alan M. Turing, electrical engineers like Vannevar Bush and Claude Shannon, physiologists like Arturo Rosenblueth and Warren McCulloch, anthropologists like Gregory Bateson and Margaret Mead, and even an economist like Oskar Morgenstern all studied information processing through feedback and what the feedback implied for biological and social processes. Feedback quickly became part of the general theory of information and communication, central not only to the psychological investigation of perception and movement but to what was quaintly called "the modern ultra-rapid computing machine."[6]

With feedback (or, more generally, cybernetics, or, still more generally, information processing), we come to an idea seminal for all those modern disciplines we call "cognitive science." Howard Gardner has traced the spectacular growth of this combined discipline in psychology. So far as this book is concerned, the concept of feedback enables us to bring together several cognitive disciplines as they bear on literary thought: physiological descriptions of the architecture and chemistry of the brain; psychological accounts of perception, memory, and cognition, particularly as they apply to reading; contemporary theories of computers and artificial intelligence, engaging problems akin to the critic's "interpretation"; and finally a psychoanalytically conceived identity unifying the behavior of Robert Frost.

For a straightforward instance of feedback, think about driving a car. Imagine that you are driving down what is for a few yards, anyway, a straight road. Imagine, if you will, that you are driving in the mountains of Crete, where no road stays straight for very long, but becomes a series of hairpin turns on the edge of the mountain. Further, there is little shoulder and no guardrails, only a shrine for a quick prayer as you tumble off the cliff. Mentally you might say to yourself, to feel safe, I should stay about a meter from the right hand edge of the road.

Accordingly, as you drive along, if you see that the distance between your right front wheel and the right edge of the road has become less than a meter, half a meter say, you feel a bit tense, and you turn the steering wheel left until the right front wheel is again a meter from the edge of the road. Conversely, if you find that distance is more than a meter, so that the left side of the car is getting too close to the rocks on the other side of this narrow road, a different source of anxiety, you turn the steering wheel right until you have brought the right front wheel again to one meter from the edge.

From your output, your steering, you are feeding back information, your perception of the right front wheel's position. You compare that information to the position you had earlier decided on. From the difference you detect between the standard you had set and the position you now see, you derive another piece of information: how far to move the steering wheel so as to position the right front wheel to achieve zero difference between its position and your standard and so to close the feedback loop.

Figure 1 diagrams that process:

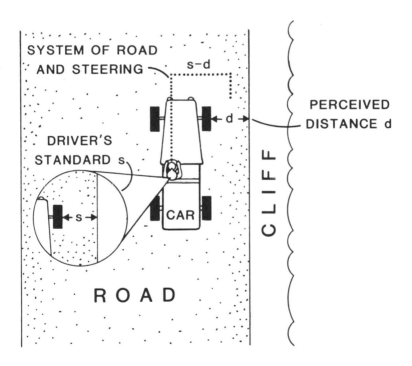

Figure 1. Driving along a road in Crete

I position the steering wheel a certain way, acting out from myself into the environment of car and road. We could think of my action in the most general terms as trying something out. Really, I am putting a hypothesis out into the world. That outer reality then feeds back to me information about what it did upon receiving my output. The steering gears, the road, the tires position the car in a certain way as a result of the way I turned the steering wheel. I get a response to my hypothesis. Then I sense whether the car is closer or less close to the right edge of the road than I want it to be, and I turn the steering wheel to right or left to bring that error as near to zero as possible.

In effect, on testing the environment, I am receiving information, my perception of the right front wheel's position d. I compare that datum to the position I had earlier decided on, my standard s. From the difference between them, s − d, I estimate how far to move the steering wheel so as to position the right front wheel to achieve zero difference between its position and my standard (s − d = 0). I may not get it right the first time, and in that case I get another, presumably smaller, s − d error signal. By trial and error (and feedback is precisely what trial and error is), I eventually bring s − d to 0 or near enough to 0 so that I feel all right about it. I minimize the error signal and so close the feedback loop.

We could schematize that process as in Figure 2.

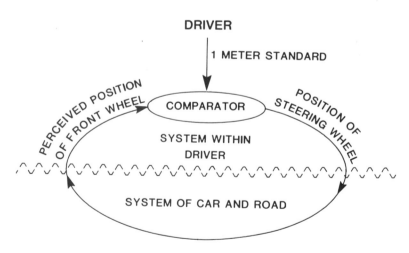

Figure 2.   Feedback diagram of car and driver

We are talking about a feedback loop, that is, a system in which the car and road feed back to the driver the results of his own actions, and he modifies those actions accordingly. More exactly, the driver, by positioning the steering wheel at a certain angle, tests the car and road. As he acts, he puts what amounts to a physical hypothesis out into car and road, and they in turn respond. He reads that response as the distance between the right front wheel and the edge of the road, and he compares that distance to his standard, the distance he wants to see, one meter. If the difference is positive, that is, if the car is more than one meter from the edge, he may position the wheel still further in the direction he already has. If the difference is negative, if the car is less than one meter from the edge, he turns the wheel back from the position he had put it in.

I realize the driving technique I am describing is rather primitive: an experienced driver really measures the rate of change in the right front wheel's position. The point is, however, that the driver compares what he does see with what he wants to see and uses that difference to correct his own output. In general terms, the driver's output is fed back to the driver's input and used to correct the output.

So far we have talked only about correcting for one's own errors. Suppose there is a puff of wind between those Cretan mountains and it pushes you to the right. Then you will have to turn the steering wheel to the left to get yourself back at the desired distance. Suppose there is a stiff wind blowing you to the right all the time. You may have to keep the steering wheel turned slightly to the left to maintain the one meter distance from the right edge of the road that feels right to you. An outside stimulus, like a puff of wind or a curve in the road, thus elicits a response, *but not in a simple stimulus-response way.* Rather it becomes part of a continuing loop of control, as in Figure 3.

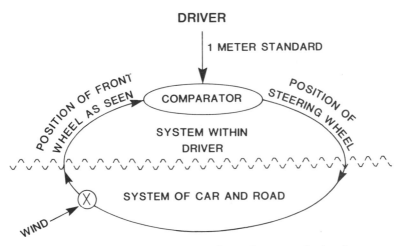

Figure 3.   Feedback diagram of car, driver, and stimulus

A puff of wind will add its effect into the feedback loop, changing the net position of the car that I see, leading me to turn the steering wheel in response.

The wind does not in and of itself prescribe a certain response, however, nor do I respond to the puff of wind in a simple stimulus-causes-response way. Rather, I calculate a response as part of the whole process of control and guidance, which now includes the puff of wind. I calculate or try out a response to the wind that will maintain my standard of one meter from the right. If there were a puff of wind *and* if the road curved at the same time so that I remained one meter from the right, I might not turn the steering wheel at all in response to the stimulus of the wind. In other words, any one stimulus has to be added to all the other stimuli and to the input being fed back toward the standard. That way, you arrive at a net change which you then compare to the standard. Control comes from the standard at the center rather than from the stimulus "out there," at the periphery.

In general, then, we do not passively respond to stimuli. Rather, we have an expectation about our world or what psychologists and neuroscientists sometimes call a "set." The brain physiologists can literally observe its activity (in the pyramidal tract system which originates in the neocortex and serves as the output system of the primary motor area of the cerebral cortex).[7] But let me put off anatomical jargon. As we change our "set," we bring to bear on our world different expectations. We therefore change the hypotheses we test against our world. The general principle is: We prepare for stimuli and actively search our environment for them.

Hence we can make driving in Crete into a generalized feedback model of human behavior (Figure 4).

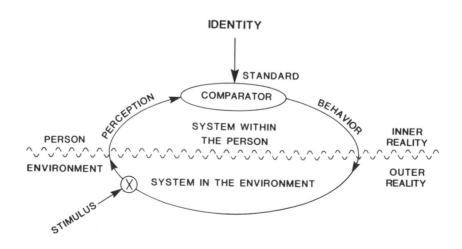

Figure 4. Generalized feedback picture of human activity

In effect, when I position the steering wheel at a certain angle, my output tests the world. By my behavior I put a hypothesis out into my environment to see what my environment will return. Then I compare that return, a perception, to my standard—the perception I want to have—and I add or subtract from my behavioral output, my "hypothesis," to elicit a return that feels right according to my standard. In other words, I seek a return that leaves me with no more error than I can comfortably tolerate. One can state this single loop mathematically in differential equations which are quite simple and familiar to engineers (but, unfortunately for my purposes, completely alien to most humanists and likely to remain so).

I would like you to notice four things about this picture. First, it involves three key elements, not two. Second, behavior controls perception not vice versa. Third, the process may look machine-like, but emotions—feelings—govern its operation. Fourth, the driving loop is more or less the same for everybody. I want to develop these four points in detail, because Figure 4 is central to, in a sense, *is* my thesis in this book.

Three elements, not two

First, there are *three* elements essential to the network. I emphasize that there are three, because psychology textbooks typically leave out the crucial one of the three when they explain feedback.[8]

1) There is the *feeding back* of the output (my behavior) through its consequences to something I perceive, a sensory input. This is what gives feedback its name, and the textbooks never fail to mention it. This feeding back is usually automatic. In driving, it is a mixture of physiological links through my hands and arms and physical links through the car's steering system and the road, links that any skilled driver has long since ceased to be aware of consciously. Feedback in this specific sense is not particularly individual. 2) There is the *comparison* between what I perceive and the standard I set, between what I want to see and what I in fact see. This comparison is, in effect, the input that leads to my behavior (output) that then feeds round again as perception (input). The comparison that gives rise to an output is the difference between the distance I would like to see between right front wheel and edge and the distance I do see after steering gears and tires and road surface have

responded to my output, that is, my steering. More generally, the comparison is the difference between what I want and what I get. My perception of that difference is probably, again, quite automatic. 3) Finally, there is that standard or reference that says, I feel safe when the car is one meter from the right edge of the road. That is a very individual thing. It is the crucial element that psychology textbooks typically leave out, although it is this reference or standard or desire or wish that sets the whole process in motion. Let me quote again brain scientist J. Z. Young, "We now find that every organism contains systems that literally embody set points or reference standards. The control mechanisms operate to ensure that action is directed to maintaining these standards."[9] A loop's standard comes from outside the control loop, not in any supernatural sense, but simply because the standard is not affected by what goes on in the loop it controls. The standard comes from some other loop in the brain. Often, psychoanalysis shows, it will be an unconscious desire that colors a conscious action.

Behavior controls perception

A second thing about Figure 4 to notice: in this picture, behavior controls perception. On that mountain road, I used the steering wheel to control my *perception* of the distance between the right wheel and the edge of the road. I was not using my vision to control the steering wheel— I was using my vision to detect the position of the car, which in turn was resulting from some combination of my steering, the turns in the road, and the wind. The perception of that relation was the end product of the transaction. Perception was what I sought.

If there had been a fog in those mountains that made the visibility so poor that I could see the car and the wheel but couldn't see the right edge of the road, and so couldn't see the position of the car relative to the right edge of the road, I would have had to pull over and stop. Just seeing the steering wheel inside the car would have been enough to control my behavior, that is, to turn the steering wheel. It would not have been enough to complete the feedback. I couldn't have maintained the distance I felt was safe. Perception was what I desired, what I wished.

We usually think that perception controls behavior, and in a limited sense it does, but if you think in terms of a total feedback loop it is really the other way round. Behavior controls perception, to cite the title of a useful book in this field.[10] Behavior serves to create the perception you desire, namely, to see that your right front wheel is at least one meter from the edge of the road.

Incidentally, the idea that behavior controls perception corresponds quite closely to Freud's definition of a wish. Perhaps, since Freud himself thought in terms of a pre-feedback, a proto-cybernetics, that should come as no surprise. He defined a wish as the desire to re-create, either by means of action on the world or by dreaming, a perception associated with a previous satisfaction.[11] The role of desire—a standard, an aim—in feedback thus corresponds to that original perception of satisfaction.

In *Beyond the Pleasure Principle* he came even closer to a modern version of feedback. In the course of considering, and rejecting, an internal "instinct to perfection," he explained it instead as a repressed instinct's persistent attempt to repeat "a primary experience of satisfaction." "It is the difference in amount between the pleasure of satisfaction which is *demanded* and that which is actually *achieved* that provides the driving factor which will permit of no halting at any position attained . . ."[12] Freud's thinking here shows that we can connect this fundamental engineering concept to psychoanalytic theory. What satisfied you before (and is therefore stored as part of your character or identity) sets the standard for what you will seek in the future and seek and seek. Often what is stored, that "primary experience of satisfaction," will be unconscious. Yet, and this is psychoanalysis' great truth, you will behave so as to meet that standard, even if it is unconscious. From a psychoanalytic point of view, then, as well as from the computer scientist's, action—behavior—serves to control perception.

Emotions decisive

The third thing I want to stress about Figure 4 follows from the second, the decisive role of conscious and unconscious wishes. Emotions guide the whole system. How I drive through the mountain roads in Crete depends upon how I *feel* as I look at those cliffs without guardrails. If I have a low anxiety level, I will not mind getting close to the edge. If I am a nervous driver, I will stay a good meter away or more. My comparison of what is fed back against my standard is both cognitive and emotional. Cognitively, what is the difference between where I am in fact and the one meter I want to see? That is, what is the difference between my standard and what I perceive? Emotionally, how do I feel about that difference? Do I feel safe or not? If I don't, I will turn the steering wheel until I feel as safe as I want to feel or can feel under the circumstances.

Because the whole process rests on what you desire, what is "correct" depends finally on how you *feel* about the external events in relation to your internal desire. The cognitive answer may be automatic and physiological, but the emotional answer will be quite individual and personal.

In other words, because feelings play such an important role in human feedback, what sets the standard is "subjective," or, to be more precise, we can think of it as identity or a function of identity.

In terms of brain science, emotions stem from one of the most ancient parts of the brain: the limbic system, and they affect all our ideas, even the most abstract and intellectual. As recently as 1952 Ludwig von Bertalanffy could describe the human central nervous system as having three more or less separate parts, arranged hierarchically. The spinal cord acts as a reflex apparatus. The ancient brain, the "palaencephalon," as he called it, the limbic system we would say today, is "the organ of depth personality with its primeval instincts, emotions, and appetites." The cortex is the organ of the "day personality," that is, the conscious I.[13]

Epilepsy demonstrates emotions arising from the limbic system itself without any particular sensory stimulus from either the body or the world. "The symptoms of patients with psychomotor epilepsy provide the most convincing evidence that the limbic cortex is implicated in the generation of emotional states, as well as symptoms of a psychotic nature." Lesions in certain parts of the limbic system give rise to epileptic discharges with the distinctive epileptic aura, "emotional feelings that under ordinary conditions are important for survival. . . . these feelings include terror, fear, foreboding, familiarity, strangeness, unreality, sadness, and feelings of a paranoid nature."[14] Furthermore, the limbic system contains the "reward" site and the "punishment-aversion system": points in the limbic system and the hypothalamus that, when electrically stimulated, provide pleasure or pain without any source outside the brain itself.[15]

A quarter of a century later, it is still clear that the limbic system gives rise to emotions,[16] but the picture is more complex. "The brain transforms the cold light with which we see into the warm light with which we feel," is the way Paul D. MacLean puts it. The brain charges raw sensory data with emotion, because there are connections from the cortex, the sensory part of the brain, into the limbic system which is involved in emotional functions and with sweating, heartbeat, breathing, and the other signs of emotion.[17]

What complicates the picture is that these connections are two-way:

Limbic functions are not only channeled into cognitive activities, but [cognitive activities] also modulate our emotions. We share with higher primates intense maternal and sibling ties . . . . we have strong emotional ties to other relatives. These emotionally charged relationships have become integrated into cognitive systems, namely, kinship structures. . . . Human emotional reactions are modulated by our limbic systems and regulated by culturally structured, cognitive processes. All human emotional expressions

and activities, ranging from lovemaking to killing, have culturally prescribed
ways to accomplish them. When conflict arises between a person's desires
and cognitive rules, the result is frequently anxiety or guilt. These qualities
may denote the linkage of cognitive and limbic systems or as Freud stated
[in *Civilization and its Discontents*], the linkage of culture and aggression.

In either case, lesions in the anterior principal nucleus of the limbic
system do suppress the association of anxiety, agitation, and aggression
with certain ideas, thereby further demonstrating the deep biological
connection between cognition and emotion.[18]

Jonathan Winson sums it up: "The limbic system is the central core
processor of the brain."[19] The hippocampus, a long, looping structure
in the limbic system, is its gateway. It receives information from the
neocortex (the temporal lobes associated with the synthesis of sensory
data, for example) and transmits it to components in the limbic system.
The hippocampus also feeds information back to the neocortex without
passing it through the limbic system. "Somehow within this loop—
neocortex to hippocampus to neocortex—and within the circuit from
neocortex to hippocampus to limbic system (with an ultimate return to
the neocortex), sensory information, analyzed in various sensory centers
of the neocortex, is brought together to record an event and remember
it."[20] The cortex forms "engrams" but these need to be integrated in the
limbic system, responded to emotionally, before they become long-term
personal memories of an experience.[21] Emotion is central to heeding and
remembering data, a literary text, for example. What we do not care
about, we neither pay attention to nor remember.[22]

Similarly, the limbic system is involved in all our judgments of satisfaction. In general, write the neuroscientists, our minds propose a given
satisfaction and posit a set of conditions that must be fulfilled to produce
that satisfaction. "The coordinated prefrontal system must render a judgment that the object of satisfaction is 'good,'" that is, that it satisfies
subjective requirements, "and that it is also 'true' (that it has all the
familiar features that make it verifiable)." For this to happen, the limbic
organized memory function has to be able to signal *error* and *novelty*,
that this does not (or does) fulfill the conditions and that this does not
(or does) compare to the satisfaction desired. "No matter how complicated a problem of adult life may be, it must always be solved through
a series of propositions and proofs, each facilitating the next, and each
organized as a miniature version of the whole. The experience of identity
integrity depends on the successful accomplishment of such coordinated
tasks."[23]

That is to say, the limbic system is a central processor. It receives pre-
organized combinations of data from the various senses, makes them

into a coherent image, connects (as it were) an appropriate emotion to that image, stores the combination for future reference in memory, and proceeds to trigger motor action on the event by higher- and lower-level systems, if that seems necessary.[24]

Considered by itself the limbic system is a "mammalian brain." We can think of our modern brains as beginning, evolutionarily, with the so-called "reptilian brain." Although an improvement on the decentralized brains of the invertebrates, it was largely a set of preprogrammed instincts to stabilize heartbeat, body temperature, breathing rate, mating rituals, and the like. To be sure, these preprogrammed instincts can become very complex, as when sea turtles return across thousands of miles of trackless ocean to the same beach where they were born. But they are unchanging programs, neither to be learnt nor unlearnt.

Mammals are more adaptive. When the first mammals evolved from reptiles some 200 million years ago, they found their ecological niche: nighttime hunting. At night, they neither competed with reptiles nor fell prey to them. Since the reptiles could not maintain their own body temperature after the sun went down, they became torpid and slept. The mammals had the night-world to themselves. To live in it, mammals evolved more complex vision (rods in the retina for low levels of light, for example), more subtle hearing, and a powerful sense of smell. Hunting in darkness, they had to be able to synthesize a world from these diverse sensory inputs. What evolved, cupped round the old reptilian brain, was the limbic system. This was the first form of our intelligence, the limbic brain as distinct from a stimulus-response brain. Its basic function was to construct a world out of the data available.

As mammals began, some 50 million years ago, to evolve monkeys, apes, and hominids, yet another brain began to develop on top of the limbic system. Living in trees, like a monkey, puts more demands upon both the senses and the brain. Sight became, finally, more important than smell. Arboreal existence required even more synthesizing power in the brain than the limbic system afforded, and the thinking, planning cortex of which we humans are so proud evolved. It evolved, however, linked to and around those earlier mammalian and reptilian brains, which preserve in us our animal inheritance. The brain stem contains the instinctual programs for maintaining heartbeat, breathing, body temperature, hormone balance, and the like. The mammalian brain keeps alive in us the needs, the synthesizing, world-building skills and, above all, the feelings of those earlier nighthunting mammals.

Paul D. MacLean, on whose account I am drawing, has isolated some mammalian functions in the limbic system. Some have called them the four F's of the mammalian brain: feeding, fighting, fleeing, and sexual behavior. MacLean finds the lower part of the limbic ring largely concerned with emotional feelings and behavior that assure self-preservation, "whereas, in contrast, the subdivision related to the septum is implicated in feeling states that are conducive to sociability, procreation, and the preservation of the species." The distinction seems to me, at least, to correspond loosely with the psychoanalytic drives of aggression (or mastery) and libido.[25]

Taste and smell connect directly to the limbic system, the reason we find foods or odors so immediately pleasurable or disgusting, I suppose, or, as with Proust, so powerfully evocative of memories.[26] Sight and hearing became more complex in primates, more directly associated with the neocortex, but in the limbic system smell predominates, even in relationships. Dogs, cats, and monkeys greet and identify one another by smell. Identifying one another by sight is an achievement of primates and especially humans who have a special site in the brain devoted to recognizing faces. Oral functions, smelling, tasting, eating, are in the limbic system closely linked to genital behavior and sexuality in general.[27] Interestingly, feelings of fear or anger can lead in mammals to sexual arousal. As for humans, Freud noted children's sexual excitement in fighting or wrestling and adults' fondness for fearful experiences[28] (like roller coasters or horror movies).

In addition to sex and survival (which reptiles share), these limbic emotions and arousals have to do with two of the specifically female developments in the transition from reptile to mammal: bearing live young (instead of eggs) and maternal nursing. MacLean was able to isolate some parts of the limbic system, those linking smell stimuli with sexuality, as specifically devoted to rearing the young. When those tissues were removed, hamsters and rats did not play, "and in addition females showed deficits in maternal behavior . . . It was as though these animals had regressed toward a reptilian condition." "The evolutionar[il]y newer parts of the limbic system appear necessary for the full expression of maternal behavior and the capacity for play." In effect, our ability to play, so central to literary experience, comes from the distaff side of evolution.[29]

Fearing, loving, desiring, playing, caring—in all these ways, our animal, maternal, mammalian, emotional brains enter into symbolic, cognitive processes:

The limbic system, those neural circuits that support and modulate our emotional behavior, structure limits for our social and motivational states. The importance of limbic input into higher cognitive functions is not restricted to language, but can be found in all symbolic expressions, be they making tools or arranging social relations. A tool's appearance and the ways to make it and use it are culturally learned and require cognitive abilities;

the ability to focus attention over sufficient time for its creation and maintenance requires tapping limbic sources.[30]

If this be true of a stone ax, how much more true it must be of a poem or a novel or an essay in literary criticism.

Once we recognize this mammalian foundation to our ostensibly intellectual activities, it becomes easier, Jonathan Winson points out, to understand dreaming. Incidentally, dreaming has seemed to many of us, starting with Freud, a model for the writing of literature and reading it—"Literature is a dream dreamed for us," I once wrote. Dreams, notes Winson, have no abstractions, only actions and pictures. Dreamers have no sense of free will—things just happen. "Language and abstract concepts derived therefrom," notes Winson, "played no part in the lower mammalian brain. The limbic-frontal cortical system governing interpretation of experience and planning operated solely on the basis of action, and this remains the case in man."[31] When we dream we tap into that mammalian brain, without plans, self-consciousness, free will, or abstractions. Possibly, when we dream, we come as close as we ever do in our lives to feeling what it is like to be a dog or a cat.

Be that as it may, this mammalian inheritance plays a key role in the processes of literature. We can visualize the limbic system as capping and linked to the ancient, reptilian brain, but connected also to the thinking, planning cortical lobes we evolved as primates and hominids. It was to these latter pathways that Morton Reiser pointed in chapter 1: sensory inputs connected to "affect systems through bidirectional cortico-limbic pathways."[32] As a psychoanalyst, he recognized in those pathways the physiological base for the associations and conflicts we carry consciously and unconsciously from infancy to the analyst's couch. Those are some of the pathways that developed during the growing and ungrowing of our brains in infancy, latency, and adolescence. In my terms, it is in those "cortico-limbic pathways" that identity resides, governing the perceptual and symbolic systems by which we write and read literature.

Hence, we can use this knowledge of the limbic system's role in the brain as a whole to understand the outer world of driving or reading or writing. Because the whole process of, say, driving rests on what you desire, what is "correct" depends finally on how you *feel* about the external events in relation to your internal desire. Even if the cognitive response to a hazard seems programmed and automatic, the emotional answer will be individual and personal. Feelings, mammalian in origin but individual in practice, govern and direct human feedback. What sets the standard, our desire, is "subjective," or, to be more precise, we can think of it as identity or a function of identity, a pathway between cortex and limbic system. Moreover—and this is the importance of the research into the limbic system—*cognition is evolutionarily, biologically, and physically connected to emotion.* Just as we grow and ungrow identity as we become adults, so we grow and ungrow those connections between the intellectual brain and the emotional brain.

In the first half of this century the psychoanalysts showed that cognition was only the tip of an iceberg, that conscious processes always had a darker unconscious underside. Now the brain scientists are showing that our hominid planning and abstracting rests on a limbic, mammalian world of raw emotion. In thinking about literature, we can no more separate emotion from the abstract skills we use in reading and writing than conscious from unconscious processes. We can use Figure 4 to image those relationships.

Low-level loops similar

That is the fourth thing I would like you to notice in the feedback picture, and for understanding reading and writing (the next chapter) it is the most important. Identity is different for each of us, but the loop governed by identity is more or less the same. We all carry out about the same physical process to steer a car so it keeps a certain distance from the right hand edge of a road. The standard, however, the distance we choose to maintain, the looseness with which we maintain it, the nervousness we may feel when we sense errors, the urgency with which we correct an error—those are individual, emotional things. They depend upon, or express or are functions of, identity.

So far as reading is concerned, as opposed to driving the mountain roads of Crete, David Rumelhart, the well-known cognitive scientist, describes it this way:

> A reader of a text is presumably constantly evaluating hypotheses about the most plausible interpretation of the text. Readers are said to have understood the text when they are able to find a configuration of hypotheses (schemata) that offers a coherent account for the various aspects of the text. To the degree to which a particular reader fails to find such a configuration, the text will appear disjointed and incomprehensible.[33]

The important thing to recognize in Rumelhart's account is that we actively test hypotheses in order to understand writing.

From the neuroscientific point of view, too, understanding writing involves the active testing of hypotheses—feedback. On the basis of his studies of brain-damaged patients, the great Soviet brain scientist

Aleksandr Luria described reading as the bringing to bear of "a sort of hypothesis," a system of associations, that "makes the subsequent reading an active process in which the search for the desired meaning and the discernment of agreements or disagreements with the expected meaning begin to assume an almost exclusive role."[34]

Understanding speech also proceeds by the rapid testing of hypotheses, according to Luria. That is, one singles out the distinctive, phonemic signs and separates them "from the unimportant, fortuitous signs that are of no phonemic significance." The process is like picking out an announcer's voice from the static on a radio.

> It is clear, therefore, that the perception of speech by hearing requires not merely delicate, but also systematized, hearing. . . . This is why the boundary between hearing speech and understanding it loses its sharp distinction. A person ignorant of a foreign language not only does not understand it, but does not even hear it, i.e., he does not distinguish from the flow of sounds the articulated elements of the language and does not systematize the sounds of speech according to its laws.

> This work must be carried out with the very close participation of articulatory acts, which, like the singing activity of the vocal cords for the hearing of music, constitute the efferent link for the perception of the sounds of speech. It consists of differentiating the significant, phonemic signs of the spoken sounds, inhibiting the unessential, nonphonemic signs, and comparing the perceived sound complexes on this phonemic basis. It refracts the newly arriving sounds through a system of dynamic stereotypes formed while the language was being learned and thus carries out its task on the basis of objective, historically established systems of connections. This deciphering of sound signals in accordance with historically established codes of spoken speech and the organization of auditory experience into new systems constitute the basic activity of the speech areas of the auditory cortex.[35]

That is, we understand speech by generating speech inside ourselves.

We know that one month old infants can distinguish phonetic differences (between p and b, say) from simple acoustic variations.[36] Evidently, then, we are born with some of the hypotheses we need for the internal speech we use in understanding language wired in. At a more sophisticated stage, we speak internally according to the grammar and syntax we have learned in childhood and school. In still a different mode of processing, we frame what we hear into a coherent scenario or model by drawing on our knowledge of the world. We frame hypotheses from all kinds of extra-linguistic knowledge, like spatial relations, contexts, social practice, probabilities, logic, motives, or causality.[37] We use these kinds of information to frame hypotheses that what we are hearing or reading confirm or disconfirm. We use all these kinds of hypotheses to make an internal speech against which to single out the meaningful elements in what we hear.

To be sure, we can describe a language formally, as linguists do, by a system like Saussure's system of opposites or Chomsky's generative transformations. We formulate such a linguistic description by studying the language as people generally use it or did use it historically. Psychologically, though, we individuals actually process language by comparing hypotheses we generate inside ourselves on the basis of that linguistic language, so to speak, with the actual flow of speech or writing that we sense "out there."

This hypothesizing goes on when we read:

> In reading there are two different levels: a level of analysis of sounds and letters, leading to ability to read words, and a level of direct grasping of the appropriate meaning of words, which is evidently connected with the integral perception of words and which can be dissociated from the act of reading words letter by letter.
>
> It is very interesting that whereas the first of these processes is connected with the dominant (left) hemisphere, the second can be a property of the nondominant (right) hemisphere, so that in this case also a complex act such as reading is performed with the participation of both hemispheres, each of which makes its own specific contribution to this complex process.

Thus Luria describes a patient who knew that a certain word she read was "something near to me, something related," but could not read letter-by-letter the name of her daughter.[38]

The point, again, is that we actively guess our way through the interpretation of language by proposing hypotheses. Nowhere, perhaps, is the functioning of those hypotheses clearer than in the study of brain-damaged Japanese readers. Neuroscientists widely agree that "The left hemisphere has a dominant role in the perception of speech codes, whereas the nondominant (right) hemisphere plays the major part in the perception of nonverbal, visual patterns." Japanese is unique in using both syllabic writing (Katakana) and pictographic writing (Kanji). A disturbance in a Japanese reader's left temporal zone (where audioverbal stimuli are analyzed) disrupts the reading of syllabic writing, but a disturbance in the parieto-occipital zones (where visuospatial analysis takes place) disrupts hieroglyphic, Kanji writing. It must be, Luria concludes, that we process different languages differently *in our very brains*. Highly phonetic languages (like Italian, German, or Russian) and languages with many conventional pronunciations (like French or English) and hieroglyphic or pictographic languages (like Chinese) must all organize our various brain functions differently. Similarly, we may process vowels in different parts of the brain from consonants.[39]

In broad outline, then, we can apply the feedback model of Figure 4 to driving a car but also to reading a poem or watching a movie[40] and, ultimately, any human activity. As Luria says, "The principle of feedback is universal in the operation of the central nervous system."[41] In terms of the brain,

> The formation of the "provisional basis of action," and the creation of complex programs of behavior; the constant monitoring of these programs and the checking of behavior with comparison of actions performed and the original plans; the provision of a system of feedback on the basis of which complex forms of behavior are regulated—all these phenomena in man take place with the intimate participation of the frontal lobes, and they account for the exceptionally important place of the frontal lobes in the general organization of behavior.

The frontal lobes, however, are not innocent of connection with the limbic system, so that the large plan is one that is emotionally as well as cognitively satisfying. Then the larger plan uses various subplans that can be more precisely localized (as with Luria's questions to brain-damaged patients).[42] According to Luria, speech—internal speech—plays a key role in this formulating and monitoring. It is through speech that we formulate a plan for a motor act and then check the actual movements with the original intention.[43]

In work more recent than Luria's, it has become possible to measure the very frequency at which we cycle or feed back some fairly specific hypotheses. For example, verbal functions take place in waves of 13 cycle per second frequency, but mental arithmetic at 15 and 17 cycles per second. In general, mentation takes place in the central areas of the brain at 13 cycles per second. It has also become possible to show how two seemingly independent functions are "electrophysiologically related" so as to contribute to one larger plan.[44] I have already mentioned the observation in the brain of a "set" that switches the expectations we bring to bear on the world. That "set" is, it seems to me, another word for the standard by which an identity governs a feedback.

The brain scientists are confirming and refining what some psychologists have derived long before from studying behaviors. In psychological circles (no pun intended), one of the best-known versions of feedback is the TOTE unit of activity proposed in 1960 by psychologist George Miller, neuroscientist Karl Pribram, and psychometricist Eugene Galanter. Test, operate, test, exit.[45] In the language I have been using: act, compare, act, cease. This picture matches that of neuroscience, although the brain scientists can draw on physical, chemical, biological, and physiological evidence.

George Kelly's "personal construct" psychology applied feedback to pure psychology even earlier than TOTE did. Kelly held that individuals developed working hypotheses to be validated or invalidated by the test of experience.[46] In effect, for Kelly, every one of us is a scientist. Kelly's "personal construct" is very like what I have been calling a "standard." For Kelly as for me, it determines what and how a person will perceive, remember, learn, think, and do with respect to the things encompassed by the construct. At the same time, Kelly imagined personal constructs in clinical terms, so that personality becomes the sum of one's constructs. Although Kelly did not propose a theme-and-variations identity, he did envision a "personality" that consists of many constructs or feedbacks, much as I envision "identity." It seems to me that Kelly's psychology has now reappeared in artificial intelligence, cognitive science, and ultimately, the physiological mode of neuroscience.

In short, the idea that we respond to the world by means of feedbacks is by no means new to psychology. As we have seen, you can even find a fairly precise description of psychological feedback in Freud. "It is the difference in amount between the pleasure of satisfaction which is *demanded* and that which is actually *achieved* that provides the driving factor which will permit of no halting at any position attained."[47] But now the brain scientists confirm that principle definitively.

Long after Freud, today's brain scientists can draw on many more discoveries, but they still come out with the general idea of a central organizing principle (an identity, I have been calling it) that governs feedbacks toward the ends that satisfy (limbically and neocortically) that identity. Nobelist Roger Sperry writes, for example, of "inner experience" having "an integral causal control role in brain function and behavior." "The events of inner experience, as emergent properties of brain processes, become themselves explanatory causal constructs in their own right, interacting at their own level with their own laws and dynamics." "The whole world of inner experience . . . becomes recognized and included within the domain of science."[48] The brain scientists are offering literary critics a utopian picture, the sciences and the humanities united round a concept of the human brain. As for psychoanalysis, let us not forget that Freud began his researches as a neuroscientist. Today's neuroscientists are confirming his dream of a psychology that would be based not only on the interpretation of actions but in the physiology of the brain itself.

6

Reading and Writing, Codes and Canons

We have begun to model what Robert Frost did when he read or wrote. In the most abstract terms, he—his identity—has a certain aim or desire which becomes a personal standard. To achieve that aim, the identity puts out behavior, which amounts to a test of the environment. The environment gives a return, thereby closing the loop. The identity compares that return with what was tried out and the standard. If they match, then the identity feels satisfied, the loop closes, and the system called Robert Frost settles down. If they do not match, if the desire continues and the identity feels dissatisfied, the Robert Frost system continues to try behavior on the environment until it achieves a match. The right side of the picture represents what you want, the left side, what you get, and as the old saying goes, What you want and what you get are seldom quite the same.

So far as reading and writing literature are concerned, the feedback picture gives us a way of describing, articulating, even perhaps explaining, how an experience, like literature, can be both shared and individual. Part will be just about the same for many human beings. Part will be unique because it answers to our highly personal standards, feelings, or "set." The feedback picture gives us a way of putting together something as individual as Robert Frost's writing a poem or Professor Six's reading of the "The Mill" with something they have completely in common like understanding the meaning of the word "miller."

Feedback through schemas lets us reject what Mark Johnson calls the "false dichotomy" between "absolute, fixed . . . standards of rationality and knowledge" or "an 'anything goes' relativism, in which there are no standards whatever, and there is no possibility for criticism."[1] Feedback through schemas lets us understand how reading can be individual without being "purely subjective"—a risk that seems to appall many literary critics.[2] In fact, people who work on the psychology of reading, so as to teach children, illiterates, or dyslexics (hardly a "purely subjective" enterprise), have for a long time used just this kind of feedback model.[3]

We can use the loop in a feedback picture such as Figure 4 to represent the processes in reading we share. We can represent what is individual, the desire, the standard, as a function of identity, and identity governs the shared loop. The psychology of writing, of course, involves an extra step and for the writing of a poem, a miraculous one that it would take another book to describe. Much, however, of Robinson's creation of "The Mill" must have been reading. That is, he writes a line. That is a kind of hypothesis he has set out. Then he reads the line he has written. That tests the hypothesis and he feels good or bad about what he has written.

In other words, we can imagine writing as reading plus. It is reading plus the hypotheses Robinson writes down in the form of particular words, lines, rhythms, stanzas—ultimately the whole poem. These hypotheses are much more Robinson's own than our ordinary hypotheses for reading. These stem from Robinson's poetic values, his vocabulary, his ideas of what will "work" with a reader, above all the sudden leaps of his imagination. Where do they come from? What is the seat of "inspiration"?

To ask is to open the whole question of "creativity," a theme that would require several books in itself. The thinking about "creativity" that I find most telling suggests that being "creative" combines three things: talent, field, and domain.[4] First, creativity involves an individual's talents and unconscious inspiration. This is the traditional concern of the psychoanalytic writer on creativity, and it is the part we most readily call "creativity." Second, creative individuals can use the techniques of their intellectual domain, as here Frost uses the techniques of poetry like rhyme, rhythm, meter, assonance, or alliteration. Less obviously, creative persons use their "field," the institutions of their discipline, to be seen and heard by others. A poet, for example, learns to use readers, audiences, publishers, editors, reviewers, awards, or foundations. Frost was adept at these matters, as anyone we call a genius must be. What we do not see and hear—and value—we cannot call "creative." Finally, then, creativity includes the recognition by that field (other people involved in the discipline) that this person's work counts and has to be accepted as part of the discipline (as Frost and Robinson were recognized). Part of our saying that Frost is "creative" is saying that a young poet starting out today would have to "know Frost," just as a young scientist would have to "know Einstein."

All I wish to say here of creativity, however, is that we can imagine writing as the reading-hypotheses preceded by a set of special and highly personal writing-hypotheses that we regularly identify as "creativity." For that reason, I will say more about reading than writing, but I believe the feedback picture of the brain in action applies to both, because it allows us to imagine how the individual talent or style combines with skills we all (or some of us) have in common.

In describing reading and writing, though, we can do more with our feedback model than simply assign what is common to the loop and what is individual to the desiring identity who sets the standard for the loop. We can describe reading in more detail by stacking these feedbacks one on top of another. In this respect, however, reading is only one instance of a principle general to the human brain. The neuroscientists tell us we humans operate in every way by means of feedback, but there are many different feedbacks and they take place in a hierarchy.[5]

They are confirming a tradition that goes back to Aristotle, the idea of the human as organism, represented by Kurt Goldstein in psychology, Aleksandr Luria in neuropsychology, Sigmund Freud in psychoanalysis, or Jean Piaget in cognitive development, an idea now updated as "General Systems Theory." The brain scientists find that, within the many coordinated feedback systems, "the different elements of the error-detection apparatus are not equally significant and that they are arranged in a hierarchy."[6]

An organism, as it develops, both differentiates and integrates. That is, it evolves new and more specialized subsystems, and it also evolves interdependencies among those subsystems so as to create overarching, interactive suprasystems. This integration necessarily gives rise to a hierarchical organization, with the levels higher in developmental achievement directing lower levels.[7]

As long ago as 1937, Sir Charles Sherrington was pointing out that the principle of "long-circuiting" through the "roof-brain" was central to the evolution of the human being and the human brain. That is, in the lowest animals, an action like a lobster's moving its antenna is controlled at the site by reflex processes. As we evolved into vertebrates, then reptiles, then mammals, "cephalization" took place. A superstructure localized in the head began to govern these lower-level activities. Sometimes the superstructure was inborn, sometimes learned, but always localized in the brain. In mammals sensory impulses get "long-circuited" to the "roof-brain" which then issues a "call" to lower-level reflex circuits to get them to respond. "The component from the roof-brain alters the character of the motor act from one of generality of purpose to one of narrowed and specific purpose fitting a specific occasion."[8] The action shifts from some overarching suprasystem associated with a general purpose to a subsystem geared to specific muscular acts.

Within that hierarchy, the various processes are relatively isolated from one another. The technique for moving an arm is separate from moving a leg or moving the eyes. This separability gave an evolutionary advantage to animals that had it, because disruption of one in a group of parallel control networks would cause only partial loss (one finger among five, one limb among four, color blindness but not total blindness). An undivided system would undergo total loss. The evolutionary advantage of hierarchical systems thus rests on what Herbert Simon calls "near decomposability": connections within a reflex subsystem are stronger than connections between reflex subsystems. Nature has separated the fast processes within a subsystem (seeing a target, keeping one's balance) from the slower (coordinating arm and eye to fire a pistol).[9]

Some fifty years after Sherrington, brain scientists continue to confirm the general idea of a central organizing principle (I have been calling it identity) that guides feedbacks toward ends that satisfy that identity. For Ragnar Granit, for example, the key terms are "purpose" and "creativeness." At the lowest level, we have the homeostatic balances of heartbeat, blood pressure, and hormonal balances controlled by the reptilian brain. Further up the evolutionary hierarchy, we have the holistic workings of organs and limbs. Further up, we have what the psychologist would call "behaviors" and still further up what the philosopher would call "mind." At every one of these levels, however, the creative purpose of a higher level directs the working of lower levels. The body uses lower processes for its higher ends so that there is what one brain scientist calls "a reorientation of purpose from level to level." "A warp of creative purposiveness is woven into the fabric of biological hierarchies with consciousness at its top level."[10] The brain, by means of consciousness, monitors its own activities. Not cell by cell, of course. Consciousness detects the overall qualities of different activity patterns. Consciousness "supervenes," fitting the brain's individual activities within an envelope of larger configurations, as the individual drops of water swirl in an eddy.[11]

"Here," writes Edward Evarts, a leading neuroscientist, "one finds remarkable agreements among scholars of widely different backgrounds, disiplines, and eras . . . that purposive movements are built on a base of reflex processes." "Reflexes and voluntary movements are not opposites," he continues, discussing the brain's control of movement. He gives the example of a Russian study of the champion pistol shots in the Red Army. As they aimed, their pistols remained immobile, even if their legs or arms or shoulders moved. In effect, reflex mechanisms, low-level subsystems, stabilized the position of each marksman's hand in space. The marksman concentrated only on his high-level goal: hitting the target. "The actual events that underlie the achievement of the goal are built up from a variety of [lower-level, semi-automatic] reflex processes."[12]

To image such a hierarchy, we can have one loop control another loop. That is, we would have one loop set the standards for one "beneath" it. If we were mathematically inclined, we could list some of the physical constraints the interlocked feedback loops would have to have. Computer scientist William T. Powers does just that in his book about such a hierarchical model for the mind. For example, a loop controlling a loop has to operate about ten times faster than the loop it controls. Powers even offers some experiments you could try out on a personal computer or simply with a rubber band.[13] Let me, however, hold my humanistic (or touristic) stance.

Suppose, for example, as I am driving through the mountains of Crete on a narrow road with a cliff and a shrine on my right, I see a large tourist bus lurching toward me in the left lane. I will want to give the bus as wide a clearance on the left as the cliff on the right. When I apply my general criteria about safety, one meter on the right no longer feels as safe to me as, say, half a meter. Another, higher loop has changed the standard for the lower loop.

More exactly, I have used a higher loop to set a new standard for the lower loop. Within the lower loop, the physical process of keeping a certain distance from the right does not change. I maneuver the steering wheel the way I usually do, but the standard for the distance from the edge has changed: I maneuver so as to keep a half meter from the edge instead of a meter. I have some similar, but higher feedback process that I use to decide what is safe on the road when there are two dangers instead of one. That higher process has set the standard for the lower loop at half a meter instead of a meter.

We could picture this combination of one feedback loop controlling another feedback loop as in Figure 5.

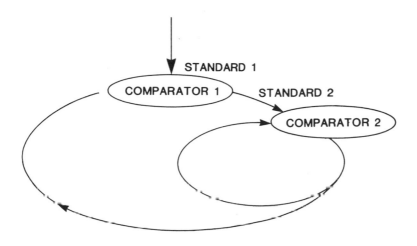

Figure 5. A feedback loop controlling a feedback loop

In general, a higher loop controls a lower one by setting its standard.

Whenever we will an action, we establish a goal. A marksman thinks of his target, an opera singer of her perfect high C, or a trapeze artist of his triple somersault. They do not think of finger, tongue, or left leg position. Subordinate reflexes handle those specific muscular details, while higher levels in the brain point all those reflexes toward one overall goal. We create "complex programs of behavior" in the frontal lobes of the neocortex. Then our feelings of pleasure from the limbic system, our enjoying the triumph of a bull's-eye or a triple somersault or a high C, these *affects* tell us the feedback has been successful.

The same principle applies to writing and reading literature. When Frost writes a poem, he thinks of the Cliff House seashore or his wall to be mended. He does not think of dotting his i's or crossing his t's or getting the subject to agree with the verb. When he heard the "mischief" in Robinson's fourth "thought," some very low-order process recognized "t-h-o-u-g-h-t" and a much higher process yielded his delight. When Professor Two encountered "wife" or "tea," he did not have to puzzle out the words. In the succinct sentences of a reader psychologist, "Verbal comprehension can be broken down into its component processes. The elementary behaviors build on each other. Sentence analysis cannot take place without lexical analysis. Text comprehension depends on sentence comprehension."[14] Two knew right away what the words were and what they meant and how they fitted the words adjacent to them. To be sure, if I had asked Two a grammatical question, he would have had to stop and think out the answer. Most of the time, though, he doesn't have to think deliberately about the syntax he is reading, he just reads. The higher processes in his brain that seek themes or recognize characters *govern* the lower processes that read letters and words and sentences. "Govern" is precisely the word the feedback engineer would use for this stacking process. It has the same root as the "kybern" (to steer) in "cybernetics," the word Norbert Wiener (or Heinz von Foerster) coined to describe the discipline of feedback he was formalizing mathematically.

One could link up feedback loops this way indefinitely, each governing one or more lower loops. In fact there must be thousands of millions of such loops in the actual brain (and loops of other types as well). When one thinks of the hypotheses and comparisons and standards in something like Frost's or the professors' reading of Robinson's poem about the miller, such a huge number of loops seems probable and even necessary. Accordingly, from the point of view of real brain physiologists, the feedback loop is but the merest sketch of the actual architecture of the brain. Nevertheless, as Roger Sperry stated in his Nobel Prize acceptance speech,[15] brain scientists have come very widely to use the principle that the events of inner experience become causal principles governing lower-level processes. Thoughts, impulses, emotions, in my terms, the response to the fed back input, the kind of thing the concept of identity addresses—these govern the processes of reading and writing all of us share.

In particular, this picture for reading and writing literature finds a parallel in the work of Sir Karl Popper and Sir John Eccles on the brain in general.[16] They describe the brain's working as interactions among three worlds: the physical-material world, cultural codes, and the world of conscious self. World 2 (self-conscious mind), acting through World 3 (mental products such as language, arts, or theories), governs and is governed by World 1 (physical reality). Being brain scientists, Popper and Eccles take into account studies of left- and right-brain, and I can only wish they had also mentioned the unconscious processes described by psychoanalysis. Nevertheless, their physiological conclusions about the brain encourage me to use even such simplified pictures as Figure 4 or 5 to think about literary processes.

We can feel confident, it seems to me, in sorting out writing and reading into three levels: identity (with which chapters 1 and 2 deal), cultural skills, and physical-physiological reality (also discussed in chapter 1). If we position at the top level identity and the emotional reactions to which it gives rise, it is possible, without overly oversimplifying, to imagine some general types of feedback loop that we would have to posit at the lower levels to explain literary and other human activities.[17]

For reading and writing in particular, we might begin by dividing the transaction into two large feedbacks.[18] First, you perform the biophysical act of reading. That is, you engage with eye and page-turning fingers or notetaking hands the little black marks that make up a text. Second, in what I will call the cultural part of reading or writing, you test and so read letters and words and sentences and poems and stories, arriving at meanings and values. If you are writing, you take the further step of using what you have read to correct (if it seems necessary) what you have written. In both reading and writing, you bring to bear the verbal know-how you have absorbed from your culture onto a physical reality. Finally, your identity compares the results of these tests and so directs the whole transaction, so as to feel good as a result of it.

To a literary critic if not to a psychologist, the physiological side of reading and writing is the easiest to talk about. As with driving, you are dealing with a physical system. In the hills of Crete, the system is the car, its steering gears, the tire, the road, but also the physical limits to my reaction time or the speed with which I can twirl the steering wheel if I try to run round those hairpin turns as if I were James Bond. We are talking here about the part of the feedback picture that converts my output (positioning the steering wheel, positioning my reading eyes) into an input. With reading (and writing), we are dealing with the physical fact of the book, its length, weight, sequence, page divisions, size of print, and the like. How quickly can my eyes scan this novel? How fast can I absorb it? How much of the wording of this poem can I remember as I start the next page? How will the page division affect my reading? Does the fine print give me a headache? The answers to such questions would emerge from the bottom of the feedback picture. They affect the answers the reader and the reading writer get from their hypotheses in quite literal, physical ways. When I look at page 111, I cannot at the same time see what is on page 115.

Literary theorists often take for granted a text's "constraining" or "limiting" its reader, and surely most writers would like to think they have that kind of control. Robert Frost certainly wrote as though he did. It is useful, though, to linger on what "constraint" might mean in reading. For example, when I am driving in the Cretan mountains, even on those hairpin turns overlooking hundred-foot drops, the cliff does not constitute a "restraint," at least in my sense of the word. In fact nothing prevents me from going over the edge—that is the trouble with driving in Crete. A guardrail might be a true restraint. It might physically turn the car back even if I tried to go over the edge. The cliff only says, in effect, if you go over my edge, even if you say a prayer as you hurtle past that little shrine, the consequences will be *very* bad.

Mostly, it seems to me, when literary people talk about texts restraining or limiting response, they are really talking about "bad consequences" kinds of restraints, not true physical restraint. The literary theorists mean, If you read it that way, you will make a mess of the text and you will look very silly. If you read "miller" in this poem as a kind of moth, you will make an ass of yourself. That is different from a true physical restraint, in my sense, at least. If you try to read the first three words of this poem as "The wife's miller," you will get gibberish for feedback. You won't feel silly, but baffled. I can imagine, however, a schizophrenic or some ingenious dadaist or even a Japanese translator playing with the idea that the miller is a moth. Indeed, during the excitements of the 1960s, a squib circulated on college campuses that claimed the significance of *Moby-Dick* was that you could use the book to chock the wheels of your car when parked on a hill and keep it from rolling down. The car might have been restrained, but nothing was restraining the student who wrote that critical essay from overturning accepted ideas about literary criticism. In this book I shall claim the term "restraint" only for real physical impossibilities: matters of the physical placement of the text, what pages a normal eye can see simultaneously, what sequence words occur in, how fast a text can be read, how much can be held in memory at once. True restraints from a text are physical-physiological things that limit the feeding back of what I put into the text.

Physiological loops constitute the solid physical foundation on which reading with the eyes or understanding spoken language builds. Most of reading, though, takes place when we apply another kind of hypothesis to the text. When I read "The Mill," I test it first—and this process is so fast and so automatic that it scarcely bears speaking of—to see whether it is English or not. For example, at Christmas 1985, I got a "Season's Greetings" from a new poet, Linda Reinfeld, and the poem began:

> 3w$yv 3w$yv
> zw082 63x/9
> zy/%x5803xz

With such a poem, I become sharply aware of the kinds of hypotheses I am applying. I bring to bear cultural hypotheses about what kinds of letters these are (not kana and not Arabic). I ask if they come together in the usual digraphs and trigraphs of English (th, thr, not yv or xz).

They do not, I am a little taken aback, and I bring a whole battery of new hypotheses to bear. Usually, at some unconscious level, I make sure the letters of a poem form words. Here they do not. I begin testing for other kinds of coherence. For example, will Reinfeld's poem become words if I type it out with my fingers in the wrong "home" position on the keyboard?

Once you or I have got the word-process feedbacks going, we can read a text very rapidly, at hundreds of words a minute. It used to be thought that we read from letters to words to sentences, but now we know that by the time we have recognized some of the words, we have established a context in our minds. This poem is about a miller and where he lives and his wife . . . and we begin to recognize other words and even complex ideas right away. Once I have that larger context I don't need the intermediate work with letters or individual words that characterizes a beginning reader. On this point, the brain physiologists confirm what the psychologists of reading have found.[19]

As a reader I establish, then, cultural feedbacks through "The Mill." This is a poem, in English, not in a challenging "modern" style. From the first moment I see the poem, but particularly after I have established that kind of cultural context, I can bring to bear on the poem various other hypotheses ready-made by my culture. These hypotheses I have internalized, and Figure 6 images the process of applying them, at least in the act of reading.

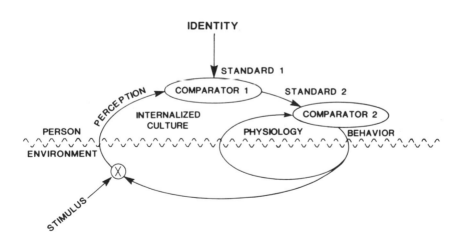

Figure 6.   Feedback controlling feedback in reading and writing

When confronted with a tour bus while driving along the Cretan cliff, my higher-level ideas of safety directed my automatic steering skills to position me closer to the edge of the cliff. The higher-level loop incorporated and made use of the lower loop. So in reading. I have internalized hypotheses from my culture about how to read. These hypotheses incorporate and make use of my loops for seeing and hearing and for dealing with size and sequence and bulk at the lower, physical-physiological level. Figure 6 shows only one "internalized culture" loop, but we have, obviously, many such cultural loops in our minds (or brains) and they overlap and coact and conflict. All are part of one person's system for dealing with the world and its texts. All answer the bidding of one identity—or at least we can think of them that way.

By these loops at an intermediate level, we can represent the skills for reading we internalize from our culture, both simple skills like reading words and sentences and more complex skills that we use for analyzing, interpreting, or judging literature.

> In the act of reading what someone has written, we enter into a kind of social relationship with the writer who has something to tell us or something to make with words and language. The reader takes on this relationship, which may feel like listening, but is in fact different in that it is more active. He recreates the meaning by processing the text at his own speed and in his own way. As he brings the text to life, he casts back and forth in his head for connections between what he is reading and what he already knows. His eyes scan forward or jump backwards. He pauses, rushes on, selects from his memory whatever relates the meaning to his experience or his earlier reading, in a rich and complex system of to-ing and fro-ing in his head, storying, reworking, understanding or being puzzled. Some successful readers say that they feel they are helping to create the work *with* the author.[20]

What Margaret Meek here describes informally as a to-ing and fro-ing is, strictly speaking, a feedback loop. Still more accurately, it is a hierarchy of feedback loops, for reading depends on the interaction of many processes.

Some are low-level processes, notes psychologist Charles Perfetti, such as the recognition of words and the encoding of word meanings. These low-level processes, however, can work only as the individual combines high-level information, semantic context, for example, with low-level information such as letters. Because ideas are the basic units of meaning, they are what readers seek by means of feedbacks, and readers are not content until they get them. To be sure, a skilled reader is efficient at context-free identification of words. Word-level skills by themselves, however, do not suffice for comprehension, because these low-level processes are highly influenced by the reader's general knowledge. It is because I know at a high level that a room-sized mill is for grinding grain, that I also know "The Mill" does not refer to a coffee grinder and the miller is not a moth. It has become increasingly clear, writes psycholinguist Eric Lenneberg, that you cannot separate human language from general human knowledge. Rather, we are talking about high-level and low-level processes in interaction. We are seeing high-level feedbacks used to govern and direct low-level feedbacks.[21]

These high-level feedback loops can represent our knowledge of language, perhaps even the formalized, algebraic grammars described by modern linguists like Noam Chomsky or Juri Lotman. Such a loop might embody the systems of narrative currently being invented by literary theorists in efforts to codify the expectations we bring to stories and novels. Literary narratologists, however, tend to situate their systems in the corpus of stories, whereas psychological narratologists recognize that "narrative competence" has to be in the mind of the reader. Children, for example, acquire a narrative competence very early.[22] Such a competence represents a set of hypotheses to be tried out in a feedback loop. Literary competence represents what we absorb from literature courses in school or college or, more generally, the interpretive communities that teach us how to read poems and stories, starting with the parents who read to us in infancy.

Having distinguished physical-physiological testing-loops from those we internalize from our culture, then, we can draw yet a further distinction in the kinds of things we bring from our culture to a text. I want to subdivide the "internalized culture" loop. I want to distinguish "codes" from "canons." I intend "code" in the strict sense: a rule that makes a message possible. That is, I want to avoid the loose sense of "code" some semioticians use, Roland Barthes, for example, or Umberto Eco. Consider, for example, the famous photograph of the Depression farm wife by Dorothea Lange to which several of the professors linked the miller's wife. I believe many semioticians would say that it is a "code" for poverty, obsolescence, or depression. But why not a code for the oppression of women? For aprons? For thinness? A code in this loose sense decrees a single, universal meaning for what is patently variable. It promotes what is no more than one person's interpretation into "the" meaning for everybody.

Instead, by "code," I mean the rules governing letters of the alphabet, numbers, grammar, recognizing a given word as that word, in general, rules that are absolutely fixed for all the people in a given culture. By "codes" I mean rules about which one can say, "No member of this society would normally claim the rule is otherwise." For example, I see the shape   A   on this line as an A. It would be very difficult for me to interpret it any other way, as a Z, for example, or some Chinese character. Indeed I learned this code so young and have used it so often it would be well-nigh impossible for me to unlearn it. I could live for a decade in Ulan Bator, reading nothing but Khalkha Mongol, and still, if I saw the shape   A   on a printed page, I would very likely think A.

"Codes" in this strict sense are indispensable, enabling, and constraining almost in the same way our bodies are or the physical-physiological loops in the feedback picture. Automatically, we put them as hypotheses into "The Mill" in order to read words, construe sentences, and arrive at meanings. The whole process is so fast and unconscious, we scarcely notice it unless we are dealing with a strange language or a poem like Linda Reinfeld's. These are the codes that fit my fellow-critics' description of what is "inscribed" on us by our culture or what constrains or limits us in "The Mill." The only such code my questionnaire overtly used in connection with "The Mill" was grammar, in Questions 1 and 2. All the poem's readers, though, used, without even noticing them, codes for deriving letters from printed shapes, for recognizing words, for imagining the objects referred to by words ("tea," "fire"), and for combining words into sentences. In effect, codes are rules that provide us with ready-made hypotheses to try out on the text. We can change this kind of rule not at all or only with great difficulty.

We have ready-made rules that c-o-l-d is "cold." We have ready-made rules that t-e-a is "tea" and that c-o-l-d—t-e-a applies syntactically the quality "cold" to the object "tea." It would be very difficult to imagine cold as other than cold, tea as other than tea, or cold tea as other than cold tea, although people might differ as to the point on the thermometer when they would say the tea is cold. All but the last, then, are codes, rules that provide us with ready-made hypotheses, rules that it is very difficult to think one's way out of, although, in application, we may arrive at different results, as in the temperature of the tea.

No member of our culture normally would disagree with the code for multiplication, although we might well disagree when we compared our answers to a big calculation like 1234567×7654321. It is in this sense that we can understand how one third of the professors made a mistake about the antecedent of "what was hanging from a beam" (and professors of English, no less). They had no disagreement about the code, that it was a noun clause, that "what" required an antecedent, only about working out the application of the code. None of us would disagree with the code for calculating logarithms or compound interest, although some of us would have trouble remembering the rules or applying them and others might never have known them.

Other codes would be hard to state at all. Given people's erratic handwriting, how do you decide that an A is an A in all the irregular scripts that people write? Yet people do, and our culture is totally agreed on these matters. *With codes properly so called, no member of our culture would normally claim the rule is otherwise than it is.* My "codes" are, in a term I shall explain a few paragraphs below, "cognitively impenetrable."

Our readers used other rules for interpreting "The Mill" as well, but they were of an entirely different order. We have seen our six professors seek unity in the poem ("each word . . . dependent on the others"). We have seen several professors resist the idea of imagining either the look of the miller's wife or a private association to her. They are, I take it, tacitly following a rule: Good reading confines itself to the words on the page. Asked for a person that the wife reminded them of, several of the professors seemed to assume that only a literary association was proper for a literary work, another rule. Almost all these professors reached for themes that went far beyond millers and weirs, themes like irony, love-death, social determinism (Four), or negativity (Six). Frost, for example, took the poem into themes of obsolescence and progress. Here again I sense a rule. Literary interpretation should move a text from its immediate subject toward more general themes.

This kind of rule I distinguish from a code, because it *can* be otherwise. You *can* say the theme of *Moby-Dick* is, This is for chocking a car on a hill. No guardrail prevents you from saying it. You won't get an A for it, but you surely *can* say it. I shall call this kind of "can be otherwise" rule a canon.

The distinction I am drawing is analogous to that proposed by the Canadian psychologist Zenon Pylyshyn.[23] Pylyshyn distinguishes between those mental capacities that are routinely affected by an individual's symbolic processes, like wishes, beliefs, or values. These are "cognitively penetrable": they change with what we know or believe, as the professors might have interpreted "The Mill" differently thirty years ago or thirty years from now. Other capacities are "cognitively impenetrable." Automatic and encapsulated, they are impervious to an individual's particular values or standards. Only these impermeable capacities can be thought of as "hard-wired" or "inscribed" on the individual's brain. By contrast, penetrable capacities are like software, programmable and subject to change. I take it, when the turn-of-the-century linguist Ferdinand de Saussure spoke of the "arbitrary" quality of the rules for recognizing letters or words, he meant something like my "cannot be otherwise."

"Codes" in my sense are "cognitively impenetrable." Codes include things like rules for interpreting shapes as letters or numbers, the fixed rules of syntax, arithmetic, or algebra, or firmly established cultural codes like "Red means stop, green means go." (No member of our culture would normally say a red traffic light means go.) "An eight-sided sign means stop." "'The Star-Spangled Banner' is the national anthem." "The Orioles play for Baltimore." "In a restaurant, you are given goods in exchange for money or a debt." No member of our culture would under normal circumstances say that the Orioles play for Chicago, or that "Stardust" is the national anthem or that department restaurants give meals away.

About canons, however, it is normal (and desirable!) for people to disagree. Canons express politics or values or beliefs, a person's "philosophy" in the loose sense, a mental "set." Mary Crawford and Roger Chaffin distinguish reading strategies that result from differences in background and differences in viewpoint. Background-canons reflect heritage, education, and life experiences. Viewpoint-canons would relate to opinions and beliefs and would be easier to change than background-canons. Particularly important aspects of personality would give rise to both kinds of canons, for example, one's psychological sense of oneself as female or male.[24]

A canon might represent the intellectual climate of an era, such as the belief common in medieval times that material reality figured a spiritual reality, a belief like Shakespeare's in a natural hierarchy among men, or the nineteenth century belief in an objective historical reality. In other words, what recent French historians call a *mentalité*, what I would call an "internalized cultural system," could be described by this kind of canon-loop between mind and physiology.

These cultural systems are not binding. As we know from such geniuses as Descartes or Nietzsche or Freud, gifted individuals can change the canons they are born into, and less gifted individuals can follow their lead. A canon could represent a national character, the American concern with dependence and independence, the French with authority, or the Japanese with the group. These too we see individuals changing and transcending. One can stand above the national character one was born into and analyze it. One can be born into a capitalist, masculinist, or racist society, but judge it, reform, and find oneself at odds with the society one was born into. Despite some metaphors popular these days among melancholy sophomores, the failings of a sexist or capitalist society are not "inscribed" permanently in our growing and ungrowing brains the way a language is.

Think of driving again. A Hungarian driver who has internalized the exuberant driving characteristic of his culture may choose to drive right up to the edge of a Cretan cliff. As a middle-aged small-town American, I feel more comfortable with a good meter of margin. We can take those cultural differences into account by imagining driving as feedback loops. There is a lower-level physical and physiological loop, which will be about the same for every normal person driving that model of car. We set the standard for that physical loop through an intermediate cultural loop, representing the biases we have all internalized from our driving culture, our various "sets." Finally each individual driver, each individual

Hungarian or small-town American, will set his or her cultural standards in his or her own way.

If we subdivide what we have internalized from our driving culture into codes and canons, we can still more closely image the relative roles of individuality, culture, and physical reality. The physical-physiological loop is the same for Hungarian daredevil and American professor. Both will have to shift into second to go up a mountain. Codes are also the same for the two. Drive on the right. Red means stop. You are supposed to halt at a railroad crossing. Either may choose to disobey the rules, but they will not differ as to what the rules are. Finally there are canons, national driving styles. The Hungarian drives with the mustachioed bravado of his fierce Magyar ancestors. The American drives to demonstrate his phallic expertise and Californian cool. The drivers have some choice about the canons, unlike the codes. The Hungarian could learn to drive like an American, the American like a Hungarian. Then, finally, there are individual drivers, Laszlo and Antal and Jane and Norm.

We are singling out, then, several features for the brains of the drivers, and several features for the six professors reading "The Mill": an identity governing a hierarchy of feedback loops with which it tests its world; within that hierarchy, codes that cannot normally be otherwise and canons that can. Such a hierarchy of feedbacks gives us a way of imagining levels of control. In particular, we can adapt our picture of an identity governing a hierarchy of canons and codes to take into account the likenesses and differences within a group like our six professors. So far as literature is concerned, codes would enable us to read letters and words, to parse phrases and sentences, and to recognize the objects referred to (a rose is a rose is a rose—in our culture). Canons would include one's tactics for interpreting, one's idea of what a poem or a fiction ought to be, one's values—all those things about which professors and other members of a literary culture customarily differ.

Interestingly, the meanings of words probably fall into the realm of canons rather than codes. People do commonly differ about the meanings of words, and dictionaries themselves differ in their phrasings. Perhaps we need to take a linguistic leaf from Saussure and regard a word (or sign) as its difference from other meanings and other words (or signs). Even so, we would find considerable variation among normal members of a culture in how such differences or words are organized in their minds. It seems to me that Saussure much overstates the case when he claims, "Language can also be compared with a sheet of paper: thought is the front and the sound the back; one cannot cut the front without cutting the back at the same time; likewise in language, one can neither divide sound from thought nor thought from sound."[25] I do not think words are physically, rigidly, attached to concepts that way. People may agree fairly well about what "horse" or "tree" bring to mind (Saussure's examples), but what about "democracy" or "God"? What about "on" or "was"?

Eric Lenneberg provides a useful counter to Saussure with his concise description of the brain as it engages language. "One of the most characteristic aspects of language is its relative 'fuzziness.'" There are no vocabulary items in which meaning is sharply defined. No phoneme has absolute acoustic boundaries. Syntax is also fuzzy, "and it is this fuzziness that makes it impossible to separate syntax from semantics, thus wedding the realm of language irrevocably to the realm of knowledge in general." Lenneberg takes us back, in effect, to the limbic system, to our mammalian brains that built a world out of our sensory data before there was any language.[26]

As readers and writers, we learn both interpretive canons and linguistic codes from our culture. When we read something like "The Mill," any one reader uses both kinds of rules, putting both kinds of hypotheses out into the poem. Psychologically, however, the two kinds of rules have quite a different status in the mind's hierarchy of feedbacks. When interpreting, one can simply choose to pay exact attention to the lifelike details of a story and stop looking for universal themes. One can put aside a search for unity and start deconstructing as easily as one can drop the Odd Fellows and join the Elks. One cannot so easily abandon seeing A as A or stop thinking in terms of subject-verb.

One kind of literary rule, the interpretive canon, we deliberately choose and learn. The other, the linguistic code, we learned willy-nilly and we can hardly unlearn it. In fact, our literary culture tolerates great variation as to whether one looks for theme or realism, character or construct, unity or disunity. You cannot apply the shibboleth, "No member of this culture will normally claim the rule is otherwise," to a canon, although you can to all kinds of syntactic transformations. A linguistic culture rests on codes. A literary culture builds canons on a linguistic culture.

When the professors read words and syntax, they did so all more or less alike. They were using codes. If I had asked them for the "theme" of "The Mill," though, I would have gotten a wide range of answers. We have seen Frost's theme, the tricks life plays on those who invest life or capital. We have seen Professor Three's idea for the poem, the treating of people as objects. I am sure others would have arrived at yet other themes. Similarly, if I had asked for the wife's motive or the miller's, I am sure I would have gotten a wide range of answers. We simply cannot apply our shibboleth, No reader in this culture would normally read it otherwise, to matters of literary interpretation.

This distinction shows a confusion in the idea of a "literary competence." "Competence" in Chomsky's syntactic sense means the ability to apply syntactic rules to make and understand sentences. These are rules that "native speakers" may not be able to articulate, but within their dialect group they do not differ in practice about what constitutes "good English." These are codes, and we use these codes to read literature.

By contrast people regularly differ about what poems and stories mean and professors argue, and are paid to argue, about what are the right rules for getting at meanings. To speak of "literary competence," as some theorists of literature do, is to equate rules for interpreting literature with rules for understanding sentences. In my terms, such a phrase lumps canons into codes. It promotes the deliberate, studied practice of a small group of people in universities with the syntactic rules all speakers of English are born into, learn intuitively, without study, internalize as children, and continue to live by all their lives.[27] If we professors treat our literary interpretations as self-evident cultural universals like syntax, we are taking ourselves very seriously indeed.

The opposite error is also possible, isolating codes and canons from the individual using them. George Dillon raises this possibility. In studying readers of Faulkner's well-known story, "A Rose for Emily," he singled out three different styles of reading.[28] Some readers elaborate the main character's traits, motives, thoughts, responses, or choices. Other readers ("Diggers," Dillon calls them) use symbolisms and depth psychology to get at the story's "secrets." A third group, the "Anthropologists," identify cultural norms and values that explain what the characters do. Dillon calls these different practices reading or cognitive styles. (I would call them interpretive canons.) He contrasts them with "deeper, unconscious entities." "At issue really is the learnability of these approaches." Presumably, Dillon is implying that I can change my style of interpretation but not my character. One is cognitively permeable, the other not.

True enough. One can learn to read for unity, for social implications, or for lifelikeness. But a critic like Professor Two is as passionately attracted to the unfolding of literary language as I am to the search for unities. We err if we make it a matter of either-or, either reading style or unconscious need. It is both-and. Two's reading style and mine parallel and express our unconscious needs as well as our cultural training. From the repertoire our literary culture offers us, each of us chose those canons of interpretation that suited our conscious and unconscious needs or the identities shaping and shaped by those needs. If we had chosen differently, we would have been showing an identity changed in at least that respect.

For working out such explorations of the individual's relation to codes and canons, most people use the familiar terms "subjective" and "objective." It seems to me, however, that they rather muddle the picture. We could say that you and I are "subjective" individuals—identities. By contrast, these hypotheses look "objective," not "subjective," because they come from our commitment to a convention, an interpretive community, a syntactic code, or even our own physiology. They stem from things outside, as it were, our "subjective" personality-selves.

In practice, however, one cannot separate self from code or canon as if they were in separate bins. Simply to label the self subjective and the code or canon objective does not do justice to the way they each involve the other. We subjects use these more or less "objective" codes and canons. We put them forth as hypotheses against which to read the text. They may come from somebody else, but when we put them out toward a text they serve *our* identities. We then hear the text reward some of these hypotheses and defeat others, but we hear individually. We apply the standards that committed us to our hypotheses in the first place to judge the return our hypotheses yield in the second.

You and I sense both a cognitive and an emotional return from the text. We find the poem delightful, moderately pleasing, anxiety-arousing, incoherent, frustrating—whatever. These feelings and emotions come about as you and I compare the return we get from the text with our inner standards for, perhaps, coherence, complexity, unity, or intensity. These inner standards are in turn functions of our respective identities. You and I may have learned them in a literature class, but they *also* express unconscious needs—otherwise we would not use them. Instead of dividing reading into an subjective part and an objective part, we can make more precise sense by saying "subjective" *uses* "objective" so that the two are really indissoluble. Finally, though, they do not represent a helpful distinction.

The feedback picture, by contrast, does let me visualize the working of Robert Frost's brain, at least in broad outline. Frost had purposes and goals at the top of his brain. I can guess at those higher goals and put them into words as my perception of Frost's identity. These goals set the references and signals for simpler reflex processes. This identity directed sight and taste and touch at the lowest levels of Frost's brain and at the edges and boundaries of his body. In the same way, his identity set standards for his literary behavior. We all share the English language, but no one will write a poem just like Robert Frost. Further, no one will *interpret* a poem just like Robert Frost.

Imagined this way, the feedback picture can refine considerably the idea of identity as a theme and variations. We can imagine a Robert Frost or a Professor Five as having a certain central theme on which he or she plays infinitely many variations. Partly, this identity operates by means of Professor Five's beliefs about mothers or Robert Frost's about the New

Deal. Partly the identity operates by means of Frost's or Professor Two's preoccupation and skill with language, at least some of which every speaker of English shares. And partly the identity operates by means of sight, hearing, and touch which are about the same for all human beings, whether or not they speak English.

In terms of identity, Professor Three was concerned with interchanging person and thing. This interest governed her use of familiar interpretive techniques. She could, for example, understand the phrase "would soon appear / The same as ever to the sight" as "heals itself." Her personality overall guided her use of shared techniques toward a particular reading that felt "right" to her. In the same way, Six used her critical skill in managing ambiguity to manage her own anxiety about deprivation. Six used techniques many critics share with her, but she used them to suit her unique identity. Two used a displacement to language that many critics would applaud, but he used it to serve his defensive needs as well as to interpret the poem. So do we all, including Robert Frost. He used Robinson's poem about the miller to develop his own sense of against-ness and balance, the small daring the large.

I too. In tracing themes in these responses, my reading of the professors' responses is as much a function of my identity as the professors' readings are of theirs (just as my reading of Robert Frost is as much a function of my identity as Robert Frost's reading of Robinson's poem is). Murray Schwartz knows me about as well as anybody does. He described my identity theme as a "delight in individual differences" combined with a "genius for unifying diverse materials." "Freedom and variety within the sameness of identity are the hallmarks of Norm's life."[29] Surely, by this time in this book, you can see the sense in Murray's reading, for this book "reads" me, Frost reads me, you read me.

That is, my conclusions, like theirs, express me as well as they express whom and what I am reading. Hence, what I am describing is a mutual interpretation. Professor One reads the poem and the poem, so to speak, reads her. I read Professor One's response and her response, so to speak, reads me. By my model of an identity governing feedbacks, I am trying to represent that systematically elusive process in words, to hold it still, at least momentarily, for *your* perusal and response. You in turn will bring to my picture skills you share with others, but you will also respond to the model in your own unique way.

We can sum all this up as an identity governing a hierarchy of feedbacks. The model embodies three basic ideas about the mind as it engages in interpretation. First, interpretation is a feedback process. Second, the feedback occurs in a hierarchy. Higher-level processes direct lower-level processes. Third, at the top is an identity. It consists of the history of a theme and its variations as they govern and permeate that hierarchy.

Within that picture of an identity governing feedbacks, we can distinguish different levels in the process of reading literature. I have pointed to four: one's personal identity; canons chosen from the culture's repertoire because they suit one's identity; codes learned willy-nilly from the culture regardless of identity; physical and physiological limits imposed by one's body and the real world, again, regardless of identity.

At the lowest level, I sense on this page a pattern of whites and blacks. Some levels up, I read an   A   as an A, I understand that   A   as part of a word like "part," and I understand that "part" in turn as part of a total sentence, which is in turn part of a whole idea. I am at the level of codes, still not clearly expressing identity. As I reach toward ideas and themes, though, I pass into the third highest loop, the canons about which normal members of a culture differ. As I reach higher and higher on the level of abstraction, my understanding becomes more and more personal: *part* is more personal than A; the sentence I take in as a whole is more personal than the one word; and my inner phrasing of the idea more personal than the sentence.

All levels ultimately serve identity, yet at every level feedback operates. Identity is the top-down agency that applies hypotheses. I put trials of meaning and context and syntax out into the text, and the text rewards my good hypotheses and defeats my poor ones, until I arrive at a total reading. Both the hypotheses and the way I "hear" the return from the text depend upon my personal standards, upon my style of reading, upon what feels like a discrepancy to me—in short, on my identity. Identity's values govern and permeate this hierarchy of feedback loops.

Identity is also a consequence. It is what is created by the continuing flow of these identity-creating experiences of trying out hypotheses and having them succeed or fail. That is, identity is what one brings to new experiences, and it is what is created by those same experiences.

The redundancy in that sentence is hard to make sense of in words, although engineers who work with feedback can describe these processes in less than a page of well-known second-order differential equations. Simple they may be for engineers, but few humanists studying the mind of a writer or reader are likely to think easily in differential equations. Words are the stock in trade of the humanist. Words, however, particularly nouns and noun-adjective phrases, can leave us with dichotomies that make it hard to think about a continuous process. Is a reading of a poem "input" or "output"? Both, really. Is a reading an action or a perception? Again, it is really a combination of the two. Objective or subjective? Is meaning inside a person or outside? These words offer dichotomies that look commonsensical, but what we need for our model is a coherent, continuous system.

Perhaps "model" is too strong. In the first instance, anyway, I intend a metaphor or a guiding principle. I am offering a picture, like Figure 4 or 6, that one can carry about in one's head with which to think about the brain as it reads and writes literature. If I put that picture in words, a person—an identity—reading "The Mill," uses hypotheses with which to sense the poem. The poem responds to those hypotheses, and the individual *feels* whether it is a favorable or unfavorable response and so closes the loop, preparatory to sending another hypothesis out around it. In writing "The Mill," Robinson used those same skills to create a text, which he then read and responded to like the rest of us, and changed according to his response.

More generally, the picture consists of:

a hierarchy of feedback loops, each providing the standard for the loop below it

    at the highest level, an identity interpreted as a theme and variations;

    at intermediate levels, loops internalized from culture, of two kinds:

        code-loops: "No member of this culture would normally believe the rule is otherwise;"

        canon-loops, rules about which people regularly differ;

    at the lowest level, a physical-physiological loop.

I would be overloading my simple picture if I claimed it "explains" how authors and readers communicate, how the mind of Professor One experiences the Robinson poem differently from Professor Six, or how the mind of Robert Frost results from the brain of Robert Frost. I do think, however, the idea of identity governing a hierarchy of feedbacks offers us a manageable picture, a working hypothesis against which to hear claims about reading and writing and Robert Frost and brains. With this picture I can visualize how "subjectivity" enters the literary process alongside "objectivity." I can realize the relation between fixed cultural codes and the mutable canons we learned in school for reading poems. I can imagine how feelings guide our cognitive responses or how the physical text relates to the emotional experience we have. The picture of an identity governing a hierarchy of feedbacks lets me pose such questions and at least begin to answer them. It lets me see the literary process far more clearly than do the usual metaphors by which we talk about literature, metaphors like LITERATURE AS CONDUIT or LITERATURE AS FORCE—metaphors to which we shall now digress.

7

A Digression on Metaphors

One of the most intriguing books I have read in recent years is George Lakoff and Mark Johnson's 1980 *Metaphors We Live By*.[1] They show that when we speak or write, we are constantly using metaphors to put abstract principles into concrete terms. The abstract principles are those that underlie our most fundamental cultural assumptions, and the terms are concrete in the simplest sensory way. In 1987 Lakoff and Johnson each produced books expanding this idea from metaphors to "image schemas" or "idealized cognitive models."[2] They are exploring a fundamental characteristic of human thought. We use basic, body images like hot-cold, high-low, or touching to structure our experience. Especially, we use these physical, body images to render abstractions in terms we can physically sense.

For example, they note in their earlier book that we customarily speak of arguments in the language of war:

Professor One *demolished* Professor Two's *indefensible* theory.

Professor Three *won* the argument.

Professor Four *shot down* Professor Five's interpretation.

Professor Six does not *attack every weak point*.

A cluster of metaphors like ARGUMENT IS WAR expresses some of our deepest feelings about what it is to engage in an argument, what it is to lose one, and what it is to stay out of one.

By contrast, ask Lakoff and Johnson, suppose we lived in a culture where the fundamental metaphor for argument was ARGUMENT IS DANCE.

Professor One and Professor Two *waltzed through* the reader-response arguments together.

Professor Three *pirouetted around* the scientific claims of experimental psychologists.

So far as the positivist view of emotion is concerned, Professor Four's paper
boogies right on down.

I take it, among other things, academia would be a much happier place.

Such metaphors let us give form to our underlying attitudes and the
metaphors in turn react upon those attitudes. We translate abstractions
like "argument" into immediate, experiential terms: fighting, eating,
forces, sizes, up-down, in-out, or part-whole, much as a poet like Frost
does. Lakoff and Johnson argue that we humans need clusters of metaphors like ARGUMENT IS WAR in order to grasp abstractions. Like a
poem, such a cluster continues and sustains those feelings. By a kind
of metaphorical logic, a metaphor may even extend a feeling to related
situations.

Such metaphors, like a Frost poem, both reflect and guide the attitudes
they express. Hence, to become aware of them is to become aware of
one's own attitudes and beliefs. That is one of the basic functions of the
"talking cure" and the reason a psychotherapist pays particular heed to
a patient's figures of speech. By saying your free associations out loud
to another person, you make your imagery and metaphors available.
You open up a way of self-knowledge and perhaps, if that is what you
want, through self-knowledge, self-change.

We have certain metaphors we use, in the Lakoff-Johnson manner,
for talking about reading, writing, and teaching literature. Like codes
and canons, those metaphors both express and form our thinking. They
both come from and give rise to the metaphors with which we think
about other, larger questions, such as how we perceive and, in general,
how our brains deal with the world around us.

We think, for example, of things going "into" and "out of" sight. In
doing so, we are treating our sight as a container. Marriage can be a
container, too, as when we speak of being "trapped in a marriage." By
contrast, when we speak of people "splitting up," we are thinking of
marriage as a whole-with-parts. At other times, we might speak of relationships as links, as in "making connections" or "breaking social ties."
"Losing your hair" treats the "you" as a center, the hair as a periphery.
A list of such schemas might include: container; part-whole; link; center-
periphery; source-path-goal; near-far; full-empty; surface, and so on.[3]

These metaphors or "image schemas" or "cognitive models" occupy
a special place among codes and canons. On the one hand, they rest on
physical realities (like hands). On the other, they express attitudes widely
shared within a given culture. For example, "In India, society is conceived
of as a body (the whole) with castes as parts—the highest caste being

the head and the lowest caste being the feet."[4] Can such a schema (body, part-whole) "be otherwise" in a given culture? Can we shed such a cultural model and learn another? I think we can. Can we learn to stop thinking of argument as war and think of it as dance? I think so. Hence, these metaphors and schemas grow from bodily realities, but they are, ultimately, canons. They are interpretive modes that our culture teaches us but that we can change.

At least, I have to think we can know and change our schemas and metaphors, for that is what I am trying to do in this book. I am asking you to recognize and accept a new model (feedback) for our existing schemas for literary experience. I think we can. I think that becoming more self-conscious about our literary schemas may enable us to think more clearly about writers, readers, books, Robert Frost, and the way our brains work with literature.

Here, for example, are some metaphorical expressions that people might use about Frost poems. I want to explore the assumptions these familiar metaphors represent. Although I made these sentences up, they are the sort of thing you and I have read hundreds of times in literary reviews and criticism:

The last lines of "Mending Wall" are *striking*.
The end of the first stanza has *real impact*.
The final scene of "The Mill" is *gripping*.
The dialogue in "Hired Man" has but a tentative *force*.

These phrasings illustrate a family of metaphors I call LITERATURE IS A PHYSICAL FORCE. It is a family from which many writers about literature actually draw:

"Much of the *power* of the images in "Dulce et Decorum Est" arises from Owen's use of simile . . ." [from a textbook].

"The precision of the images in *striking* the core of human feeling is splendid" [student paper].

"[The most important word is] dead. [It] is right at beginning of poem & *puts weight on everything that follows*" [one of the forty-four anonymous professors].

"[The most important word is] what. [It] *brings reader in*" [one of the anonymous professors].

Naturally, we hear these same metaphors in our critical classics. In a famous passage of the *Preface to Shakespeare*, Dr. Johnson remarks, "It will be asked how the drama *moves* . . .", and goes on to an even more deliberate use of the physical force metaphor: "So *powerful is the current of the poet's imagination that the mind which once ventures within it is hurried irresistibly along*."

Now this implies a simple picture of text and reader, just—

$$\text{Text} \xrightarrow{\text{acts on}} \text{Reader}$$

The text is the active one in the transaction. It *does* things to its readers. This is what I have been calling the "text-active model" of literary response, far and away the most widespread among the people who write today's literary theory.

In a variation of this LITERATURE IS FORCE metaphor, we speak of writing as guiding or controlling us:

By his irony, Frost carefully *directs* our feelings.

"Once by the Pacific" *defines* a range of possible responses.

The imagery of "The Death of the Hired Man" *limits* the grief we feel.

Again, although I have made these examples up, they typify what literary critics and reviewers write. As in the title of a recent, highly successful book, they assume "textual power."

This metaphor, LITERATURE IS CONTROLLER, has grown into the most widespread school of criticism in German-speaking countries, *Rezeptions-ästhetik* as developed by literary theorists like Wolfgang Iser. *Rezeptions-ästhetik* is the study of a literary work through its "reception" (*Rezeption*, not response, *Wirkung*).[5] "Reception" takes readers in relation to a work, not as individuals, but collectively. Often a reception theorist considers how the work's audience taken as a bloc responded at various points in history. One *Rezeptionsästhetik* study looked at some 900 novels circulating in France in 1856 to explore what people expected when they picked up *Madame Bovary* in 1857. The critics considered no actual readers, notice, but the novels readers were reading in 1856. Texts. In other versions of *Rezeptionsästhetik*, critics take the position that one can presume a large part, at least, of the collective response by looking at the text itself, sometimes (but not always) focusing on just the reader implied or posited by the text.

In other words, *Rezeptionsästhetik* mostly presumes a literary response from some literary text. In its most influential form, it builds on what I call a bi-active model for literary response: a text sets limits on its reader's experience but it also leaves gaps within which each reader can freely imagine. Surely this is a very commonsensical view of the literary process. Wolfgang Iser writes, for example, "If communication between text and reader is to be successful, clearly the reader's activity must also be *controlled* in some way by the text."[6] I believe Iser does not regard the responses of real readers as relevant for theory, but if he were to consider Frost's and the professors' readings of "The Mill," he would account for the likenesses by saying the text controls its readers. He would account for the differences, I assume, by saying the various readers are simply filling in the gaps in the text where they are free to do so. Naturally, they fill in those gaps differently and unpredictably.

Iser paints a more complicated picture than the simple text-active, LITERATURE IS FORCE model. His *Rezeptionsästhetik* presupposes a two-27. Commemoration of the storming of the Bastille   000way interaction:

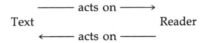

                              ——— acts on ———→
              Text   Reader
                        ←——— acts on ———

This two-way, bi-active model with its two separate arrows implies that one can separate the reading transaction into two pieces. In one a reader does something to a text, and in the other a text does something to a reader. In this second half you have exactly the same text-active model as in other, simpler LITERATURE IS FORCE metaphors. In other words, although *Rezeption* critics sometimes use the language of feedback, they are usually not using a real feedback model. In real feedback the "action" of the text comes wholly in *re*action to what some actual reader brings to it.

The text-active model and the metaphors associated with it admit still other variations. For example, literary people often speak of a book as another person, usually in a dialogue:

"The Mill" *asks us* to imagine grief within the mind of a simple working woman.

A Frost poem typically *invites us* to infer larger, abstract meanings.

"The Mill" *requires* that we know something about industrial changes in the early twentieth century.

"*Goodbye Columbus* [the film] is clearly not a work which *knows* its own vulgarity" (Stanley Cavell).

Here too, as with *Rezeptionsästhetik*, the implied model (LITERATURE IS ANOTHER PERSON) is two-way—bi-active—hence more complex than the ordinary LITERATURE IS FORCE metaphor that rests on a simple text-active model. This cluster has text and reader interacting like two equal parties in a dialogue or a struggle.

Nevertheless all three, LITERATURE IS FORCE, LITERATURE IS CONTROLLER, LITERATURE IS PERSON, have something in common as opposed to the feedback picture of Figures 4 or 6. In the feedback model, the text only does something *because* we do something to it. By itself, a text is inert. The answers we get from a text depend upon the questions we ask. A text "does" something only as part of our asking. In these three metaphorical clusters, however, the text does something all by itself. A text is an independent entity with, as it were, a will or at least an effect of its own. All three treat a film or a poem or a story as either a knowing, speaking Other or a physical force vis-à-vis its audience, but, no matter which, an Other who acts on you and me.

Another common family of metaphors treats the literary work as a thing in itself but made up of parts that can be separated from one another like different numbers in a sum:

Referring to God at the end *puts* religious meaning into a seaside storm.

The repetition of the proverb in "Mending Wall" *detracts from* the tragic feeling by *reducing* the pessimism of the poem.

"The tragedy has *lost half its beauty*" (*The Spectator*).

"There is no scene which *does not contribute* to the aggravation of the distress or conduct of the action, and scarce a line which *does not conduce* to the progress of the scene" (Samuel Johnson).

Following Dr. Johnson, you could say a line *subtracts from* or *cancels out* or *becomes a factor in*—and so on through all the modes of arithmetic.

This metaphor also lends itself to various figures based on following recipes or filling prescriptions:

Form and content *combine* to produce a unified effect.

"There is a *certain* romantic *element in* each [of Shakespeare's tragicomic romances]. They *receive contributions from every portion* of Shakespeare's genius . . ." (Edward Dowden).

Hence, a branch of this family of ISOLABLE PARTS metaphors treats the literary work as the result of some arithmetical operation in which, say,

Flashback technique *adds* a whole new dimension to the poem.

Alliteration is only one of many *factors* that produce the poetic effect.

"In addition to appealing to our senses with images, authors also appeal to our intellectual ability to connect the literal meanings of language (what the dictionary definitions *add up to*) with imagined or figurative meanings."

This last example comes from a textbook and reminds me that some textbooks and courses in literature build on a radical extension of the metaphor, LITERARY EXPERIENCE IS ISOLABLE PARTS. The class spends a couple of weeks on "point of view," several periods on "theme," another segment on "character," a week on "structure." Inevitably, such courses treat each technique as a part that can be marked off from the total literary work or experience.

Implicit in the idea that a poem or play can be divided into parts is the idea that the text is a whole *within* which are isolable parts. Thus some ISOLABLE PARTS metaphors shade over into the group Lakoff and Johnson single out as the system, LINGUISTIC EXPRESSIONS ARE CONTAINERS. Alternatively, a fine paper by the linguist Michael Reddy identifies this group as "The Conduit Metaphor."[7]

In this model, people speak of literature as containing or holding or delivering something. Words surround meanings the way books enclose pages. For example,

Frost's poems *contain* a great deal of wisdom.

There is a lot of truth *in* "The Mill."

Think of the student question that an enthusiastically analytic professor is most likely to hear, "Do you really think Shakespeare *put all this stuff in there?*"

But even readers who have more experience say things like,

What you *got out of that line* is certainly not what the rest of us *took away from it.*

Poetry *captures* feelings *in words*.

Professor Two's words are *hollow*.

Frost's poems *have* a great deal of moral *content*.

I don't like poems that *deliver messages*.

Frost *filled his writings* with his farming experiences.

"Art is inherently, inescapably, *loaded with*—indeed made of—ideology" (Wayne Booth, summing Bakhtin).

[The wife's appearance?] "No clue *in* poem" [one of the anonymous professors].

Day after day I hear one or another of my non-reader-response colleagues insisting at me, "The meaning is right there! *in* the words on the page!"

The basic assumption is an ancient one: words have an inside and an outside. The meaning is inside the word, whose outside consists of its physical sound or shape. The outside is physical, and the inside is psychological. A writer puts something from his psyche inside this outer container, the text. Then the text delivers its contents the way a truck or a pipeline would. Alternatively, the reader digs a meaning out, but, of course, you can only "get" the meaning that is already there.

If *Rezeptionsästhetik* is the critical school built on the LITERATURE IS CONTROLLER metaphor, semiotics is the school that rests on LITERATURE IS A CONDUIT. Reviewing for the *New York Times*, a professor of philosophy defined semiotics as "the study of signs; it is interested in anything that *carries meaning*."[8] Like the *Times'* reviewer, semioticists themselves use container metaphors. Here, for example, is Roland Barthes describing the way myths mean:

> The signifier of myth presents itself in an ambiguous way: it is at the same time meaning and form, *full on one side* and *empty* on the other. As meaning, the signifier already postulates a reading, I grasp it through my eyes, it has a sensory reality . . . , there is *a richness in it* . . .
>
> When it [the meaning] becomes form, the meaning leaves its contingency behind; it *empties itself*, it becomes impoverished, history evaporates, only the letter *remains*.[9]

In the idea that a signifier is full of meaning or an empty form, Barthes is adapting the conduit metaphor into a full-fledged theory of language. It is a highly determinate theory in which a signifier dictates its own interpretation: it "postulates a reading." In general, in the world posited by this kind of criticism as by the LITERATURE AS FORCE metaphors, words and signs *do* things. Here, "The meaning leaves its contingency behind."

Hence, if I try to render these figures of speech in a picture, I get something not very different from the LITERATURE IS FORCE schema:

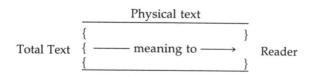

There is a pre-packaged meaning that the text as a whole simply delivers like the Post Office. Alternatively, the reader works to "get" a meaning that is already "there." It is in this sense, I take it, that Barthes' signifier "postulates a reading."

In general, these metaphors combine and interact to create still other metaphors. For example, LITERATURE IS CONTAINER shades easily into an idea of literature as containing something valuable within itself, literature as carrying a treasure or a precious possession, the "heritage" of our civilization. We combine LITERATURE IS CONTAINER with LITERATURE IS FORCE in metaphors like:

> I got *a bang out of* "Mending Wall."
> I get *a lift from* Robert Frost.

An apostrophe from De Quincey's essay on *Macbeth* combines the IS-OLABLE PARTS metaphor with the CONTAINER, as he addresses Shakespeare:

> O mighty poet! Thy works . . . . are to be studied . . . in the perfect faith that *in them there can be no too much or too little,* nothing useless or inert . . .

One of the anonymous professors, answering Question 2, stating the antecedent of "What else there was," combined CONTAINER, ISOLABLE PARTS, and LITERATURE IS FORCE:

> It refers to that "something" that pervades the room,
> fills it with suspense. Not knowing what that something
> is is *half the reason* for its *powerful effect.*

One could go on and on—after all, it is impossible to talk without metaphors.

We also use these clusters of metaphor with a certain logic. Sometimes one such metaphor entails another. Sometimes a group of such metaphors are subsets of one larger, less articulated metaphor. I think that is true here with LITERATURE IS OTHER, LITERARY EXPERIENCE IS ISOLABLE PARTS, and LITERATURE IS CONDUIT. For me, each implies a certain picture of the literary transaction.

LITERATURE IS ISOLABLE PARTS divides something that is made up of one and the same words into form and content, sound and sense, imagery and plot, or text and meaning. We use the ISOLABLE PARTS metaphor to image to ourselves theme or imagery by treating them as different parts of the text—isolable. By contrast, the feedback metaphor pictures one book acted on by different systems responsive to one self. Theme or imagery then become different ways of looking at a book. We bring hypotheses or guesses about theme or imagery to it, and we are rewarded or not. Both models or metaphors can represent the success we feel when we come to a book looking for one specific thing, realism, say, or deconstruction. In the separable parts model, we are likely to feel, "I have 'found it,' " a separable it. In the feedback model, we are likely to feel "I have succeeded in 'doing it,' " deconstructing the text, for example, or finding realism. The feedback picture translates into verbs, while LITERATURE IS ISOLABLE PARTS divides the book or the interaction between book and reader into separate things—nouns.

LITERATURE IS FORCE suggests a simple cause-effect or stimulus-response model. The book and our experience of the book, signifier and signified, words and meaning, are sharply bounded from each other. One is cause, the other effect. By making the book either an outside force or another person, the whole family of LITERATURE IS OTHER metaphors separates the literary work from its reader or hearer. LITERATURE IS CONDUIT divides a book into a meaning and the text's directly observable parts, like sound, shape, size, or arrangement. It, too, isolates a literary work from its readers and hearers. They, separate beings, get separable meanings "out of" the containing text, and that text is as separate from its audience as a carafe is separate from the drinker.

All these different systems of metaphor thus presuppose various divisions. They either divide the work of literature within itself or they mark off audience, maker, and work from one another. Literature is either isolated in a self-other way—literature is isolated from its readers and hearers—or literature is made up in itself of isolable parts. It seems to me, then, that LITERARY EXPERIENCE IS ISOLABLE PARTS is the general metaphorical principle that entails the other two.

There are, of course, other figures of speech for literature, but this large and pervasive family of metaphors suggests one fundamental attitude. Literature is distinctly other and separate. At least we *can* isolate it. These metaphors all voice one basic attitude, and it runs counter to the sense of literature as a process in which writer and book or book and reader animate one another in a continuous system.

One thing that interests me in these metaphors for reading and literature is the way they also crop up in non-literary contexts. For instance, many introductory psychology textbooks discuss the effects of heredity and environment on human intelligence, and particularly the controversy over applying I.Q. tests to disadvantaged minorities. In the quotations that follow, I have italicized the phrases I want to single out from a particularly popular textbook:[10]

> In addition, they [those who spoke for the disadvantaged] argued that intellectual attitudes are *much more determined* by nurture than nature. In

their view, differences in intelligence, especially those between different ethnic and racial groups, are *determined predominantly by* environmental factors such as early home background and schooling.

There is evidently a genetic component in the *determination* of intelligence-test performance. But heredity alone does not *account for all of the variance* in intellectual performance. There is little doubt that environmental factors also *play a role*.

The evidence as a whole dictates the conclusion that *both* genetic and environmental factors *play a role* in *determining* IQ variations within groups. On this point there is wide agreement.

. . . the genetic interpretation does not imply that environmental intervention—in home or school—will have no *effect*. There is no one who denies that environmental factors *are responsible for some proportion of* the between-group variance.

All this sounds sensible, if somewhat ponderous, quite in the manner of social science textbooks. I see the underlined passages, however, as resting on a certain number of assumptions, parallel to the common metaphors for literary response. This textbook builds from the same deterministic picture as LITERATURE IS FORCE, but the author applies the picture to psychological causes for a response rather than textual ones. In particular, forms of the word "determines" occur four times in these brief quotations. The passages insist that heredity and environment determine, cause, or are responsible for, variations in intelligence. In effect, the model is:

$$\text{Stimulus} \longrightarrow \text{leads to} \longrightarrow \text{Response}$$

The author makes the further assumption that one can isolate stimuli like heredity or environment, dividing, if necessary, the response they cause into a proportion due to one stimulus, a proportion due to a second, and so on.

$$
\begin{array}{l}
\text{Stimulus \#1} \longrightarrow \text{One fraction of response }\} \\
\text{Stimulus \#2} \longrightarrow \text{One fraction of response }\} \quad \text{Total} \\
\text{Stimulus \#3} \longrightarrow \text{One fraction of response }\}
\end{array}
$$

Then these fractions add up, as it were, to the total response. Diverse causes combine to form one effect. In another context, obviously, one could have several different stimuli leading to several different responses:

Stimulus #1 ──────→ Response A
Stimulus #2 ──────→ Response B
Stimulus #3 ──────→ Response C

As I see it, this model of the human being, widely used by conventional psychological experimenters, combines the LITERATURE IS FORCE metaphor with the LITERATURE IS ISOLABLE PARTS and extends them to all human activities. Events can be separated into causes and effects (or independent and dependent variables). One can isolate these variables from one another, and one can isolate the experimenter from what he or she is studying, much as conventional literary criticism isolates the text from its reader. Similarly, it is good experimental practice in psychology to carry on research by breaking a large question down into smaller ones, that is, smaller correlations of stimulus to response or of independent to dependent variables. From the attitudes these metaphors express proceed some of the most useful assumptions of psychological research. Traditional psychologists define them as the very essence of the "scientific."

The passage shows still another intriguing variation on STIMULUS IS FORCE. At one point the author asserts, "The evidence . . . dictates the conclusion that . . . " At other points he expresses conclusions this way: "There is little doubt that . . . " or "On this point there is wide agreement" or "There is no one who denies that . . ." Now these are two quite different pictures of psychologists' response to evidence. In the first the evidence determines the outcome, just as a stimulus determines a response, or a text a meaning. In the second, the psychologists do. Indeed the second is in principle rather like the feedback pictures of chapters 5 and 6.

The author slides back and forth between these two completely different processes for psychologists' agreeing because, presumably, he does not feel the issue is a serious one. He senses no real difference between evidence dictating a certain conclusion and people agreeing about it—and that would follow from the basic assumption of STIMULUS IS FORCE. If a stimulus forces a response, then "The evidence dictates the conclusion" and "There is no one who denies" are just two ways of saying the same thing.

You could collect hundreds of such metaphors in psychology or sociology. Indeed our textbook author could have been echoing one of the great gnomic statements of twentieth century social science, by two of its stars, Clyde Kluckhohn and Henry A. Murray: "Everyone is *in certain* respects (a) like all other men, (b) like some other men and (c) like no other man."[11] Here again, their word "respects" as well as the neat division into a, b, and c express an underlying belief that either humans or the way we look at humans can be—and for research purposes, should be—broken into distinct and separate parts.

In these passages, social scientists are trying to use the idea of isolable parts to think scientifically about mind and brain. The same metaphors crop up in informal psychology also. Here, for example, is a passage from a philosophical book, a history of phenomenology often quoted in literary circles. I have italicized the phrases I want to point to in this passage which describes how phenomena are built up ("constituted") in consciousness:

> A first illustration of such a constitution can be the experience of getting oriented in a new city, whose "picture" gradually *takes shape in our mind.* Having arrived at night and having lost all our bearings in retiring to our quarters, with only a very confused idea as to how we got there, we may find ourselves awaking in a strange bed with the task of building up a new space pattern . . . . Perhaps the most important process here is how the "empty lots" of our new spatial pattern *are more and more "built up"* by corridors, stairs, streets, and houses that *establish themselves* more or less firmly until the pattern *gets sedimented,* usually after a good many upsets, which break up the first outlines as a result of disorientations, "getting lost," and similar adventures.[12]

The opening phrase, "takes shape," is ambiguous. It could admit the feedback process, but others as well. "*In* our mind" suggests the mind as container, and that "our" suggests a uniformity among minds, but neither phrasing urges the position strongly. "Are more and more 'built up' by corridors" however, decisively posits a passive mind on which active corridors and stairs and streets act. Stairs and streets "establish themselves" on, again, a passive mind so that a pattern "gets sedimented," like the sands of the sea settling on deeper, earlier—and passive—sands.

Most curious, however, is the final reference to upsets, disorientations, and getting lost. These are the testing, comparing, and revising of hypotheses, from which one actively builds just such a picture of the world. The last phrases describe a feedback. The passage shifts between a city's imposing itself on a passive mind and an active mind trying to map that city. Presumably the question, Which is active, the stimulus or the mind?, does not feel like a live issue to this author any more than to the psychologist. Neither sees a difference between events imposing and people agreeing on conclusions.

I get the same feeling when I read an interview with the most influential literary theorist of today. The interviewer asked Jacques Derrida, "Do you believe [that any interpretation is as good as any other] and how do you select some interpretations as being better than others?" He replied:

> Derrida: I am not a pluralist and I would never say that every interpretation is equal but *I* do not select. The interpretations select themselves. . . . I would not say that some interpretations are truer than others. I would say that some are more powerful than others. The hierarchy is between forces and not between true and false. There are interpretations which account for more meaning and this is the criterion.
>
> Interviewer: You would reject then the view that meaning is any response whatever to a sign? that meaning is determined by the person who reads the sign?
>
> Derrida: Yes, of course. Meaning is determined by a system of forces which is not personal. It does not depend on the subjective identity but on the field of different forces, the conflict of forces, which produce interpretations.[13]

Derrida is using a classic stimulus-response model. To be sure, Derrida is responding to this particular interviewer, who may have muddled matters by drawing some red herrings across the trail of "meaning" and "interpretation." That is, I know of no one who maintains that "any interpretation is as good as any other" or that "meaning" is "any response whatsoever to a sign." Certainly not me.

Nevertheless, Derrida's whimsical answer to these confused questions states a firm commitment to the metaphor of LITERATURE IS FORCE. At the same time, when he acknowledges that "there are interpretations which account for more meaning," I catch a fleeting glimpse of inter-pre*ters*, some persons supplying better and worse interpretations. On the other hand, Derrida rules out such a person when he insists that "interpretations select themselves." I wonder how he would account for our forty-four professors. Or Robert Frost.

Behind Derrida (despite his intricate critique and "reinscription" of the turn-of-the-century linguist), I see Ferdinand de Saussure. It seems to me that Derrida, like many of today's literary theorists, has rather uncritically adopted Saussure's notion of "signifying." "Signifying" in Saussure's sense posits a text-active model based on the metaphor, LIT-ERATURE IS FORCE.

Saussure defined the act of communication as twofold. A speaker draws on a communal storehouse of language (*langue*) for his individual speaking (*parole*). The hearer then automatically associates the sounds he hears with the concepts prescribed by *langue*.[14]

In Saussure's account of understanding language, the receiver is passive and communication automatic. The "speaking-circuit" has "an active and a passive part: everything that goes from the associative center of the speaker to the ear of the listener is active, and everything that goes from the ear of the listener to his associative center is passive." In understanding, "Through the functioning of the receptive and co-ordinating faculties, impressions (*des empreintes*) that are perceptibly the same for all are made (*se forment*) on the minds of speakers."[15] In speaking language, *parole*, Saussure of course allows for the individual's psychology in choosing words from the system of *langue*, but he allows no such freedom in understanding language.

In this picture of a person's understanding language, texts simply signify. Active texts insist on meanings, which inactive, unthinking readers take automatically into their thoughts. LITERATURE IS OTHER. Also Saussure's version of language imprints itself on its hearer's mind—LITERATURE IS FORCE. Either way, there is no room here for the individual responses of Professors One through Six. Many of today's literary theorists have taken over Saussure's picture whole, and to that extent much of current literary thought is committed to various forms of the LITERATURE IS FORCE or LITERATURE IS ISOLABLE PARTS metaphors. The idea that a book forces a certain response seems natural enough, for it has been customary to think that way for a century or more.

If for no other reason than habit, the assumption of "signifying" luxuriates in literary circles these days. Similar assumptions abound in experimental psychology and elsewhere in the social sciences. Nevertheless, "signifying" or STIMULUS IS FORCE or LITERATURE IS ISOLABLE PARTS are not self-evident assumptions to be made unquestioningly. If we start our investigation of reading or the relation between intelligence and heredity or signifier and signified by assuming isolable parts, we will have ruled out systems thinking from the start. We never will find out if a continuous process would serve better as a model. Once we have isolated a poem from its reader, we cannot at the same time talk about it as it functions in a feedback process. Conversely, once we have agreed to talk about the poem as part of a system, we can no longer talk about it in isolation. Hence, STIMULUS IS FORCE or LITERATURE IS ISOLABLE PARTS or LITERATURE IS FEEDBACK typically pre-empt, without ever making it explicit that they are doing so, alternative models of literature or the human being. As for the actual behavior of Robert Frost or the forty-four professors, I believe we can better explain it by the feedback picture than by "signifying" or other forms of LITERATURE IS ISOLABLE PARTS. If, however, we automatically assume the traditional, "signifying" model, we will have barred that possibility from the start.

Any intellectual discipline has to begin with some sort of model of the human being. It may do so explicitly or tacitly, but before someone working in the discipline can make any statement at all, he or she has to have made some kind of model of the human—at least of the person making the statement. Different disciplines use different models as different researchers seek this or that result.

Saussure, for example, sought a purely formal grammar. He hoped to create an account of language that would have to rely no more on human psychology or sociology than an algebraic expression does. To that end he made the very bold assumption that language, formally defined, was a ready-made cognitive system in the brain of the individual speaker. "Language exists in the form of a sum of impressions deposited in the brain of each member of a community, almost like a dictionary of which identical copies have been distributed to each individual."[16] This is an assumption that, if suitably updated, would hold good today. A variant occurs in Chomsky's thinking, and I have incorporated my own version in Figures 4 and 6.

Saussure, however, tried simply to catalog the data of a given language or *langue*, and for Saussure, who derived from an etymological tradition, what stood out about language was the meanings of single words. As in that sentence about language deposited in the brain, he created essentially a one-to-one, dictionary model of language. We hear "tree" and we think —tree-concept—. He even draws a tree to indicate what we think of when we hear "tree." Although he refined this simple model to say that "tree" only means tree because the "tree"-word differs from other words the way the tree-concept differs from other concepts, he still created a one-to-one conception of language. He offers a very clear model. "Language can also be compared with a sheet of paper: thought is the front and the sound the back; one cannot cut the front without cutting the back at the same time; likewise in language, one can neither divide sound from thought nor thought from sound."[17] Essentially Saussure sees language as a lexicon that lists a series of statements like, value A signifies value B. That is, the value A (the system of differences associated with language-stuff A by a *langue*) signifies value B (the system of differences associated *by that language* with thought-stuff B). He thus committed himself to the position that one could build up the larger system of language from these smaller constituents, and some decades later Chomsky was to show that was not possible.

Chomsky also sought a formal grammar, but he chose to inquire at the level of the sentence. How is it that you and I can understand infinitely many new sentences, sentences that we have never heard before, that may never even have existed before? Nobody ever taught us how, yet we can do this extraordinary thing. Similarly, how is it that anybody, including quite young children, can make up an infinity of new and satisfyingly grammatical English sentences?

These are psychological questions, but Chomsky, like Saussure, wanted to hold off the psychological question in order to achieve a purely formal account of language. That is, he sought a system of abstract rules. The rules would be free of any context except the sentences to which they apply. They were to generate all the grammatical sentences in English and none of the ungrammatical ones in the same way the rules of the theory of numbers will generate all the numbers.

He and his associates formulated rules that would assign structural descriptions or markers to sentences, and these markers indicated a procedure by which such a sentence could be produced or understood. As with Saussure, however, it is difficult not to think of this formal system as embodied in the mind and brain of the speakers that use it. Although Chomsky kept a certain distance from the psychological parts of his quest, others have undertaken the psycholinguistic research his project leads to. Finally, as many have said, Chomsky's project may be impossible. It may be that one cannot posit such a set of rules apart from the human mind and the social context in which they operate. Nevertheless, Chomsky's hypothesis has led to a rich variety of research into the way adults understand language, how children acquire language, and what abilities must be innately present in our brains for us to be language-using animals. So far as human psychology is concerned, all this goes well beyond the automatic process of "signifying" that Saussure posited.

Chomsky and Saussure modeled the human as having language devices built into the mind, so that one signifier would evoke its signified (Saussure's dictionary) or so that one could learn how to make sentences (Chomsky's LAD—language acquisition device). By contrast, experimental psychologists traditionally "black box" the internal operations of the psyche to concentrate instead on measurable externals, "behaviors." They assume that the experimenter is isolated from the experiment, and they do so despite phenomena well known in psychological circles such as the Rosenthal effect[18] (in which the experimenters' biases change the numbers that come out of the experiment). As the old story has it, American rats, confronted with a maze, rush here and there in a flurry of energy. German rats, confronted with the same maze, sit down and try to work out a world-system.

Psychologists accept these limitations in hopes of creating a "scientific" psychology, and today's psychologist has indeed achieved remarkable rigor. There has been a price, however, and I believe it has been a high one. The price was scope. Scientific though it may be, no one would seriously claim that modern psychology has arrived at any large truths about human nature or demonstrated any comprehensive model of the human being. Instead, psychology as we know it has concentrated on the precise testing of a great many small hypotheses. Often a psychologist's conclusions are even limited to some one particular experimental technique.

Today the avant-garde in psychology has become willing to consider the internal workings of the mind in, for example, reading, and we have a new wave in psychology, "cognitive science." (As I was writing this chapter, I received an alumni magazine informing me that my alma mater[19] had just reorganized its Department of Psychology into a Department of Brain and Cognitive Sciences.)

A different new wave is "social construction" psychology. Psychologists like Kenneth Gergen, Keith Davis, or Peter Ossorio recognize that knowledge is a social and cultural phenomenon: "The terms in which the world is understood are social artifacts, products of historically situated interchanges among people." Even in the natural sciences, "What passes for 'hard fact' . . . depends on a subtle but potent array of social microprocesses."[20] If that is true of physics, how much more so of psychology. We need to recognize that psychologists, like all scientists, are persons when they do psychology. Hence, a psychology, to be adequate, must account for itself. It must be a reflexive discipline.[21] In my terms, the psychologist must be able to analyze his or her own work in terms of Figure 6. What are my hypotheses? To what extent do I share them with my interpretive community? To what extent are they the way they are because of my own inner needs? Because of my culture? Because of my gender?

The British psychologist, N. E. Weatherick,[22] insists that "A genuine science of psychology will have to confront the phenomena of consciousness and of human agency." When it does, "The question to be answered will be what sort of thing is it that can do what we know human beings can do and experience what they can experience and at the same time constitute itself in the kind of physiological structure we know organisms to consist of?" In other words, academic psychology has defined itself up to now by a particular methodology. Psychology is "the scientific study of behavior," and "scientific" means the establishment of statistical correlations between a dependent variable (like a response) and an independent variable (like a stimulus). Weatherick is saying that the time has come for psychologists to make a science out of human experiences and the way the human brain is constructed so as to have those experiences. Hear, hear.

If the psychologists are trying to make a "science," what are we literary critics and theorists trying to do? I have been proud to see my profession move from a genteel, somewhat snobbish "appreciation" in the early 1950s of a canon (primarily white, English, and male) to a challenging intellectuality of interpretation, questioning, and theory. In particular, in recent years, I have watched my colleagues in literary criticism seek for real intellectual rigor in their understanding of the creation and interpretation of literature. There are times, though, darker moments when I think we are only hoping to say smart things about poems or stories, and any theory will do, if it enables us to publish more and perish less.

My disappointment comes from the unwillingness of most of my fellow professors to question the simple text-active model. Even such highly sophisticated literary theories as *Rezeptionsästhetik*, semiotics, and deconstructionist criticism all, in their rather different ways, depend upon the old metaphor of LITERATURE IS FORCE. *Rezeptionsästhetik* purports to give an account of readers' responses, yet it does so by means of the text-active, LITERATURE IS FORCE principle. To retain that principle, reception critics and theorists ignore the responses of actual readers. Deconstructionists seek to discover the ways in which a text undercuts its own ostensible meaning. "Any literary text," writes J. Hillis Miller, " . . . already misreads itself,"[23] and we have seen Jacques Derrida attribute meanings to a system of forces divorced from persons. Semioticians also claim to derive their meanings from texts, as though they were dispassionate explorers of new territory.

All these otherwise highly subtle and complex theories seem to depend upon a simple text-active model of response or meaning. "The Mill" constrains its readers. Texts cause responses. But we have seen that "The Mill" does *not* constrain its readers. That is too simple. We need to find a way to imagine readers both limited *and freed* by a poem.

As literary criticism becomes more philosophical and philosophy more like literary criticism, this issue shades over into "doing philosophy." The phenomenologist we sampled wants to imagine how the mind is both passive and active as it engages the world. Yet he seems unaware that that is precisely what a feedback picture describes, an individual who both acts on the world and is therefore and thereby acted upon *by* the world. What I feel my world of the humanities needs is more aware-ness of the picture now receiving confirmation from explorations in the brain itself. An identity governing feedbacks provides an image for the more complex concept of literary response that we need for explaining real readers. It is a picture far more congenial to humanists (or, I should think, postmodernists) than the older psychology that emerged from stimulus-response behaviorism.

As I look at today's intellectual scene, literary theorists seem to me to divide into those who have collected or at least looked at actual readers' relatively free responses and a much larger number who have not. Those who have looked at free responses seem to me unanimous in finding that readers have the decisive role in making texts mean. Those who have not looked at actual responses make the text the cause of response.

The problem may be that many of us assume that responses in the classroom are like the private responses of a reader in an armchair. They are not. The answers one gets to an armchair question like 5, "Whom does [the miller's wife] remind you of?," differ sharply from the relatively uniform responses one gets from a specific inquiry like Question 1, a grammatical question you might find in any literary textbook. The re-sponses to 1 look alike. They give an impression of uniformity. One can see, however, from the later, more open questions, that the processes that led to those uniform answers were in fact different for different individuals. Most literature teachers use a socratic method that requires pointed questions looking for specific answers like 1, not questions look-ing for "free" associations like question 5. Hence many teachers get the impression that texts elicit uniform responses from their students when in fact it is their questions that evoke the uniformity.

We have glanced, and only glanced, at a sampling of today's cognitive sciences and "poststructuralist" humanities. They seem to me to divide according to whether or not they rest on the idea of STIMULUS (or LAN-GUAGE, or LITERATURE) IS FORCE:

Linguistics

Chomsky and post-Chomsky Psycholinguistics	Saussure

Psychology

Cognitive Science Psychoanalysis	Experimental

Literary Theory

Reader-active   Text-active

In this book, I am urging my fellow laborers in the vineyard of literary theory toward the more modern side of this paradigm. My politics being what they are, I have made it the left side.

I hesitate this late in the century to say that those on the left are "true" or "right." After all, it is precisely my position that the truth—the answer you get—depends upon the question you ask. I would suggest only that the disciplines on the left seem to me to offer a richer set of hypotheses with which to approach experience, a set more likely to yield comprehensive and satisfying answers. No doubt, they will in their turn be replaced by other hypotheses, other feedbacks.

In the meantime, though, *is* that feedback picture more accurate than other models in the study of literature based on isolable parts and, if so, why?

For one thing, feedback accords with what we know or think we know about the psychology of perception, cognitive psychology, artificial intelligence, and, most importantly, brain physiology. At least in broad outline, we see, hear, move, recognize, and know through some sort of hierarchy of feedbacks like that in Figure 6. Obviously, Figure 6 grossly oversimplifies, showing only two networks. The brain consists of millions, perhaps thousands of millions, of feedback loops.[24] Moreover, they do not function in a simple hierarchy, but with complex releasings and inhibitions at the same level, with loops that cut across and up and down the chains of command, and with feedings back both up and down what is really a heterarchy. Some students of the brain talk about "coalitions," systems that straddle the boundary between brain and environment, including some of "out there" along with some of "in here," neither part able to function without the other.[25]

In general, then, the brain physiologists, the psychoanalysts, the cognitive scientists, the "social construction" psychologists, the cultural anthropologists—perhaps even, if read a certain way, the literary deconstructionists—a variety of social and human scientists suggest that we are *not* separable from our human and physical surroundings. We are born into a community and we grow up by interacting with the world around us, a world we share with other humans. To assume that we can separate ourselves from that world—as these ISOLABLE PARTS metaphors assume—may obscure or even falsify what we think we know about the relationships among ourselves as individuals and the world and the culture we share with our fellow humans.

The feedback picture, even in grossly simplified form, fits better with what we think we know about the brain and its relations with the world. It fits better with what we know about the psychology of reading: "Understanding always involves the operation of many levels of hierarchically organized schemata."[26] Indeed, identity-governing-feedbacks fits better with what we know about any and all of our comprehensions. These seem to me the most solid reasons for preferring feedback and its associated metaphors to figures of speech and thought based on STIMULUS IS OTHER, IS FORCE, or IS ISOLABLE PARTS. There is, however, another reason, a more immediate one, for preferring the feedback picture.

Feedback does better with the relation between our professors' answers to Questions 1 and 5. That is, Question 1 called for an "objective" answer to an "objective" question, and Question 5 asked for a "subjective" imagining. Question 1 asked for a fact, if you will, and 5 for an opinion, and the other questions spanned the scale of "subjectivity" in between.

My quotation marks express my belief that "objective" and "subjective" are a version of the ISOLABLE PARTS metaphor—and a particularly confusing version. By contrast, the feedback picture allows us to ask whether there is a continuity between our statements of fact and of opinion and, if we find a continuity, to explain it. Indeed, I thought I could trace a continuity between the professors' answers to 1 and to 5, just as, in our exploration of Robert Frost, we were able to see a continuity between Frost's writing, reading, and his saying. To be sure, in order to look for such a continuity (or identity), I have assumed that one *can* trace a theme through all the variations of Frost's behavior. In doing so, I am again acting out the feedback picture: putting a hypothesis out into the world and seeing what return I get from it. Specifically, my hypothesis is that I *can formulate a unity* for Frost's behavior. Not that "there is a unity in" Frost's behavior—that would be a quite confusing conduit metaphor.

In this instance, I think I get a good return on this hypothesis, good enough, anyway, to justify trying it in other situations such as the professors'. Can I trace a continuity between Professor Six's answers to factual questions and questions that ask her to project or imagine? Yes, I get good feedback when I try that—at least I get what seems to me good feedback.

Were I to assume that Professor Six's answers were simply the result of the Visiting Fireman's visit, of individual lines in the poem, or of my questionnaire, I would be assuming that one could isolate her answer to my first question, treating it as independent of her answer to the last. Surely one *can* do that—psychologists do it all the time—but it seems to me a less fruitful assumption (and just as self-fulfilling) as the assumption of continuity.

Turning the literary process around, making the reader the active one instead of the text, marks a profound change in literary theory. Nevertheless, as Stanley Fish has pointed out, even a massive change in literary theory will not change literary practice, if the theory is an attempt to describe or explain (as opposed to prescribe) what critics do.[27] Here, I believe I am *de*scribing in a "metacritical" way how people read texts. I am not *pre*scribing how they should read them. Nothing I say here precludes essays about individual texts or author's biography or literary history. Nothing here will privilege a reading that shows unity and structure over one that shows deconstruction and disunity, or vice versa.

I do claim, however, that if we understand the act of reading as an identity governing a hierarchy of feedbacks, we will be able to think more clearly about writing and reading literature. We will be better able to map out what we are doing as critics and teachers. We can use more telling metaphors to talk about writing and reading. We will hear the metaphors we already have differently. And that's what we shall be doing in the next chapter.

8

Literary Process and the Personal Brain

We have arrived at a picture of the literary process that makes Robinson's poem into forty-five different, private experiences for Frost and the forty-four professors. The same picture will nevertheless let us see how Robinson "communicates" to these private minds—the first move in this chapter. In the second, we shall use the picture to chart what we are doing by various typical moves in the classroom. Finally the picture of an identity governing a hierarchy of feedbacks will enable us to see what we are doing when we "read" the identity of a Robert Frost.

We can imagine a Robert Frost or, for that matter, a Professor Five by means of a certain central theme on which he or she plays infinitely many variations. Partly the identity manifests itself in Professor Five's beliefs about mothers or Professor Two's preoccupation with language or Robert Frost's about the New Deal. We could call these Five's, Two's, or Frost's "values," and they are really a side of personal identity. If we want to focus on literature, we would call them canons of interpretation and literary value that were chosen by Two or Five or Frost from a variety of canons our literary culture offers. At a somewhat lower level, identity operates through codes, the everyday skills that every English speaker uses. Identity sets the standards for the canons, and we can think of the canons as using—setting standards for—the codes. Finally, there is the physical text addressed by those codes and canons.

Imagined this way, the feedback picture refines our conception of how Robinson "communicates" to his reader. The literary process begins with Robinson's writing as an expression of his identity. How might I say the identity of E. A. Robinson? I would put it this way: the ironic, unspeakable contradiction between the material world and the spiritual or psychological. I am thinking of the kind of thing he says in "The Man Against the Sky":

> But this we know, if we know anything:
> That we may laugh and fight and sing
> And of our transience here make offering
> To an orient Word that will not be erased,
> Or, save in incommunicable gleams
> Too permanent for dreams,
> Be found or known.

Out of some such sardonic tension between an abstract, indifferent eternity and a suffering humanity, Robinson wrote the tale of the miller's wife. He made a poem from the cruelty of the material world, the despair of the psychological self, the uncaring surroundings, and the wry, ironic tone in which I infer his bitter laughter at the fight put up by the miller and his wife against their economic doom.

Robinson draws on techniques personal to him and characteristic of at least some of the poets of his era, his relentless rhyming, his abstract, elliptical choice of words, the mingling of narrative and lyric, his sense of dramatic timing, above all, the ironies that he dares to leave unspoken, although I do not always feel these silences as he apparently hoped I would. These tactics I call canons. Through these canons the poet draws also on the less personal skills I call codes: English grammar and syntax and phonetics, his vocabulary, or the rules of scansion or rhyme. Out of a hierarchy of feedbacks, finding English words, framing English sentences and rhymes, finding the sudden drop into an irony that feels right to him, E. A. Robinson created a thing: the physical text of "The Miller." This new piece of the real world feeds back various results to Robinson. It "feels right," or it doesn't. People admire it—or they don't. The poem "works"—or it doesn't.

Then Robert Frost reads Robinson's poem out of *his* hierarchy of feedbacks, both private and communal. Governing that hierarchy is Frost's identity, the small known managing the big unknown (rather different from Robinson's abstractions which become deadly ironies). Out of his own processes of feedback, framing grammatical sentences, choosing this word or that, listening for sentences that can only be sounded one way, in general, sensing what feels right to him, Robert Frost also creates a thing, not an external thing but his internal experience of Robinson's poem.

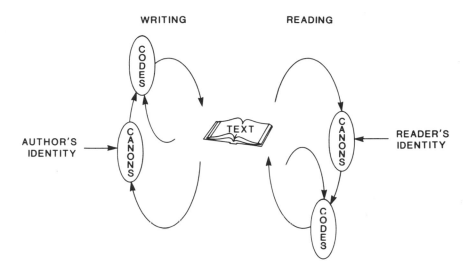

WRITING READING

AUTHOR'S IDENTITY

READER'S IDENTITY

Figure 7. Writing and reading

As we have seen, the whole process involves Frost's unique identity setting standards for the canons he shared with some readers (like Pound and Robinson), but not all readers, and his identity setting standards for the codes he shared with all readers of English. Frost's re-creation of Robinson's "The Mill" quite resembles his own creation of a poem. When he reads, he draws on the same canons and codes with which he writes. When he writes, he judges what he writes through the same reading process he uses to read a poem by another poet.

Thinking like a reader, Frost wrote to Robinson about a play of Robinson's he liked: "It is good writing, or better than that, good speaking caught alive—every sentence of it. The speaking tones are all there on the printed page, nothing is left for the actor but to recognize and give them."[1] In other words, Frost liked Robinson's lines because Robinson had caught the sound of the sentence before the sense, and this Frost valued above all other qualities in poetry: "The sound of sense, then. . . . the abstract vitality of our speech . . . pure sound—pure form."[2] Frost found in Robinson's lines the same "good speaking caught alive" that he tried to give to his own readers. Frost, in other words, reads Robinson's lines with his own ear for the unstudied rhythms of ordinary speech. To read Robinson, he used the astonishing knack with which he wrote his own colloquial poetry and which he prescribed to other writers: "The reader must be at no loss to give his voice the posture proper to the sentence." "Never if you can help it write down a sentence in which the voice will not know how to posture *specially*."[3]

Yet obviously Frost also read Robinson with skills all speakers of English have in common: reading A as A, m-i-l-l-e-r as miller, grammar, syntax, and rules like vocabulary, Americanisms, the rules of scansion or rhyme that many, but not all, readers shared with him. To read, Frost used the same skills with which he wrote. He read as he wrote and he wrote as he read.

So do we all. Many years after Frost wrote on Robinson, I thrust under the nose of Professor One a physical thing, a mimeographed text of "The Mill." She looked at that physical object by means of *her* system of feedbacks, some of which she shared with Robinson, some with Frost, some with me, and some of which were peculiarly her own. She tried out this or that hypothesis on the text, and it felt right to her, it worked for her, or it didn't, that is, it felt identity-fulfilling to her or it didn't, and she applauded or didn't, accordingly.

A feedback model of the reading and writing of literature thus provides for *both* the author's unique expression of self *and* the reader's. It allows for *both* author's and reader's individuality *and* their sharing of semantic codes, taught techniques, interpretive communities, or, in general, the features of reading shared by many readers.

Professors One and Two probably have much the same physical way of scanning and looking at letters and lines. They probably share similar ways of interpreting English. They can go, for example, to the annual meeting of the Modern Language Association and debate interpretations. They may even have similar ideas about mills and oceans and literature. But they may have very different beliefs about their fellow human beings, about what sounds good, or how one should read. Sharing *some* processes of interpretation, necessarily low-level processes, makes it possible for them to communicate. Their difference at higher levels *guarantees* that they will experience the poem differently.

Robinson and Frost and One and Two could all talk to one another about "The Mill" because they share low-level modes of processing language. They share cultural codes *and* they experience the poem differently, individually. One need not resort to such dramatic strategies for alienating individuality from culture as this statement, "My language is not mine, just as my unconscious is not mine."[4] One might ask, as Freud asked about a dream (for a dream seems even more "Other" than language), Whose is it then? "Unless the content of the dream . . . is inspired by alien spirits, it is a part of my own being," wrote Freud.[5] Obviously, my language is mine—*and* yours *and* Frost's *and* our whole culture's. One belonging does not exclude other belongings. Rather, feedback gives us a way of thinking about the way language belongs to each of us as well as to all of us. It does not follow that it therefore belongs to none of us. The fact is that we do experience things differently, but we also share and communicate. We even teach.

The scene: a typical classroom. Big windows that give lots of light. Institution-colored walls. The characters: a teacher standing at the front of the room. A dozen or more students sit in various degrees of attention or slouch. Behind the teacher, a blackboard bears a single word like a prophecy against the clouds of half-erased past learning. The smell of chalk.

Except for that, there is, of course, no such thing as a typical classroom. What is outside those windows? A grey river with a grey sky? Dirty snow on brown grass? Blue skies, red brick, and palm trees? The writing-chairs. Are they the wooden ones with decades of the grooved emblems of student loves and loyalties? Or are they the impervious kind, over whose formica surface boredom manages to triumph? (At Florida, where school colors dictate decor, the right-handed writing chairs are blue, the left-handed orange.) The walls, are they cinderblock with a "nice" pastel or cracked yellow paint over plaster? This is a public room and it wears the signs of it—of them.

The students. Are they wearing puffy down jackets that make them look like the Michelin tire man? Or Dolphin shorts? Today's cast: The Smart Ones (specialty indeterminate, but you notice them first), the Pretty Girl(s), the Hunk(s), the Poet (he/she will let you know), the Aristocrat (accent tells), the Con Man (or Woman), the Angry One, the Confused One, the Ones that Need Help, the Ones You Don't Remember. I recognize them all. Always the same, and always very, very different. As for the teacher—typical? How could there be such a one?

The class, however, is the familiar "introduction to literature" course, which typically tries to teach beginning college students "how to read" (really, how to interpret, or at the very least, how to pay close attention to language). The script might include:

Teacher: To what does the clause "what was hanging from a beam" refer?
Teacher: To what does the clause "What else there was" refer?

A teacher might use questions like the Visiting Fireman's 1 and 2 with right-wrong answers to "get into" the poem. Probably these would elicit some argument from the students followed by a settling on the same kind of answers as the professors gave.

A more interesting script might go:

Teacher: Is Robinson saying the wife wants to leave no mark?
Student: Yes.
Teacher: Why? Why does she want that, do you think?

This question would surely elicit a discussion from most students of the wife's motives, although there is little indication of them in the poem. More sophisticated students might talk about the wife's obeying a thematic necessity, Robinson's theme here being, perhaps, the taking control of one's destiny, even if you have to nullify it, as the miller had to. The wife leaves nothing whatsoever behind, less than tea leaves or ashes or the miller's gear. Still more sophisticated students might question the question. We aren't dealing with a realistic portrayal of people.

Teacher: How does "weir" fit into the poem as a whole?

This might elicit a theme of trying to possess or hold on—an economic theme for the poem. The weir tries to hold back the inevitable flow of the water. Other containings in the poem: the teapot, the mill, what else there was, what was hanging from a beam, and so on.

Teacher: How does the word "velvet" change the poem? Suppose he had said "starry ebony"?
Teacher: How about the word "ruffled"? Suppose he had said "rippled"?

Surely middle-level students would arrive at a theme of cloth or clothing. These two might elicit in another way a unifying theme of holding on, the dam, the miller, the teapot.

Teacher: What is the effect of Robinson's saying only indirectly what happened to the miller?

Here again, we might get a theme of things getting away from us. The poem, as it were, mobilizes our own efforts to get, to have, to hold, to possess.

Teacher: How does "no form" fit in?

This question might get a "deconstructive" response, that this is a formal poem. It has a lot of form, that is, metre, rhyme, and stanza divisions.

The very form of the poem deconstructs the poet's claim that a fear can have no form. Or something like that.

My point is simply this: the feedback-and-identity picture lets those of us who teach literature ask ourselves more tellingly what we are doing by any given classroom move. We can use the model to sort out and rethink what we are doing.

For example, some teaching of literature consists simply of exposing the student to the world of letters. "For Wednesday's class, read 'The Mill.'" In terms of the feedback picture, that move simply places students in contact with what Figures 4 and 6 call "Environment" or "Outer." The teacher expects the students to use on "The Mill" the hypotheses they already have for addressing texts. The teacher can go further, posing, in the manner of many textbooks, "Study Questions" (like those in the scripts above). Such a teacher provides the student with ready-made hypotheses to try (as my questionnaire did).

A reader just beginning school learns how to use hypotheses to put shapes together to form letters, letters to form words, words to form sentences, sentences to form the whole poem. In first grade, we learned to find the sound or meaning of an unknown word. A few grades later, we were able to infer the meaning of a word from context even if we had not seen it before. A more sophisticated reader learns how to use hypotheses to assign meaning to a whole text.

Any modern criticism requires us to pay close attention to the language. Hence any critical move could well begin with routine, right-wrong questions, like "To what does the clause 'what was hanging from a beam' refer?" or "To what does the clause 'What else there was' refer?" Similarly, basic reading addresses matters of cause and effect or motivation, like, Why does the wife want to leave no mark? A more advanced reader uses this close attention to language and event to try out on a poem hypotheses like: You will be able to read the poem as referring to more than its ostensible subject, the obsolescence of millers. These large hypotheses correspond to various "interpretive communities" or schools of criticism. New Criticism: You will be able to shape the poem into a unity. The New Critic asks questions like, How does "weir" fit in to the poem as a whole? Once you have done so, you will not be able to find an unnecessary word in this poem, and any changes you make in details will change the whole, probably for the worse. As in the questions about "velvet" or "ruffled." Suppose he had said "starry ebony"? Suppose he had said "rippled"? Even within that unity, you will probably be able to find an irony cross-cutting the poem, making it more complicated to put together (like the "velvet" water one of our professors mentioned).

Phenomenological criticism: you will probably be able to find a reference in the poem to its own creation. Often such a reference will seem to cut across the ostensible sense of the poem or "deconstruct" it—deconstructionism. "How does 'no form' fit in?" When it is a poem of rather strict form.

At this higher level of teaching interpretation, a "critical school" or "interpretive community" tries to provide the student with hypotheses with which to address *any* text. At a still higher level we try to give students the ability to hypothesize hypotheses which will give the best return from this particular text. When we teach literary theory, we take as our texts the hypotheses we see professional interpreters applying to a text, and we hypothesize about the hypotheses themselves.

Notice that in our teaching scenario we mostly are addressing the *hypotheses* a student brings to a text. The identity-governing-feedback model lets us visualize how different levels of sophistication in teaching literature correspond to different levels of abstraction in the hypotheses we apply or discuss. The identity-governing-feedback model can be helpful in visualizing other kinds of teaching, as well, because the teaching of anything, particularly at advanced or even secondary levels, mostly follows this pattern. Whether the class is dealing with a poem by E. A. Robinson, an experiment with mice and mazes, or a computer program in LISP, the teacher works with the hypotheses by which the student addresses that particular piece of experience. At any given moment a teacher may be giving a student hypotheses or suggesting hypotheses for finding hypotheses or testing a hypothesis to sense the return. All are familiar strategies in teaching. All use the students' responses. All seek a homogeneity of response—right answers. A "misreading" (according to the feedback picture) would correspond either to a wrong hypothesis or to a right hypothesis wrongly applied or to a poor return perceived as a good return.

Typically this kind of right-wrong teaching uses only those responses that can be generalized, shared, or otherwise made available to all the students. It deals with students almost entirely in the plural. We expect all the students just to come up peaceably with the same reading of the poem, the same results from the mice in the maze, or the same output from the LISP program.

As feminists have been pointing out, there is nothing sacred about this mode of teaching. (It may come simply from men's being the overwhelming majority in the professoriat.) Learning or research or teaching that tries to get as briskly as possible to the "right" answer is not necessarily more right or true than other styles. It may be that the nine year old girl student of programming who interacts back and forth with her computer as a person is applying a different hypothesis from the nine year old boy who uses the "top-down, divide-and-conquer" strategies of "good programming." The boy and girl are applying different hypotheses at a very high level: How do you best relate to what you are studying? Sherry Turkle, the sociologist who has studied children and computers, contrasts the boys' style, "hard mastery," with the girls' "soft mastery," the mastery of the artist as opposed to the mastery of the engineer.[6]

Similarly, feminist studies suggest different styles of science from that implied by the SEPARABLE PARTS metaphors. Increasingly, psychoanalysts conclude that boy babies differentiate themselves from their mothers more harshly than girls do. They aggressively thrust free from this differently sexed parent. They come away from this experience with a "masculine" way of relating to other people and to inanimate reality. Typically, in this kind of parenting, the boy will be more separate— more aggressive, more abstract, and more categorical—than the girl. She, by contrast, continues her connection with the, for her, same sexed first love, the mother. A science committed to the idea that the scientist is sharply separate from what he studies would be male. A science that acknowledges the involvement of the scientist in what she studies would be female. This more feminine, or feminist, science would admit extensive interactions between the knower and what is known. What is needed, though, is a science of which we have yet no inkling, one that would transcend this distinction.[7] Possibly Third World cultures, where learning is oral and repetitive and classes consist of chanting the lesson aloud represent yet other styles of knowing and therefore different kinds of hypotheses to be brought to bear on a subject-matter.

The identity-and-feedback model lets us see how our ways of teaching are masculine or feminine in these (culture-bound) senses of the terms. In providing a student with a poem, an experiment, or a program and with hypotheses for working with them, we teachers provide the raw materials from which students will fashion an experience. Like Question 1 in the Visiting Fireman's questionnaire, this kind of teaching looks "objective," because the teacher stands back to let the student create his or her own learning experience. In its separateness, this is a "masculine" way of teaching.

In fact, however, if the identity-and-feedback model is right, whether the hypothesis is used at all, or whether any given application to poem, experiment, or program feels right to the student, will depend on his or her identity. The student's identity will govern the use made of the raw materials and the hypotheses the teacher gives, just as an artist's identity would govern the use of pigment, canvas, and scene. The learning is, as learning must always be, "subjective." In fact, it seems to me, teaching and learning answer better to a "feminine" kind of knowledge than a "masculine."

One can, of course, sidestep the students' personal response. Teachers sometimes say, That belongs after hours, outside of class. One can treat a class as a homogeneous group whose knowledge, methods, and interpretations approach uniformity. This is what happens in most classrooms, and it has worked well for centuries now, millennia perhaps.

In recent years, however, in the teaching of literature at least, another way of using responses has arisen. A teacher addresses the nature of the reading process itself instead of some particular hypotheses associated with one or another school of criticism. By asking questions like, What does the miller's wife look like? (when the poem doesn't say) or Whom does she remind you of?, a teacher addresses a student's experience of a poem. The questions elicit a student's feelings instead of some interpretive strategy learned in school. The model enables us to get beyond the familiar oppositions of true-false, right answer and wrong, "objective" and "subjective." Sometimes.

In our script, the teacher asked, "What is the effect of Robinson's saying only indirectly what happened to the miller?" That question looks as though it were asking students for their feelings. Actually, however, the teacher has distanced the personal response, because the question assumes a uniform response, "*the* effect." The questioner did not ask, What is the effect on *you* of Robinson's method? How do *you* feel? And, of course, the word "effect" assumes a cause-effect, stimulus-response, text-active model. Contrast a teacher's asking, "What do you make of Robinson's saying only indirectly what happened to the miller?"

The feedback picture lets us see how this kind of teaching to the student's feelings complements the more traditional kind. A reader-response teacher does not talk about the interpretive hypotheses coming out of the right side of the student "comparator" so much as the "return" on the left. Instead of asking, say, how the word "velvet" relates to the rest of the poem, a teacher might ask students to notice specifically what emotions they sense as they read "velvet" (how a given return *feels* as opposed to how it *fits*). Such a teacher might (but need not) go further. The class might explore how a given hypothesis or return fits the identity of some student reader so far as it has appeared in the classroom,[8] much as we have noticed how concerned Two is with language and Four with mothers.

In asking about feelings in this kind of response-centered class, we do not eliminate the idea of a "misreading." I do ask, however, that the one who proclaims a "mis-" make the rule explicit that makes the mis-a mis-. Too often, we teachers take the rightness of one answer for granted, part of a residual belief, I think, that modes of reading are self-evident, not to be questioned, eternal verities, linguistic competences, rigid codes, "objective" readings, signifieds simply emerging from signifiers, interpretations dictated by texts. In effect we extend too automatically into theory what is merely a convenient convention in teaching. It is a convenience, sometimes, to sidestep individual responses to treat a classroom of diverse people as a homogeneous group. That does not mean that they really *are* a homogeneous group.

Feedback (as in Figures 4 and 6) lets me picture the relation between these two rather different teaching strategies. A teacher can address the experience of a particular student. A teacher can examine the right and wrong applications of hypotheses. Reader-response teaching explores the top of Figure 6: processes of comparison and the standards each individual brain applies.[9] The traditional teaching of how-to-read-literature deals with the two loops: putting out hypotheses and getting returns from them. By addressing the hypotheses with which one reads, the traditional teaching of literature directs attention *away* from the person applying the hypotheses. Reader-response teaching does just the opposite. Reader-response teaching addresses that person as uniquely phrasing and applying hypotheses, asks how he or she feels, and listens to what he or she says when those hypotheses are applied. Questions 3, 4, and 5 on the questionnaire were typical reader-response questions. Hence reader-response teaching points *away* from a critique of the hypotheses themselves or the ways they are applied. The two kinds of teaching are different, but not inconsistent. They are part of one model, as in Figure 6.

As that picture suggests, these two kinds of teaching are essentially independent. Neither substitutes for the other. Emotional sensitivity does not substitute for skill, nor skill for sensitivity. Rather, each should complement and supplement the other. If they do, then there is no reason why one cannot equally well teach chemistry or psychology or computer programming from student responses. Indeed there is every reason one should. Would not a chemist, a computer programmer, or a psychologist (surely!) do better for knowing also how they feel about their crafts, why this technique or that suits their personal needs, and what a given task might be doing or not doing for them psychologically?

To be sure, these two modes, teaching hypotheses and teaching sensitivity, cast the teacher in contrary roles, permissive and corrective. I cannot find any reason, however, why two teachers or even one could not apply both methods as they seemed appropriate. Professors Two and Three, who like to concentrate on language, could do the regular teaching only, the conventional classes. Professors Five and Six, who were more sensitive to the personal element in their responses, might like to try to focus on responses only, as reader-response classes tend to. Or just one teacher could consider responses alternately as a function of the person and of the hypotheses chosen and applied.

We have for a long time accepted the idea that students learning, say, chemistry should have hands-on experience of the physical acts that textbooks summarize. Why not have emotions-on experience of the same? Why should that be any more of a private matter to be excluded from the classroom than the bodily practice of heating test tubes, writing to floppy disks, or training mice in mazes?

When this theorist of literature, however, ventures so far from his poems and stories as chemistry and computers, I make it very clear how far this book has wandered beyond the quirks and quiddities of Robert Frost. This is, as I warned you at the outset, a book more about brains than about Robert Frost's brain. It is, moreover, a book drawing to its conclusion. One conclusion is: we have learned something new about this book's cornerstone concept—identity. Let me recapitulate.

When Frost or the professors read the Robinson poem, their brains (or identities or more loosely, "the subjective") entered the feedback loop in at least four different ways. First, identity or the brain was the agent. Frost sat down to read the Robinson volume, to turn the pages, to scan the lines. Even the professors, although my questionnaire fed them the hypotheses with which to approach the poem, read and applied those hypotheses in as individual a style as they would later write their replies. Second, the poem did not simply return an answer to Frost's or the professors' probing. The "answer" was not the same for them all. Frost and each of the professors *heard* an answer but heard it with his or her own set of ears, own linguistic usage, and own inner sentences. (As we have seen, we understand the sentences we hear or read by generating "inner sentences" to test the input sentence against. Understanding language requires the active generation of linguistic expectations.[10] We heard the questionnaire, and we heard "The Mill" answer the questions we asked of it—both in the idiom of our forty-six identities. Identity was the consequence of that experience as well as what determined the style of the experience.

Third, identity or the brain compared that return to inner standards. What sounded "right" or satisfying or incoherent to each of us in the poem's answers to those hypotheses depended on the standards each of us applied. Questions 4 and 5, for example, seemed to many of the professors to go "beyond the text." To others, the questions seemed reasonable. Just about all the professors shared the canon that one should conform one's reading to the text, but they applied that standard individually. They all shared the belief that one must (at least for starters) read a poem to bring out its coherence, but what seems coherent to one may not seem so to another. What pleases passive One may not please fearful Five. What suits Frost's sense of "the sound of the sentence" may differ even from what felt right to Robinson. What suits Four as an answer to question 1 may not suit Two's more finely honed sense of grammar. All these criteria demonstrate individual identities applying individual standards to the return from hypotheses that may be individual or may be shared.

Finally, identity enters into the perception of identity. To put someone's identity into words, you must apply (as I did in chapters 1 and 2) the hypotheses for interpretation your interpretive community offers. From my community, I take hypotheses that combine the personality theory of psychoanalysis with the hypothesis-testing feedbacks of "cognitive science."

As a "top-down" agency, identity acts, as it were, on the hierarchy from the top down to the lowest level, generating the hypotheses that control this hierarchy. Identity asks questions of the text or of the world, listens for the answers, and decides if they are tolerably in accord with the hypotheses or insufferably off. Identity in this sense is the active principle of the self. Identity is agency.

Identity is also passive, however, or bottom-up. As we have seen in chapter 5, these experiences of trying out hypotheses and having them succeed or fail are identity-creating experiences. That is, we are both what we bring to those new experiences and what is created by those same experiences. Identity is consequence. In chapter 1, the brain scientists told us how. We grow many more brain cells in infancy than we can use, and we un-grow them in adolescence. Both the growth and the un-growth depend upon the way we exercise those cells. Hence the form of our physical brains result from the experiences we have. Our brain holds the traces of our preferences. Those activities we favor will get and keep neurons. Those activities we avoid will not. This inscribing of experience goes on all our lives. All our lives we add identity to our brains.[11]

Identity is also a representation, and that is the third element. My formulating a theme and variations for Frost or the professors is just as much my act of representation as their reading of Robinson's poem is theirs. When I say "fearful" Five, then, I am phrasing *my* reading of his standards for apprehending loss and anxiety, inferring them from the answers he wrote down and phrasing them in the light of my own standards and hypotheses. We need to remember there is another identity in the picture, one who is representing the identity of the professor under discussion. Just as their representations are functions of their identities, so my representations of them are functions of mine.

Identity is all three: agency, representation, consequence. If you are fond of mnemonics, as I am, you will see that we can represent these three terms as ARC. Identity ARCs out into the world which feeds back its responses to the self. Identity thus enters a feedback picture of reading (and, I should think, any kind of perception or interpretation) in at least four ways. Identity frames the hypotheses and tries them out, identity hears and absorbs the return, and identity *feels* the discrepancy between that return and one's inner standards. Finally, *my* identity phrases the identity which does these things.

In other words, we have to imagine that every statement of an identity itself presupposes someone—with an identity—who is doing the stating (as in Figure 8).

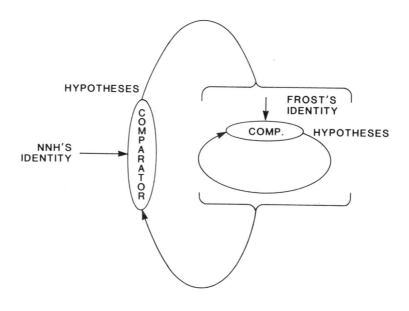

Figure 8.   An identity interpreting an identity

This picture simply applies to the perception of identity the same feedback principle (Figure 4) as for the perception of a literary text or anything else.

NNH puts forward a hypothesis about another person, Robert Frost. Part of my hypothesis is that I *can* interpret Frost as an identity theme and variations guiding various feedback systems. Part has to do with the particular theme I have derived from my reading of what Frost said and did. Part has to do with my own knowledge of how infants and mothers differentiate, how paranoia works, how people defend against their fears and wishes. Then I see and hear what Frost wrote and said and did (that is, I perceive the real world) and that real world rewards or defeats my hypotheses. I can then change the hypotheses until I reach a representation of Frost that feels right to me. The hypotheses I put forth, the way I hear the results, and the feeling I get from the process are all functions of my identity, my talent for unifying freedom and variety within a sameness, as Murray Schwartz said.[12] You have had evidence aplenty to confirm his reading, but ultimately you will arrive at your own. My own identity can only be known as someone perceives it through this same process.

I can never have some ultimately "true" knowledge of Frost, because it is always *my* knowledge. Your view of Frost will *necessarily* differ from mine, even if we share the same psychological and psychoanalytic hypotheses and even if we apply them as carefully as can be. In effect, our readings of Frost must differ, just as our readings of "The Mill" must differ, because *we* differ.

But suppose one person were to interpret that same person. Figure 7 pictures how one person (NNH) interprets another person's (Frost's) identity. If I were to cross out Frost and write in NNH, it would picture me as I interpret my own identity. As in any other situation of self-observation, I imagine myself split. Here, I become both observer and observed, subject and object. I am on both sides of the picture.

When I try to read my own identity, however, that very act of interpretation is part of the me I am trying to read. Identity is both what is being interpreted and what is doing the interpreting. Hence I cannot actually split myself, only imagine myself split. I can no more arrive at some final, "true," or "objective" account of my own identity than I can of Robert Frost's. Ultimate self-knowledge is as impossible as ultimate knowledge of another person. Both are, in a philosophical term, "systematically elusive." There is an ultimate limit even to the self-knowledge a psychoanalysis can give.

Perhaps you could say that to search for an identity is to deconstruct the identity one is searching for—I am not sure. I *am* sure that you could say that the search for identity engages one in an infinite regression, like looking for the square root of two. The infinity of the regression, however, does not imply that there is no such thing, any more than the unreachability of a final value proves there is no square root of two.

Postmodernist theorists like to speak of "the death of the subject" or the "disappearance of the self." The theorist typically argues as follows:

Because what I think and do depends on codes (linguistic, cultural, political) which *I* did not choose and over which *I* have no control (shades of Saussure), there really is no I worth talking about. Jonathan Culler's customary clarity enables him to stand as example for a host of others:

> . . . as meaning is explained in terms of systems of signs—systems which the subject does not control—the subject is deprived of his role as source of meaning. I know a language, certainly, but since I need a linguist to tell me what it is that I know, the status and nature of the 'I' which knows is called into question . . . Although they [the human sciences] begin by making man an object of knowledge, these disciplines find, as their work advances, that the self is dissolved as its various functions are ascribed to impersonal systems which operate through it.[13]

As we have seen, though, it is this division into I *as opposed to* the codes, the self *as opposed to* the Other, subjective *as opposed to* objective, these SEPARABLE PARTS metaphors, that cause the confusion. They do not account at all well for facts like the professors' and Robert Frost's readings of "The Mill." The forty-six readings do involve shared codes, and about some of these codes we had no choice at all (syntax or letter A). Many of the codes, however, "could be otherwise." All of them can be applied in individually different ways—as functions of an identity—and were so applied. The theorists dissociate codes from self and then give the codes autonomy. If we do that, though, we can no longer explain those forty-six different applications of the codes.

But isn't identity itself determined? Isn't the self therefore less than its surround? Aren't we all just products of our genes, our upbringing, and our culture? (The way signifieds are the products of signifying.) Identity is agency and consequence *and a representation of identity*. The first two are deterministic, but the third is no more determined than the professors' readings were determined by "The Mill" or—and this is closer to the deconstructionist position—than "The Mill" was determined by their readings. Both those phrasings oversimplify.

Identity is an agency, directing feedbacks. It is the consequence of the feedbacks it directs. And it is somebody's representation of that agency and consequence. One has to juggle, keeping all three of these terms in use at once, to make this model of identity work. To drop any one of the three muddles the model.

In particular, if one ignores the limits or the paradoxes required by identity's being a representation, one will quickly create a deterministic, naively realistic version of the theme and variations self. Someone's phrasing of an identity theme will turn into a prison one cannot get out of. Then, if one ignores identity's being a consequence, one will imagine a "transcendental signifier," a self that, as it were, floats free of the guy wires of reality. No. Identity is constantly being created by the very feedback loops that identity governs. Also, because identity is a representation (a fiction, if you like), it is always de-centered. It is always between an interpreter and what is being interpreted.

If two things are in a feedback relationship (reader and text, self and environment), then, to understand their interaction and indeed the things themselves, we need to address the processes by which, in their very relating, each defines the other. If we isolate a reader from a text or a rule for interpretation from people's applying it, we falsify the process. We lead ourselves into the futile paradox by which Ambrose Bierce defined "mind" in *The Devil's Dictionary*:

> MIND, *n.*   A mysterious form of matter secreted by the brain. Its chief activity consists in the endeavor to ascertain its own nature, the futility of the attempt being due to the fact that it has nothing but itself to know itself with.[14]

Obviously, if mind is "matter," an "it," it cannot know itself. If, however, mind is a process, a verb, it can process the concept of itself. To be sure, it will carry out that process with at least the same limitations as it processes other concepts and maybe still others arising from the difficulty of confronting one's own unconscious processes.

Since identity represents a process—a process of being, of interpreting, of experiencing—any effort to freeze that process into a static formula is bound to fail, even though one needs to state an identity in order to get feedback about that statement. Identity is a process, but language being what it is, we have difficulty representing it other than as a product: some statement "arrived at." Yet every such statement must be provisional, none final, each only an invitation to an exchange of ideas about that identity.

Differences about identity become like arguments about texts. As some wit has described them, literary disputes take the following form:

> "I went to Niagara Falls yesterday."
> "No, I did *not!*"

We could extend the analogy:

> "I had a great time yesterday."
> "No, I did *not!*"
>
> "This is a great poem."
> "No, it is *not!*"

"This poem is about economics."
"No, it is *not!*"

If we apply the picture of an identity governing feedbacks to these statements, we can see that they all involve comments ostensibly about an "out there," but the "out there" is governed by an "in here." How, then, can we settle such disputes? That is what keeps literary critics publishing and not perishing.

If there is no settling these matters, then "the truth" becomes something other than "the" truth. We can turn to the ideas of the German theorist, Jürgen Habermas. He defines truth or validity as the claim that we make whenever we make any claim: I can justify what I am saying if we talk long enough. He imagines an "ideal speech situation" in which people can talk free of any kind of domination (like professor over student, boss over employee, man over woman, critic over author or text, or state over citizen). For Habermas, consensus arrived at in that kind of free discourse is our best guarantee of truth.[15] "The truth" about identity is like "the truth" about literature: a process, a continuing discussion, something open, not closed.

Much contemporary thought about literature, despite sophisticated postmodern disclaimers, finds a "the" truth independent of the human beings who arrive at it. Theorists separate a book from the humans in whom such relations as "meaning" exist and function. By contrast, few indeed are the literary theorists who have studied the "free" responses of actual readers. Presumably that is why the ideas of the cognitive psychologist who studies actual readers differ so from the "signifying" texts of literary theory: "The meaning of a text is in the mind of the reader. The text itself consists only of instructions for the reader as to how to retrieve or construct that meaning."[16] Notice the verbs.

Often, literary theorists try to think about reading with nouns that seem to describe the separate elements of the reading process well—"the" text, "the" reader, subjectivity, competence. But nouns that serve us so well to class individuals serve poorly to describe an interactive process like reading. Nouns require that something be here or there, so or not so, objective or subjective, self or other. None of these forced dualisms works well to describe the dialectic of a feedback process, because they lead to the LITERATURE IS ISOLABLE PARTS metaphors. These metaphors, we have seen, do not particularly help us toward answers for the two basic questions this book addresses. How do we read and write individually? How alike?

I have been developing an image of the literary process as a brain or identity arcing hypotheses out into the world through a hierarchy of feedbacks. A writer like Robinson uses his personal themes and his literary canons and codes to write a poem about a miller. He writes in a "creative" mode, and we all know how complicated a concept that is. When he judges what he writes, however, he reads like any other reader. Once Robinson has finished making the poem, Robert Frost uses *his* personal themes and *his* literary skills to make that poem into a satisfying experience for himself. Similarly Professor One and the rest use their quite different values but similar skills to make the poem into an experience which is both like and unlike Robinson's or Frost's.

We can use this model of author and reader as identities governing levels of feedback, then, to understand that likeness and that difference, the separateness and individuality of our writings and readings and the way we also share them. Our next question, then, ought to be, Can this model yield better metaphors for talking about the literary process?

9

Hearing Ourselves Think

This book asks two basic questions about the brain, particularly as said brain (or mind) engages literature. One, everyone writes literature differently, and everyone responds to literature differently. How can we explain or articulate that? Two, if everyone creates individually and everyone responds individually, then how is it also true that we do in fact share our different experiences of language?

Trying to answer these questions has taken us on the one hand into the solidity of the body and on the other into the airiness of metaphor. As for the body, we have been asking how one might think about the individuality of a given person in terms of what the cognitive psychologists and the neuroscientists tell us about our brains.

Our brains individuate more during our development than do hearts, pancreases, or our other organs. The brain grows in childhood, and it un-grows as we approach adolescence. In the process, each of our brains becomes a somewhat different brain, and out of that individual brain comes a personal style—an identity. The brain is the organ of the unique mind by which we read and write in individual ways.

From identity and the brain we digressed to the metaphors we use to talk about writing and reading and about the way our brains do these things. It seems to me that those metaphors rest on a misleading model. I cannot provide you—no one can provide you with a comprehensive model of the way the brain works in reading and writing. Cognitive psychologists and brain scientists, however, can provide you with better metaphors for those literary acts. Hence, my answers to this book's two questions take the form of a sketch which one can use to picture to oneself the acts of reading or writing or, in general, using language. I am offering, simply, a better metaphor with which to hear ourselves think.

To arrive at that metaphor, I am asking you deliberately to draw on the scientific and technological knowledge of our own time. Once, when I was expounding this idea, someone from the audience asked me, "Do we really shop for metaphors this way? Do we pick and choose our metaphors? Don't metaphors just happen?" I don't think so.

In his *Essay on Man*, for example, René Descartes drew explicitly on the engineering of his day, as a metaphor for the "nerves," "muscles and tendons," and "the Animal Spirits" of the human machine. He compared them to "the grottoes and fountains which are in our royal gardens." In the late medieval period, miners invented more sophisticated pumps to get water out of their mines. As a result, it became possible for us to imagine the heart as a pump instead of as a furnace, the way centuries of physicians, following Galen, had been picturing it. In the nineteenth century, evolution offered a metaphor to economics with which to understand and justify the rise of capitalism. Or, some say, *laissez-faire* capitalism provided a free-market model for understanding the origin of species. "It is impossible to imagine how anyone could have made sense of the heart before we knew what a pump was," remarks Jonathan Miller, the physician-director, in the book based on his artful television series *The Body in Question*. "Before the invention of automatic gun-turrets," he continues, "there was no model to explain the finesse of voluntary muscular movement."[1] Furnaces, crucibles, ovens, pumps, free markets, and gun-turrets are all intrinsically useful. We sometimes forget they have another use: they let us image ourselves to ourselves.

In our own time, as with Dr. Miller's gun-turrets, all kinds of information processing devices have become metaphors for mental processes. If I say to you, "Descartes *turns me on*," you understand immediately that I am comparing myself to a television set or some other electrical machine. If I say to you, "Jacques Lacan's book *does not compute*," you recognize that I am saying it doesn't make sense—but perhaps only in terms of the obstinate categories of computer logic.

The point is, we can and do communicate by means of metaphors drawn from the engineering of our day, even if our knowledge of science is sophomoric. Indeed this may be the true value of science for nonscientists. It gives us ways of grasping more important things, things that cannot be handled by the mathematics of science but by the metaphoric logic that governs our thinking and feeling about love, beauty, misery, work, talk—or literature.

There is, I have been saying, a better metaphor for thinking about "Mending Wall" than saying that the poem controls our response or that it contains meanings which it then delivers. Identity governing feedback is a more accurate metaphor in the same sense that "The earth turns" is more accurate than "The sun rises." I am not so naïve as those seventeenth-century gentlemen in the Royal Society who wanted to do away with all metaphors in order to ensure clear, scientific thinking. We need metaphors to think. Indeed we cannot think without them. The clearest and most rigorous thinking, such as the scientist's use of mathematical models, is itself a comparison, hence metaphorical. As we have heard Frost say, "Isn't science just an extended metaphor: its aim to describe the unknown in terms of the known? Isn't it a kind of poetry?"

We can, however, have better and worse metaphors. Consider "The earth turns" and "The sun rises." Both metaphors oversimplify our picture of the universe, but one agrees with our other knowledge better than the other. One gets better feedback from the planetary world. In that sense, one is a better figure of speech than the other.

To picture our brains' dealings with "Mending Wall" or "Once by the Pacific" as an identity governing a network of feedbacks yields better metaphors than any picture of language or literature as fence, pipeline, force, recipe, or, in general, some isolable parts or isolable Other. Furthermore, is there any profound difference between interpreting "Mending Wall" and interpreting the *New York Times*? Or between language and other kinds of stimuli? If not, then a picture of our experiencing Frost's poem must apply to any kind of language, indeed any stimulus at all. With a better model for poems, we should be able to think better about perception and knowledge of every kind. Conversely, a better model of perception and knowledge offers a better model of writing and reading poetry.

We can bring to the matter of reading the robust ideas coming from the contemporary psychological view of perception, from cognitive psychology, artificial intelligence, and brain physiology. It is because the neuroscientists and the cognitive psychologists have gotten beyond stimulus-response that we literary critics can better model our response to "Mending Wall." We can begin to think in terms of a continuing, circling dialectic in which our brains change and choose what the world does to us even as the world does it. "Dialectic," however, is a difficult abstraction, while we can understand information processing feedbacks from telephones, radios, televisions, computers, and a hundred other devices around us every day and, of course, from our own bodies. In us, as in lesser organisms, chemicals like the hormones and neurotransmitters maintain a whole series of equilibria through feedback.

As we have seen, we habitually use other metaphors that make human beings and our literature into isolable parts. In asking you to think in systems and processes instead of entities, verbs instead of nouns, I realize I am asking you to get past the deeply ingrained metaphors for reading and writing to which we digressed in chapter 7. To what metaphors, then, do Figures 4 and 6 lead?

Listen to the differences as we go from "The Robinson poem *struck me*" to "I *was struck by* the Robinson poem" to "I felt after the Robinson poem *as though I had been struck.*" One way to move toward clearer metaphors for the processes of literature is to speak about feelings. They are, after all, what literature is all about. More precisely, they are the sensing instrument by which identity governs the feedbacks we use in reading and writing. When you talk about your feelings you get round the doubtful metaphysics of the CONDUIT metaphor or LITERATURE AS ISOLABLE PARTS.

To be sure, even those questionable metaphors describe satisfactorily certain experiences or sensations. I really do feel sometimes as though a poem has struck me. Fine. Let's say right out loud that that's what we are using that figure of speech for. Let's (as in the third sentence above) make it explicit that the metaphor is an attempt to describe certain feelings. Listen to the difference between "There is a meaning in 'Mending Wall' that I just can't get out" and "It feels as though there is a meaning in 'Mending Wall' that I can't get out." By saying our feelings directly, we can yield to the force of habit and continue to use the traditional language. We unpack the old metaphors and do not commit ourselves to the old model.

We could also try translating those same feelings into another metaphor. That is, feeling that one can't get a meaning "out" expresses a certain persistent drive and its frustration. One could say "Reading 'Mending Wall' is like finding a paperback with the pages glued shut." Hearing "like," I make the inside-outside premise of the CONDUIT metaphor explicitly a metaphor for a feeling. This metaphor treats the poem as a container, but only in relation to a desiring human being. The metaphor deals with the frustrated, digging feeling one gets with an obscure poem. Or, if you feel the poem is not obscure but too obvious, "Interpreting 'Mending Wall' is like trying to read a paperback with the pages falling out all the time."

Sometimes one can improve a metaphor just by clarifying it. "I *got that idea from* Frost criticism" comes across more accurately as "I *got that idea by reading* Frost criticism."

The first sentence phrases Frost criticism as a conduit that contains or delivers ideas. The second puts the texts of Frost criticism in relationship to a reader. Frost criticism is a thing in itself but my getting an idea is something *I* do.

Here are various ways to describe my writing this paragraph:

Holland can only use English.	Holland is trapped by English.
Holland exploits paradoxes.	Holland is exploited by paradoxes.
Holland plays with metaphors.	Metaphors make Holland playful.
Holland begins his sentences with sentence modifiers.	Sentence modifiers begin Holland's sentences.

The figures of speech on the right are language-active or text-active. Those on the left are person-active, and I wrote them with the feedback picture in mind. True, the confusions those on the right bring are a matter of degree. The last is less of a muddle than the first. Even so, compare—

Sentence modifiers begin his sentences.

Holland begins his sentences with sentence modifiers.

The first thing I come to in one of Holland's sentences is a sentence modifier.

The last says right out what is happening to the I. The first makes the sentence modifiers the active agent. The second attempts to infer my process of writing. (A copy editor, after all, might have inserted all these sentence modifiers—no, probably not.)

The confusion is minor, not to say minuscule. Nevertheless, it is the beginning of the much more substantive confusions we saw in chapter 7. Poems that "invite," novels that "absorb," and signifiers that "signify" all subsume a text-active model. In general, it seems to me, one should look with suspicion at phrasings that treat language as an agent. Acknowledging that the person is the active one in any use of language seems to me truer both to scientific psychology and to everyday experience. Moreover, making the person the agent leads to a proper family of metaphors.

That is, clarifying one's metaphors or spelling out the fact that one is talking about feelings are useful steps, but only a beginning. We can also seek out those metaphors for speaking and thinking about literature that are just plain better than others. I want to get past the old habits. I want to convert our pictures of an identity governing feedbacks into metaphors that involve more fruitful assumptions and a better model of the person.

Consider these:

Robert Frost *built* his readings on the foundation of his classical education.

Robert Frost *constructed* his readings . . .
Robert Frost *developed* his readings . . .
Robert Frost *created* his readings . . .
Robert Frost *crafted* his readings . . .

We could equally say,

Robert Frost *completed* Untermeyer's interpretation.
He *mended* it.
He *filled the gaps in* it.
He *made improvements on* it.
He *complemented* it.

Another family of metaphors:

Robert Frost's reading of Robinson is a beautiful *performance*.
Robert Frost's reading is an elegant *show*.
Robert Frost's reading is a makeshift *construction*.
Robert Frost's reading is an impulsive *scribble*.
Robert Frost's reading is a highly visible *achievement*.

And another:

Holland *limited* his response to "Mending Wall."
Holland *controlled* his response.
Holland *defined* his response.
Holland *shaped* his response.
Holland *inflated* his response.

The traditional metaphors image people as passively being hit or poured into. I would trade them for language that expresses the craftsmanship, skill, dexterity, mastery, artistry—or clumsiness—that we bring to reading and (more obviously) writing. We even bring a craftsmanship to moviegoing and television watching. I would call the metaphorical family LITERARY PROCESS AS PERFORMANCE. Or: WRITING AS ART, READING AS CRAFT. This brings American "reader-response criticism" closer to Germanic *Rezeptionsästhetik*. German critics have long recognized that the production of meaning is a "performance." "Literary texts," says Wolfgang Iser, "initiate 'performances' of meaning rather than actually formulating meanings themselves." "Without the participation of the individual reader there can be no performance."[2]

The metaphors I have instanced are not new, but when we look at them *as metaphors* we can see they build on a different idea of the literary process and a different picture of the human animal from the CONDUIT or ISOLABLE PARTS metaphors. Instead of treating the human as passive material to be worked over by words as though by the secret police, we can image a human being as the governor implicit in the cybernetic, feedback picture. We steer ourselves through the material world. I like John Dewey's term "transact." We transact cultural and physical realities, much the way we carry on affairs. A term like "transact" or these figures of speech I am recommending—that Frost *used* his knowledge of the classics or that Two *controlled* his response by referring to language— these build on the feedback picture of human action.

I believe metaphors from feedback will work better in our speech and thought than the simpler, text-active models on which semiotics rests or, finally, *Rezeptionsästhetik*. Although Iser recognizes that we perform meanings, it is nevertheless the text that initiates the performance, and "What is important to readers, critics, and authors is what literature *does* and not what it *means*."[3] For the German critic, it is the text that acts. For the American reader-response critic, this one at any rate, it is the reader that initiates the performance.

Robert Frost, when he reads (as when he writes), is an artist, and certainly when he was on stage he was a performer. He is *using* his skill with language to make interpretations and judgments just as Itzhak Perlman *uses* an E-string or Alex Katz applies burnt umber. Similarly, Professors One through Six are drawing on their critical know-how to read Robinson's poem or to establish grammatical antecedents, much as a carpenter used saw and skill to create the table at which they wrote. So too Professor Holland *uses* his ability to read for themes or his psychoanalytic training to interpret Robert Frost and the six professors. Or seven.

If we think of reading as performance, we can hear the confusions entailed by the metaphysics of isolable parts. Does it make sense to say that part of hammering a nail comes from the hammer, part from the carpenter? Would it make any more sense to say that 35% of a Jackson Pollock painting comes from Pollock and 65% from the properties of Duco paints? When we break the process down that way, we falsify it. Similarly we falsify reading if we say that "some" of Professor Three's reading comes from her vocabulary and "some" from her characteristic desire to crack a joke.

In considering a performance, can one isolate a violin from the artistry of the performer? Sort of . . . "Itzhak Perlman was playing his Stradivarius." Isolating the violin will help us understand rosin, resin, and resonances, but are we then understanding the performance? Does isolating the violin help us understand the way Perlman and his instrument come together to make a concerto we hear as Perlman-playing-his-Stradivarius? Imagine a simpler task, the making of a table. Can you sunder the carpenter, the plan, the saw, and the skill? Of course you can, so long as they are not interacting. If you decide to study the making of a table, however, they all become inseparable parts of one system.

There may be a difficulty inherent in using nouns to think in feedback terms. Herbert Simon (the only psychologist to win a Nobel Prize) notes that, in the development of modern science, substituting a process description (verb) for a state description (noun-adjective) has played a central role. Often, it has turned out that complex situations can be simply described by means of the kind of differential or difference equations that describe feedbacks, and this is not accidental. To adapt to its environment, any organism must be able to convert its imagining of a desired state into a process for reaching that state and vice versa. Hence we require an interaction of state descriptions and process descriptions, noun-descriptions and verb-descriptions, to describe the processes of feedback that go into reading and writing and every other kind of human activity.[4]

Perhaps an uncertainty principle comes into play any time you isolate some element like a canon or code or an identity. Once you lift one item out of the whole feedback system, you can no longer use it in accounting for the whole transaction the feedback was designed to explain. You can only talk about the single element. That may be a useful thing to do—it surely *is* useful to discuss codes and canons and identities per se—but we should not confuse it with explaining or talking about the transaction as a whole. If you were analyzing how I write a paragraph, you would do well to study my vocabulary or my oedipus complex. If you were studying how I read a paragraph, you might test my knowledge of grammar or ask me to associate to an inkblot. But only if you put me and my skills together into a functioning system could you truly study how I write or read.

In these metaphors or pictures of the literary process, reading is like writing, and this model offers us an answer to what literary circles find a troubling question these days. What is the authority of a text? We have seen that the text does not "control" our response to it. We have seen that Frost and the professors read according to an interpretive community which serves as an authority for certain canons of reading. But what is the authority of the text itself over the individual reader?

Behind the insistence on the question lies a fear, a fear that if the text does not have "authority," literary criticism will lapse back into its *fin-de-siècle* impressionism—anything goes. Two decades ago, when the New Criticism had its heyday in university teaching, "its major critical tenet . . . [was] an insistence on the primacy of the text over the individual response of the reader as the legitimate determiner of literary understanding and value."[5] The text, in short, was the authority. It determined meaning, although how it did so, as a psychological matter, critics didn't particularly ask.

In this fear we are meeting again what Mark Johnson calls the "false dichotomy" between fixed standards of knowledge and "'anything goes' relativism."[6] If we "perform," "craft," or "build" a literary experience by feeding back canons and codes through it, however, there is no dichotomy, because there is no one "authority." We are dealing instead with a complex process of construction by an individual using shared codes and text. Text, cultural codes or canons, and the individual all coact in a complex system of checks and balances.

If reading is like a musical performance, obviously the text resembles the score. To quote the psychologists again, "The meaning of a text is in the mind of the reader. The text itself consists only of instructions for the reader as to how to retrieve or construct that meaning."[7] A text is like a score in that we read it in order to create the work in our heads in order perhaps to create a public performance (analogous to literary criticism). Ultimately the score does not "control" that performance, because we could imagine, I suppose, some avant-garde performance artist at the Brooklyn Academy of Music who would use the score only as pieces of paper to be tossed about the stage or projected as a backdrop for some altogether different enterprise. Even performers who set out to "follow the score" will differ considerably in what they finally do. Ultimately, I think the score provides instructions so that *we* can compare different performances.

To get at the "authority" of a literary text, I think it is even more useful to analogize to the instrument being played. The Stradivarius affects Itzhak Perlman's re-creation *re*actively, the way a chisel acts back on a carpenter's plans or as bronze both enables and limits a sculptor. We sense the text feeding back our ideas to us, as if we were active, creative musicians trying this riff or that as we compose with a synthesizer. In this sense, the literary text is like the instrument, the instrument is like the score, the score like an instrument, the literary text like either or both. All coact in a system of checks and balances. All depend on the human being to "initiate the performance."

If we think of Professor Six as *using* Robinson's poem as an instrument with which to make a poetic experience, we can understand how even her "objective" answers express "subjective" concerns, for the same argument applies to the codes and canons of chapter 6 as to the text. They, too, are like a musical instrument or score. The English whose codes we learn as children, the interpretive communities to which we belong and whose rules we choose, the classroom or laboratory or armchair in which we read—these are things we use, like the text itself. The text, the interpersonal situation, or the rules for reading are all in a feedback with a self that is like an active, creative artist. They serve us like instruments, and like instruments their *re*action shapes our action.

Yet we are also free, like artists, no matter how bound in by tradition or rules, to write and read with a personal style. The text, the rules, the codes, are like musical instruments on which we play variations of our identity themes. We are makers when we read. Indeed we cannot do otherwise. That was why even the professors' "objective" answers were functions of "subjective" concerns.

We, as individuals with individual styles, create literary experiences that evidence those styles. In writing and reading, we *use* our English. We *use* a text. We *use* the methods we have learned in school. We *use* the canons of the interpretive community to which we have allied ourselves. We *use* the classroom or reading room or theater or conference in which we are writing or reading.

Finally, in using all these things, we re-create our personal identities (understood as agency, consequence, and representation), our own continuity in time. Every time we close one of those feedback loops, moreover, we add another iota of experience to our identity. We grow. We change. We are the consequence of what we do. As Frost says in "At Woodward's Gardens," "It's knowing what to do with things that counts."

If understanding is like speaking and reading is like writing, if all four are artistries, then hearing a metaphor is as important as making one. At least as important as any particular metaphors we choose is the way we hear the metaphors we and others already use. Even if we use old-fashioned words like "signifying" or metaphors of conduits and containers to describe Frost writing like Frost or Professor Six reading, we can hear those words and metaphors with a different picture in mind.

We do, after all, continue to say "The sun rises" and "The sun sets," but we hear those idioms differently from our sixteenth-century ancestors. They saw the sun lifting itself up above the earth. When I watch a sunrise or hear someone say "The sun is setting," I imagine, and I can almost feel, the earth's slow turning under my feet. I understand, in a way no fifteenth-century reader could, John Updike's tanning tourist (in "Island Sun") "whose back is gilded each time the planet turns." I hear, in a way Chaucer never could, Archibald Macleish's lines about a body in a grave:

> To feel the always coming on
> The always rising of the night.

To read such poems, we need not learn Kepler's tables or Newton's equations. We need only keep in mind a general picture of the earth turning in a Copernican sky. In the same way, we need not learn the differential equations that describe feedback loops to update our thinking about brains. We can simply listen to what we and others say about the self with some simple picture like Figure 4 in mind.

Listen, while remembering that image of feedback, to these passages from Frost. In the early poem, "The Trial by Existence," he images life as a continual testing, revising, being rewarded—in his virile word, "daring."

> Even the bravest that are slain
>   Shall not dissemble their surprise
> On waking to find . . . .
>   that the utmost reward
> Of daring should be still to dare.[8]

The bravest thing in life is "daring"—I hear "testing"—and the best reward is to be allowed to continue that openness. Frost seems almost to anticipate feedback.

Then, in the much later "White-Tailed Hornet," Frost writes about the instincts of animals and how we marvel at them as unerring. We are wrong to do so, he writes.

> Won't this whole instinct matter bear revision?
> Won't almost any theory bear revision?
> To err is human, not to, animal.
> Or so we pay the compliment to instinct,
> Only too liberal of our compliment
> That really takes away instead of gives.[9]

I hear Frost saying that instinct consists of thinking without the possibility of corrective feedback ("revision"), hence a lesser thing than being able to "err," less worthy of our compliment than human "daring" and correcting.

Frost's own writing often takes on that quality of testing, or so I can read these lines:

> You could not tell, and yet it looked as if
> The shore was lucky in being backed by cliff,
> The cliff in being backed by continent.

Often I sense that one polarity, basic to many of Frost's polarities, is the difference between being open to testing or feedback and the closed, certain mind. Thus, I can hear the final voice, the "other," of "Mending Wall" as the kind of person who uses feedbacks not to date, but only to confirm what he already knows. When the I of the poem tries to let the wall down,

> He will not go behind his father's saying,
> And he likes having thought of it so well
> He says again, 'Good fences make good neighbors.'

Hypothesis tried, feedback bad, close system, clunk. "He will not go behind"—he will not try a deeper, stranger supposition.

To understand these lines of Frost's, I have been cupping, like a hand against my ear, the idea of an identity governing a hierarchy of feedbacks. More obviously, we can use that model to listen to critical statements about response. We can hear simple statements like "It's funny" differently. We can hear them as "really" saying, "When I hear that, I laugh." "People feel amused by that cartoon." "I find this article funny." When the music critic on the radio announces he is going to do a program on "spirituality *in* music," I hear him using a container metaphor. When, in his next sentence, he says, "Of course, whether there is spirituality in the music or not, depends on whether you can hear it," I think to myself that I am listening to a rather confused music critic. That is, his "spirituality *in* the music" states a container metaphor, but when he makes the listener the arbiter and achiever of "spirituality," he shifts to a quite inconsistent performance metaphor.

At a much more sophisticated level of thinking, here is an introductory passage from a recent book applying contemporary literary theory to Renaissance texts:

As interest shifts from the meaning of the text to the principles governing its act of signification, that meaning both breaks apart and expands beyond the text's "proper" boundaries. The text no longer seems to speak with a single voice of its own . . . Literature . . . becomes a system in which the text . . . coalesces into an endless process of textual production.

This is an active text indeed, but on what evidence? If I take the clue of "signification," it is on Saussure's say-so. The writer goes on to force a startling but seemingly inevitable dichotomy:

The choice seems to be all or nothing: the totalizing concept of the individual, who, in the person of author or reader, appropriates the text and imposes closure upon its meanings; or a corresponding "dehumanization" of the text, the reduction of its meaning to impersonal procedures of writing, at once aleatory [i.e, by chance] and rigorously determined.[10]

That is, swept up in his own rhetoric, the writer insists that either the text "signifies" or the author does, not both. If, like all good moderns, we recognize that environments affect people, then we will be led to say, as some of the authors in this collection go on to do, that a Shakespearean tragedy is simply the product of Renaissance writing procedures. Driven by our own insistence on a text-active model, we will have turned Shakespeare into a mere funnel with cultural input at the big end and literary output at the small.

One of the finest of our contemporary critics, Geoffrey Hartman, writes of one critical mode currently in vogue, deconstruction:

There are many ways of describing the force of literature. The priority of language to meaning is only one of these, but it plays a crucial role in these essays. It expresses what we all feel about figurative language, its excess over an assigned meaning, or, put more generally, the strength of the signifier vis-à-vis a signified (the "meaning") that tries to enclose it. Deconstruction, as it has come to be called, refuses to identify the force of literature with any concept of embodied meaning and shows how deeply such logocentric or incarnationist perspectives have influenced the way we think about art. We [conventionally, before deconstruction—NNH] assume that, by the miracle of art, the "presence of the word" is equivalent to the presence of meaning. But the opposite can also be urged, that the word carries with it a certain absence or indeterminacy of meaning. Literary language foregrounds language itself as something not reducible to meaning: it opens as well as closes the disparity between symbol and idea, between written sign and assigned meaning.[11]

Conventionally, says Hartman, we tend to think of language as "saying" or meaning things instead of language as language—sounds, shapes, the surfaces (so to speak) of words. He is setting out to invert or neutralize that tendency. When, however, he inverts the traditional priority of language over meaning (signifiers' signifying signifieds), he does so in a quite traditional CONDUIT metaphor: "The word carries with it a certain absence or indeterminacy of meaning." Similarly, in the sentence, "Literary language foregrounds language itself . . ." he resorts to the text-active tradition. He does so again when he describes the signified trying to enclose the signifier or says of literary language that "it opens as well as closes. . ." Indeed, the whole statement rests on a premise, "the force of literature." Hartman reverses the direction of that force, but he does not question the idea that language does exert a force.

Even so, Hartman recognizes that we, in some kind of feedback process, bring "logocentric or incarnationist perspectives" (hypotheses?) to bear. He says, as I would, that these "perspectives have influenced the way we think about art." I would go further—the hypotheses we bring to bear *are* the way we think about art. Yet this half-glimpsed feedback model is inconsistent with the text-active model on which the thought as a whole depends. As with other critics we have considered, the dichotomy between person-active and language-active theories of literature remains suppressed or ignored. Text-active vs. reader-active is not a live issue.

What I am suggesting is that one can sort out the intricacies of modern critical theory by setting them against this model. One can hear, really hear, what Hartman is saying by hearing it through the idea of an identity governing feedbacks. When I hear it that way, I realize that I am hearing not so much new theory about the way literature means as new values applied to traditional theories.

Hartman's is a complex statement, but the same kind of listening applies to more commonplace remarks. We can better hear the usual statements we make about writers by interpreting them against this guiding metaphor. "Robert Frost's poetic style comes partly from his mother's interest in symbolism, partly from his own classical background." We are accustomed to thinking of *part* as meaning something like "roughly a half" or "44/100" or "some," part of a thing—a noun. With a better guiding metaphor, we can hear those *parts* as themselves parallel processes of feedback within a larger system. Sometimes Frost wrote by means of his mother's symbolic codes. Sometimes he used the codes he learned from the Greek and Roman classics.

We can better understand our explanations of what we do when we teach literature. "I always ask them just to analyze the words on the page"—teachers who say that "really" mean they encourage the student to make use of one particular kind of hypothesis in the feedback process of reading and no other. The teacher was willing to work with hypotheses about verbal patterns, the words-on-the-page, but not to test, say, what the author might have intended or how the students felt.

"The text determines its meaning." By that text-active form, it seems to me, a literary speaker attests to a feeling of the rightness and inevitability of "the" meaning and an unawareness of his or her own role in creating that meaning. In that form, this now-traditional critical view uses a stimulus-response model. But we can hear the sentence another way: When you bring your codes and canons and personal identity to bear upon a text, the text reacts and what you hear as meaning is that reaction. In that sense, it is true that the text determines its meaning, but only in that sense.

The point is to hear ourselves think. I am, in the terms of George Lakoff and Mark Johnson, trying to change a "cognitive model" or an "image-schema," one of those half-cultural, half-physical metaphors by which we construe our world. I would like us not to think of literature in terms of isolable parts, stimulus-response, or an objective Other "out there" forcing itself on a subjective "in here." Instead, I would like us to accept that we understand poems and stories (and the rest of the world) by our personal use of cultural and physical guesses.

This is not to say that our experience of literature is merely whim. Philosopher Hilary Putnam argues:

> Our conceptions of coherence and acceptability are . . . deeply interwoven with our psychology. They depend upon our biology and our culture; they are by no means 'value free.' But they *are* our conceptions, and they are conceptions of something real. They define a kind of objectivity, *objectivity for us,* even if it is not the metaphysical objectivity of the God's Eye view. Objectivity and rationality humanly speaking are what we have; they are better than nothing.[12]

George Lakoff in turn extends Putnam's argument:

> He is not saying that we cannot have correct knowledge. What he is saying is that we cannot have a privileged correct description *from an externalist perspective.*
>
> The problem is the external perspective—the God's eye view. We are not outside of reality. We are part of it, *in* it. What is needed is . . . an internalist perspective. It is a perspective that acknowledges that we are organisms functioning as part of reality and that it is impossible for us to ever stand outside it and take the stance of an observer with perfect knowledge, an observer with a God's eye point of view. But that does not mean that knowledge is impossible. We can know reality from the inside, on the

basis of our being part of it. It is not the absolute perfect knowledge of the God's eye variety, but that kind of knowledge is logically impossible anyway. What *is* possible is knowledge of another kind: knowledge from a particular point of view, knowledge which includes the awareness that it is from a particular point of view, and knowledge which grants that other points of view can be legitimate.[13]

As a philosopher, Mark Johnson adopts the same position: "Whether it be for human events or for words and sentences, meaning is always meaning *for* some person or community. Words do not have meaning in themselves; they have meaning only for people who *use* them to mean something."[14] *Use.* That is the image-schema (or cognitive model) I would like you to make part of your thinking. We craft, we perform, we construct a literary experience. We use poems and fictions to make experiences.

Murray Schwartz wrote me about this book, that it is "a utopian project, like psychoanalysis, in its desire for full awareness." True. I would like us to share Nietzsche's awareness that our findings of goodness, beauty, or truth express our own need to make our world understandable. I regard his likening this book to a psychoanalysis as a still greater honor and compliment, even if no book can possibly live up to it. Yes, I am being utopian, but if you will bring to your thinking about literature, the image of an individual identity using cultural codes and canons and physical actions to test a text (Figures 4 and 6), I can ask no more.

Frost says (in "Etherealizing"):

> A theory if you hold it hard enough
> And long enough gets rated as a creed.

He could surely have said that of my theory that the human being is an identity governing feedbacks. It has become a creed. I believe it is true, although I almost blush to write "true" at the latter end of our super-skeptical century. In my better moments, I claim no more than that it is a guiding metaphor against which to hear other descriptions and explanations.

Paradoxically, however, the process of feedback is a metaphor for metaphoring. We can use the feedback picture to image metaphor building itself. We hypothesize—put out—a metaphor, and according to the feedback we get from the world and from our fellow humans we conclude it is a good metaphor or a bad one and revise it accordingly. It is in this sense that a good metaphor is "true," and truth (in our skeptical century) no more than a good metaphor.

That is, this theory defines truth as what gives good feedback when we try it out on the world. My image of the I is just one more hypothesis to be put out into the world, and, when I say it is "true," I am simply saying I get a good return from it. (I do not, unfortunately, mean royalties.) That "good return" constitutes the truth of this book, and as the circle of this book closes I can summarize what has made that feedback seem good to me.

Conclusions

I was able to read Robert Frost as managing his fears of the unlimited and unmanageable by manipulating limited, knowable symbols. In chapters 2 and 3 I traced that identity theme against three kinds of variations: particular poems, Frost's opinions and life, and Frost's readings of the poems of others. I believe one could as successfully interpret all Frost's different activities as variations on such a centering theme, one, to be sure, supplied by me as part of my own identity theme. Similarly, chapter 4 showed that I could interpret, as themes and variations, the readings of a group of college professors, although I knew much less about them than I did about Frost.

For me, the important thing about the professors' responses to the poem was that I could trace in their seemingly "objective" answers to "objective" questions the same theme-and-variations identity that showed more clearly in their "subjective" responses. That said to me that we can understand *both* "the subjective" and "the objective" in *both* reading and writing in terms of one process. That process, rather than being either subjective or objective, describes the way any reading is necessarily always both. Furthermore, we can think about it in minimalist terms. We can imagine that process in a way that suffices for our literary purposes but is unlikely to be overturned even by our rapidly expanding knowledge of the way the brain works.

Chapters 5 and 6 described that process. A de-centered identity (the theme and variations with which one can phrase Frost or a professor) governs a hierarchy of information processing feedbacks. Then, in reading or writing, we test a book by three kinds of hypotheses: physical acts, codes, and canons. We perform the acts of writing or reading with our eyes and fingers, and we recognize such things as size and shape and sequence that physically "cannot be otherwise." These physical acts enable us to write and test writings with "cannot be otherwise" codes from our culture, codes like the shapes of letters and numbers, the spelling codes by which we form words from letters, social symbolisms like flags and traffic lights, or the rules of grammar or syntax by which we form sentences from words. Finally, we use canons, the "can be otherwise" rules of a particular classroom, "interpretive community," or social movement that say you should read and write these sentences or use these words a certain way. All three kinds of loops serve the conscious and unconscious desires of a personal identity.

Phrased that way, I have looked at the process from the bottom up, from the ground of physical reality through two kinds of cultural reality. We could equally well move from the top down. My identity *uses* canons of interpretation, which *use* the linguistic and cultural codes I share with you, which in turn *use* the physical acts of reading and writing.

At the very highest level, governing those "can be otherwise" and "cannot be otherwise" hypotheses, are we: our identities. At the top of the hierarchy that reads and writes are our personal tastes, values, morality, style, or character—all of which I intend in the term "identity," for that is what identity refers to: the pattern of our choices. To phrase an identity, I prefer the technique of reading for a theme and variations. The theme is the sameness I can trace through Frost's writing, reading, life, and opinions. The variations are the necessary differences we will find as we pass from writing to reading to life to opinions. I prefer to assume a single theme, but you might wish to phrase several, and, of course, there may be other ways altogether of phrasing an identity. The crucial thing is to find a way of putting into words a person's style as manifested in their choices.

In imagining identity at the top of a hierarchy of feedbacks, we give three aspects to identity: agency, consequence, and representation. Identity is what governs the feedbacks and acts through them on the text. Identity is also the result of that action, the memory, as it were, of what has happened to the I as a result of all these actions and re-actions. Identity in these two aspects is something that was inscribed in the pathways between Robert Frost's neocortex and limbic system as he grew and ungrew nerve cells and synapses in childhood, adolescence, and thereafter.

Finally, and simultaneously, identity is something I read in Robert Frost and the professors, just as if I were reading a text. It is an interpretation, a construct. It is de-centered, something between me and Robert Frost rather than simply something in me or in him. It is itself a hypothesis feeding back a return.

This book is, like all books, such a feeding back of information. In these pages, starting with chapter 1, I am asking two basic questions about the brain, particularly as said brain (or mind) engages literature. One, when we speak and we write, we make up sentences in an individual style—or at least somewhat differently from anyone else. We also hear and interpret in an individual style the sentences others speak and

write—or at least we hear and interpret somewhat differently from anyone else. How can we imagine that individuality in an intelligible way?
Two, if it is true that we make up sentences in an individual style and
that we understand the sentences others speak and write in an individual
style, then how do we explain the obvious fact that we do communicate?
How do we manage to share our private experiences of language? How
do we teach? How do we write literary criticism?

To these two questions, this book proposes answers, which are, in
the framework of the book as a whole, hypotheses for you to test against
your own experience of literature and language. First, what engages
literature in the literary process, what writes and reads, is an identity
that is different for each of us. By thinking of identity as a theme and
variations and as agency, consequence, and representation, we can imagine the individuality of speakers and hearers or writers and readers in
a coherent way. (Indeed, those who like uncertainty may find it too
coherent.) Second, in engaging language, each unique theme-and-var-
iation identity uses hypotheses to test a text through feedbacks. These
hypotheses are the same for many or all of us.

We create and respond using bodies, codes, and canons. Whoever
has the same kind of bodies, codes, or canons as we, can use them to
understand our sentences or to make up new sentences that we in turn
will be able to understand. Insofar as we share these interpretive skills,
we will understand things the same way, and we will also understand
them differently because identities are different. Always, already, before
there ever was language, it was in the nature of the animal that we
would simultaneously understand and misunderstand each other, because we are both different from and the same as our fellow humans.

It was in chapters 5 and 6 that I developed this model, and I put it
graphically in Figures 4 and 6. If you were to remember anything from
this book, I would like it to be those pictures. They will serve for imagining all kinds of mental processes: perception, action, memory, or
knowledge, as well as our creation and re-creation of literature. With
them we can hear ourselves think.

The feedback picture allows us to understand what feels like the "constraint" of a text or culture. Although we sometimes feel them that way,
words or culture do not restrain us like guardrails or prison bars. Rather,
people reach into the cultural storehouse of their vocabulary or their
neighborhood and take out ideas—be they from science or literature or
street culture—for expressing their experience. What isn't there, you
can't take out, and that is one limitation from the social world around

us. What contemporary literary thought does not offer me, I cannot profit from. That is why feminist literary criticism is so important.

Feminist critics have pointed to the "immasculation" of women readers. In a decisive account,[15] Patrocinio Schweickart points to the dilemma, "The woman reader . . . realizes that the text has power to structure her experience." Without buying into her text-active metaphor, I can readily accept the other half of the picture Schweickart draws: "However, her recognition of the power of the text is matched by her awareness of her essential role in the process of reading. Without her, the text is nothing— it is inert and harmless." Precisely. Schweickart goes on to explain what the text's "power" is. The woman reader has read many authoritative male texts. As a result, "She has introjected not only androcentric texts, but also androcentric reading strategies and values." The psychoanalytic term "introjected" is exactly right: a reader takes into his or her mind the tactics that work for a given text, and the return those tactics yield when fed back. As a result, "This androcentricity is deeply etched in the strategies and modes of thought that have been introjected by all readers, women as well as men."

It is not so much that the text has "power." Rather, to get anything out of masculinist texts, you have to use masculinist strategies to read them, and eventually those strategies become the way you read. That is why feminist writing and reading are so important in the feedback picture. They provide writings from which to introject feminist, instead of masculinist, canons for reading, and thus, writes Schweickart of the feminist reader, "In the end she succeeds in extricating herself from the androcentric logic of the literary and critical canons." Canons *can* be otherwise, if our cultural storehouse offers us alternatives.

What we *can* take from the storehouse, we use. We use books, we use language, customs, and values, we use the polity, we use the physical world around us, our own bodies, our minds, our race, our sex, our gender, and our age to achieve our individual aims, values, and standards. Nevertheless, "using" things is the second kind of limitation we get from culture. The things we use—language, customs, values, polity, body, mind, race, sex, gender, age, and physical world—both enable and inhibit us in achieving those aims. They free and limit us as Frost's use of country imagery both freed and limited him. There are things you can do with colloquial speech and country imagery and things you can't. There are things you can do with masculinist canons for reading and things you can't, things that male readers often need. Metaphors of social "forces" or "inscribings" make it hard to imagine that curious mixture of limitation and freedom.

The re-action from what we try to do, the return from the codes and canons we apply and what we apply them to, completes the feedback, and the cumulating history of those feedbacks is our identity. "History" admits a useful ambiguity. We are what "really happened," but we are always the story of what really happened, rather than some Aristotelian essence or Kantian thing-in-itself. Identity is what happened *but* also the representation of what happened. In that double sense, we *are* the feedbacks we have performed in our lifetimes. In that sense, but that sense only, we are "determined" by language and culture. Only in that "reactive" sense do texts have "power."

This whole matter of power led me in chapter 7 to digress into the kinds of metaphors we use for thinking about language and literature. It seems to me we need to hear ourselves think. We need to listen to ourselves and the fictions we are subscribing to. If we do, we can improve the metaphors with which we have been describing ourselves to our-selves or imaging such things as the writing and reading of literature or the "impact" of society or the relation between the brain of Robert Frost and his writings.

If you or I incorporate Figures 4 and 6 into our thinking, we become able to assess and to improve the models or metaphors with which we customarily think about writing, reading, and other types of perception. With reading in particular, we can get past the old claim that texts impose meanings or control responses. We can do better than the simple division of reading into a subjective and an objective part. Rather, one can picture (as in Figure 7) the process by which authors communicate with readers in a world of private minds. One can picture (as in Figure 6) the relation between the limits imposed by cultural codes and those imposed by the physical world. Figure 6 lets us understand what is, in the profoundest sense, the dialectic between brain and world or between individual and society. What seems puzzling at first becomes clear: how a reading can be determined both by the text and by the reader. Similarly, we can tease apart the process by which a reading is both culturally determined yet individual. The minglings of individual and culture, text and re-sponse, become, in the light of a new guiding metaphor, understandable. We can think better about teaching.

Conversely, if we isolate an author or a reader from a text or a rule for interpretation from people's applying it, we make the whole literary process harder to understand. Often, it seems to me, contemporary thinking about literature falls into this error, through clinging to the Saussurean idea of a signifier that signifies a signified. This is the text-active model with a vengeance. What has happened is that critics have taken Saussure's formal or logical description of language and substituted it for the psychology of speaking and understanding.

"Signifying" simply does not correspond to the psychological pro-cesses that actually go on when we speak, write, hear, or read, any more than number theory corresponds to what goes on in our heads when we balance our checkbooks. Logically,

$$\begin{array}{r} 142,857 \\ \underline{\times 7} \\ 999,999 \end{array}$$

But that equation has practically no relation to

> Seven times seven is forty-nine, write nine, carry four—seven times five is thirty-five, add four, write nine, carry three—seven times eight is fifty-six, add three, write nine, carry five—seven times two is fourteen, add five, write nine, carry one—seven times four is twenty-eight, add one, write nine, carry two—seven times one is seven, add two, write nine—quit.

—or whatever goes on in *your* mind when you do that arithmetic.

If the formal description and the psychological were the same, we would never make mistakes. If "signifying" corresponded to the psychological processes of language, we would never misunderstand one another. We would never have had to learn to read or even to talk. Language would have taken care of all that by itself.

We humanists often resist over-simple pictures of the human, yet we stumble into them again when we trap ourselves in outmoded psychological assumptions. I am thinking, for example, of the simple stimulus-response, cause-effect model of the human being associated with the more behaviorist forms of "scientific" psychology. Some Marxian theorists likewise picture the individual as mere clay molded by historical pressures. Conversely, religious and political conservatives speak of an isolated "free" (undetermined) individual. It seems to me the sciences of our age have for many decades outmoded the simple split of subject and object or the simple process of signifiers' signifying. These are flat earth theories that look incontrovertibly commonsensical—until you try to detail them or fit them into other knowledge. We need to get beyond these nineteenth-century models.

Nevertheless, many literary people continue to write as though meanings or emotions or even deconstructions are "in" the poem, or that the book "out there" dictates what students say about it, or that Frost's poetry comes "out of" a series of historical determiners or codes inscribed by society. It seems to me that these traditional beliefs and metaphors persist because they meet deep personal needs. People need to project their feelings out into the world, finding a justification or cause outside themselves. "It's funny," not "When I read that, I laugh." "'The Mill' moves me" or "'The Mill' is moving," instead of, "Something in me responds deeply to 'The Mill.'" Every response to art tests (and may, in testing, threaten) something very profound to each one of us.

From this perspective, by LITERATURE IS ISOLABLE PARTS and the metaphysics that accompany that metaphor, we express an attitude toward boundaries. Brains engaged in laughing or writing poetry or reading a novel are crossing boundaries, both the literal, physical boundaries between reader and text and the much more general boundary between self and not-self.

Boundaries are at the very root of our being. From the point of view of child development, our most important early achievement is just that: finding a boundary. As Daniel Stern phrases it, "The infant discovers that he or she has a mind and that other people have minds as well."[16] We each have to learn that I am an I, separate from a mother who is also an I but whose nurture surrounds me to form an environment. It is precisely the ability to accept the separateness of self and other that allows us to become selves at all. This second, psychological birth hatches our attitudes toward all boundaries. Are divisions rigid and hostile or loving and giving? Is separateness lonely or satisfying? Are boundaries real and forever or only provisional, constructive, even imaginary? Later, adult feelings about boundaries are likely to sustain our most primal sense of what it is to be a separate being, and to question boundaries may well feel as though one were tugging at the very roots of selfhood.

Hence, "Good fences make good neighbors." Some people need to feel that boundaries are clear and strong, decisively marking off male from female, say, parent from child, true from false, or thou shalts from thou shalt nots. Strong social, verbal, and logical distinctions between ideas, classes, races, and sexes *feel* right. They provide an emotional hard hat.

We often feel that literature takes our boundaries down. We are "absorbed" by a story. When, however, we use ISOLABLE PARTS to express that feeling, we separate ourselves from what we once were, fused or at one with the story. We, in effect, recapitulate exactly that early childhood development. It seems to me that is the reason the ISOLABLE PARTS metaphor persists as a basic and needed way of thinking about literature or, in the largest sense, human experience. It is, perhaps, a particularly masculine need.

Nowadays, we are seeing our technology work a profound change in the way we live in our world and our selves. Traditional ideas of here and there or now and then dissolve in an electronic world in which information is neither here nor there but continually twinkling and circling along telephone lines between computer data bases, themselves only more and more loops of cycling electrons. Even my money is just some computer's memory, and "Reach out and touch somebody" means, in the world of today's advertising slogans, telephoning them. Much of the time we no longer live in a world of discrete objects here and there, like the famous rock that Dr. Johnson kicked to show the solidity, the out-there-ness, of experience.

In this psychological sense, a growing technology fundamentally challenges our inner and outer boundaries. Our science is sweeping us along willy-nilly, ever more rapidly into a world of continuities and systems and processes in which the traditional dividing lines against which one could read "here" and "there," "now" and "then," or "she" and "I" are no longer available to us. These changes in our concept of the world seem to me rapid beyond any human control, inevitable and irreversible. We are all in systems and processes together, and we need ways to think about ourselves and the things around us as parts of systems, always, already in interaction. The distinction between subject and object has—not "disappeared," that wouldn't express it—it has ceased to be as useful as it once was.

How this change in *Weltanschauung* feels to you will depend on your own deep feelings about boundaries. As for me, I feel a conflict. Consciously, I want to see the walls come down. Yet I know that, deep down, I feel more secure with boundaries firmly drawn. Perhaps that is why, despite all my efforts, my phrasings sometimes lapse from my conscious belief in feedback into an older, more simply deterministic idiom that, at some deep level, my psyche craves. Perhaps that ambivalence toward boundaries is why I feel so drawn to the feedback picture. I hold it, Frost would say, like a creed, because it allows me to visualize boundaries but see them crossed, transcended, and finally understood as more imagined than physical. The picture of an identity governing feedbacks lets me do that while I am myself comfortably bounded and distanced by the abstraction of the model. It satisfies the part of me that wants to stand outside and "know" things without being a part of them. And surely this new guiding metaphor makes the minglings of individual and culture, text and response, self and object, knowable.

Even so, there is a residual mystery, which may be a modern form of the old mind-body or mind-brain problem. An identity is always someone's putting an identity into symbolic form. Hence an identity is always arrived at by the very process one is trying to describe—identity governing the testing of hypotheses. Identity is de-centered, as in Figure 6, even, perhaps, deconstructed. At any rate, the concept of identity sets a limit to our knowledge. We can never step out of the ways our bodies and minds know things. We cannot have a "God's eye" view of things, because we can never step out of our selves. And we can never finally know those selves.

Within that horizon of knowability, I am urging on you today's ways of thinking about mind and brain as they make and re-make literature. You could say the point of this book is no more than a series of metaphors that reflect the revolution in psychology called "cognitive science." Cognitive science offers us new and better ways of describing how Robert Frost or Edwin A. Robinson wrote and how poets and professors read them.

What of the brain, though? What of the soft, cream-cheesy three-and-a-half pounds of neurons and synapses inside Frost's craggy cranium with which we began? What does neuroscience say to a literary critic? Cognitive science is psychological. It therefore lends itself nicely to theories of literature, and that is why I have rested much of my case on cognitive science. Brain science is physiological, though, and therefore harder to use in thinking about literature, especially the readings and writings of an individual like Robert Frost. Nevertheless, we know that, in the feedbacks governed by identity, the brain structures experience and experience structures the brain. When we talk about Robert Frost's style, readings, critical opinions, or identity, we are talking ultimately about the brain of Robert Frost.

There are, it seems to me, three fundamental ways in which the special architecture of the human brain expresses itself in literary actions. First, it is a fundamental principle of today's neuroscience that the brain operates by means of feedbacks and, specifically, a hierarchy of feedbacks. Once we accept the idea of such a hierarchy we become able to sort out what is individual, what is cultural, and what is physically constrained in our reading and writing. We can understand how it is that we each read differently yet use common canons and codes and texts, and therefore share, at least partly, those highly individual experiences.

Second, in contrast to the pre-programmed responses of reptiles, the limbic system of the mammalian brain enables or inhibits actions through emotions: desire, anger, fear. Moreover the limbic system coacts with the neocortex and its plans and abstractions, to construct a world, both the real world in which mammals survive and the fictional worlds we humans create and enjoy in literature. At root, then, literature rests on a pre-verbal habit of constructing worlds, something visceral, emotional, and personal rather than an act of purely linguistic interpretation.

Third, somewhere, somehow in those connections between limbic system and neocortex is human identity. In the growing and ungrowing of the brain, some connections arise and are favored; others die off or never come into being in the first place. Written in the very fibers that linked his hominid brain with a mammalian brain capping his brainstem was the essential Robert-Frostness of Robert Frost, waiting to be read by the essential you-ness of you and me-ness of me. It seems safe to assume, moreover, that some of the feedback loops that Frost used in writing and that we use in reading him were established in the growing and ungrowing of his brain, in those same links between neocortex and limbic system. Some are primitive and hard-wired, the ways we govern our senses, for example. Others are cultural codes, like the way we recognize letters. Others are cultural canons: how we read poems, what we value in them, the metaphorical structures by which we perceive the world and which Frost must echo or challenge, the ways Americans think and read and write. Some of these loops we can change and un-learn. Others are there for the duration. All provide ways the brain governs the reading and writing of literature.

To be sure, we know less about the brain than we do about the behaviors studied by cognitive and other psychologists. We are seeing in this decade, however, a powerful convergence of cognitive science and brain science and even that frail cousin of academic psychology, psychoanalysis. Starting from very different kinds of evidence, the three disciplines now confirm one another.

Psychoanalysis, resting on the necessarily personal interpretation of clinical evidence, offers least in the way of proof but most in the way of detailed explanations of some individual's behavior (of, say, Frost's specific reaction to "Miniver Cheevy"). Brain science offers the strongest proofs for its conclusions, physical, chemical, and biological evidence, but those conclusions apply to many, often all, brains. They lack the detail of psychoanalytic interpretation. The proofs of cognitive science are strong (but statistical and inferential, not directly physical like the brain scientists'). The cognitive scientists' explanations of behavior are also strong, but they operate at the level of many human beings rather than one. Yet that is what literary studies finally address, the individual writer and the individual reader.

We can combine brain science, cognitive psychology, and psychoan-alytic theory into one model: a personal identity governing a hierarchy of feedbacks that use shared codes, canons, and physical realities to make experiences, literature among them. Then we can use such a picture of the human being to address writers and readers in both their indi-viduality and the qualities they share with some or all of the rest of us. When we do, it seems to me, we have to re-examine some of the as-sumptions literary critics cling to most tenaciously. The idea that texts mean apart from some emotional human being making them mean, the idea of the "free play of language," the idea that codes or other symbolic orders can be isolated from the human being using them—these we need to rethink in the light of what we now know about human psy-chology and the human brain.

As I said at the outset, this is not a book about Robert Frost. Yet so gently has Frost lent himself to my odd little book about the ways brains do literature, it is only fair that he should have the last word.

His 1932 poem, "Build Soil," is a dialogue between two shepherds in the manner of a pastoral by Horace. Frost touches on politics and other subjects, and, as in "Mending Wall," he contrasts the two men's attitudes toward boundaries. One is a commercial, post-cutting, fence-mending farmer. The other, the more liberal, is a farmer-poet, who says,

> The world's one globe, human society
> Another softer globe that slightly flattened
> Rests on the world, and clinging slowly rolls.
>
> * * * *
>
> We are balls,
> We are round from the same source of roundness.
> We are both round because the mind is round,
> Because all reasoning is in a circle.

Frost seems to be hinting at something quite elusive here. I say "Frost," because this speaker seems more like Frost himself than the "castaway of commerce." I side, perhaps too decisively, with the poet. It seems to me that in describing the mind as round and reasoning as circular, Frost is hinting that the round world answers us according to what we ask of it. Our knowledge is circular, because we have to dare and then learn how our dare comes out. That is why we can only learn, in a sense, what we already know, or at least what we already know enough of to surmise. Frost seems to me to be phrasing, with a poet's art, feedback.

The earlier "Mending Wall" had a puzzling line about the stones the two men pick up: "And some are loaves and some so nearly balls." Once upon a time, mesmerized by the classical psychoanalytic system of symbols, I would have convinced myself those stones referred to phallus and testicles, respectively. Now the later poem, "Build Soil," and a newer psychoanalysis allow me a more generative intuition to wrap around the old one. I read in Frost's loaves and balls two beliefs about thinking. One: thought is a circling—a feedback, if you will. The other: thought is as straight as a loaf of bread, logical, with entailings and inevitabilities following one upon another. Certainly thought feels that way sometimes.

Our different styles of thought, loaf or ball, create the walls between humans that ward off threats as illusory as marching pines or as grandly real as oceans. They create walls within humans as well. They reflect deeper, emotional attitudes toward walls and boundaries. Certainly there has been a wall in literary criticism: the reader-response critics on one side; traditional New Criticism and seemingly new "theory" on the other.

One side tests poets and professors. The other marches along a logical track.

As between loaf and ball, I consciously choose ball. I am a critic whose image of the human rests on feedback. "We are round," as Frost says. Frost, however, is, as any poet must be, on both sides of that wall. That is why we need poets so. Frost lets me open my made-up mind, my settled feedback loops, to the ambiguities he makes possible for me. He lets me try hypotheses. He lets me see that, for all my belief in feedback, there must also be a sense in which our thought streaks as unrelentingly as an arrow from premise to, as here, conclusion. He lets me find an older, hidden part of myself that doubts the ball and still believes in the loaf. He leaves me wondering, at myself, at him, at thought, at this world we think about. Is it noun? Is it verb? He leaves me reading and writing, daring, he would have called it, guessing say I, as I guess and guess again.

Notes

1 Thoughts about Brains

1. So popular is this fantasy that the Curt Siodmak story has been filmed four times: *The Lady and the Brain* (U.S., 1944); *Donovan's Brain* (U.S., 1953); *Vengeance* (Germany, 1962); *The Brain* (Germany-Great Britain, 1965).

2. Douglas R. Hofstadter, *Gödel, Escher, Bach: An Eternal Golden Braid* (New York: Basic Books, 1979) 341–346.

3. Colin Blakemore, *Mechanics of the Mind*, BBC Reith lectures 1976 (Cambridge and New York: Cambridge UP, 1977) 1–9.

4. Aleksandr Romanovich Luria, *Higher Cortical Functions in Man*, 2d ed., trans. Basil Haigh (New York: Basic Books, 1980) 19–20.

5. Jonathan Winson, *Brain and Psyche: The Biology of the Unconscious* (Garden City NY: Anchor Press/Doubleday, 1985).

6. Morton F. Reiser, *Mind, Brain, Body: Toward a Convergence of Psychoanalysis and Neurobiology* (New York: Basic Books, 1984) ch. 6.

7. Jay E. Harris, *Clinical Neuroscience: From Neuroanatomy to Psychodynamics* (New York: Human Sciences P, 1986) 29.

8. Harris, *Clinical Neuroscience*, 35–36.

9. Roger Sperry, "Some Effects of Disconnecting the Cerebral Hemispheres," *Science* 217 (24 Sept. 1982): 1223–1226.

10. Dale Purves and Jeff W. Lichtman, *Principles of Neural Development* (Sunderland MA: Sinauer Assoc., 1985) 153, 359–363.

11. Sandra Blakeslee, "Rapid Changes Seen in Young Brain," Science Times, *The New York Times* (24 June 1986): C1, C10.

12. Dale Purves and Robert D. Hadley, "Changes in the Dendritic Branching of Adult Mammalian Neurones Revealed by Repeated Imaging *in situ*," *Nature* 315 (30 May 1985): 404–406.

13. Blakeslee, "Rapid Changes."

14. Christopher E. Henderson, et al., "Increase of Neurite-Promoting Activity for Spinal Neurons in Muscles of 'Paralysé' Mice and Tenotomised Rats," *Developmental Brain Research* 25 (1986): 65–70.

15. Deborah M. Barnes, "Brain Architecture: Beyond Genes," Research News, *Science* 253 (11 July 1986): 155–156. Report of a conference, "Brain Beyond Genes," New York,

2–4 June 1986, Institute for Child Development Research, 330 Madison Ave., New York NY 10017.

16. S. S. Easter, Jr., et al., "The Changing View of Neural Specificity," *Science* 230 (1 Nov. 1985): 507–511. A highly readable account of this and other recent discoveries about brain development is Richard M. Restak's *The Infant Mind* (Garden City NY: Doubleday, 1986).

17. Richard C. Anderson, Rand J. Spiro, and William E. Montague, Preface, *Schooling and the Acquisition of Knowledge*, ed. Richard C. Anderson, Rand J. Spiro, and William E. Montague (Hillsdale NJ: Lawrence Erlbaum, 1977) ix.

18. Howard Gardner, *The Mind's New Science: A History of the Cognitive Revolution* (New York: Basic Books, 1985) 109.

19. Richard C. Anderson, "The Notion of Schemata and the Educational Enterprise: General Discussion of the Conference," *Schooling and the Acquisition of Knowledge*, ed. Richard C. Anderson, Rand J. Spiro, and William E. Montague (Hillsdale, NJ: Lawrence Erlbaum, 1977) 415–431, 416.

20. Noam Chomsky, Review of *Verbal Behavior* by B. F. Skinner, *Language* 35 (1959): 26–58.

21. David E. Rumelhart and Andrew Ortony, "The Representation of Knowledge in Memory," *Schooling and the Acquisition of Knowledge*, ed. Richard C. Anderson, Rand J. Spiro, and William E. Montague (Hillsdale NJ: Lawrence Erlbaum, 1977) 99–135, 100.

22. David E. Rumelhart, *Introduction to Human Information Processing* (New York: Wiley, 1977) 169.

23. Bryan Kolb and Ian Q. Whishaw, *Fundamentals of Human Neuropsychology*, 2d ed. (New York: W. H. Freeman, 1985), 513–545.

24. David Marr, *Vision: A Computational Investigation into the Human Representation and Processing of Visual Information* (San Francisco: W. H. Freeman, 1982).

25. Morse Peckham, *Man's Rage for Chaos: Biology, Behavior, and the Arts* (Philadelphia: Chilton, 1965).

26. Paul Hoffman, "The Next Leap in Computers," *New York Times Magazine* (7 December 1986): 126–133, 130.

27. John Z. Young, *Programs of the Brain* (New York: Oxford UP, 1978) 17, 265.

28. See note 3 in chapter 6.

2   Reading Frost

1. *The Poetry of Robert Frost*, ed. Edward Connery Lathem (New York: Holt, Rinehart, and Winston, 1975) 250. The poem originally appeared in *The New Republic* (1926). Frost annotated it, "As of about 1880." Although often reprinted, it has received only moderate attention from critics. The following approximates a complete list, although, given the large bulk of Frost criticism, I make no guarantees. Brian Barbour, "Frost's 'Once by the Pacific,'" *Explicator* 37.4 (1979): 18–19; C. Hines Edwards, "Frost's ONCE BY THE PACIFIC," *Explicator* 39.4 (1981): 28–29; Robert F. Fleissner, "Robert Frost, 'Once by the Pacific': The Moorish Genesis," *The CLA Journal* 23 (1979): 160–171; Robert F. Fleissner, "Frost and Lanier: An Immediate Literary Source of 'Once by the Pacific,'" *Papers on Language and Literature* 16 (1980): 320–325; R. F. Fleissner, "Frost's ONCE BY THE PACIFIC," *Explicator* 40 (1982): 46–47; D. S. J. Parsons, "Night of Dark Intent," *Papers on Language and Literature* 6 (1970): 205–210; Laurence Perrine, "Frost's ONCE BY THE PACIFIC," *Explicator* 41.3 (1983): 44; John Oliver Perry, "The Dialog of Voices in Frost," *South Atlantic Quarterly* 81 (1982): 214–229, 226–227; Judith P. Saunders, "Frost's ONCE BY THE PACIFIC," *Explicator* 39.4 (1981): 29–31. I have written on the poem myself, "A Touching of Literary and

Psychiatric Education," *Seminars in Psychiatry* 5 (1973): 247–257, but the essay did not find its way into the literary bibliographies.

2. Fleissner (1979) 161.

3. Stanley Burnshaw, *Robert Frost Himself* (New York: Braziller, 1986) 252, citing John McGiffert, "Something in Robert Frost," *English Journal* 34 (1945): 469–471. McGiffert's pre-*Concordance* counts are slightly off.

4. Louis Mertins, *Robert Frost: Life and Talks-Walking* (Norman OK: U of Oklahoma Press, 1965) 6.

5. Reuben A. Brower, *The Poetry of Robert Frost: Constellations of Intention* (New York: Oxford UP, 1963) 89.

6. For the general concept see Aaron H. Esman, "The Primal Scene: A Review and a Reconsideration," *Psychoanalytic Study of the Child* 28 (1973): 48–81, or Wayne A. Myers, "Clinical Consequences of Chronic Primal Scene Exposure," *Psychoanalytic Quarterly* 48.1 (1979): 1–26. For details, see Harold P. Blum, "On the Concept and Consequences of the Primal Scene," *Psychoanalytic Quarterly* 48.1 (1979): 27–47; Henry Edelheit, "Crucifixion Fantasies and Their Relation to the Primal Scene," *International Journal of Psycho-Analysis* 55 (1974): 193–199; Henry Edelheit, "Mythopoiesis and the Primal Scene," *Psychoanalytic Study of Society* 5 (1972): 213–233; Wayne A. Myers, "Split Self-Representation and the Primal Scene," *Psychoanalytic Quarterly* 42.4 (1973): 525–538.

7. *Poetry*, ed. Lathem, 379–380.

8. *Poetry*, ed. Lathem, 191–196, l. 143.

9. *Poetry*, ed. Lathem, 252–253.

10. Elizabeth Shepley Sergeant, *Robert Frost: The Trial by Existence* (New York: Holt, Rinehart and Winston, 1960) xxi and 433–434.

11. Sigmund Freud, *Jokes and their Relation to the Unconscious* (1905c), *The Standard Edition of the Complete Psychological Works of Sigmund Freud*, trans. James Strachey, with Anna Freud, Alix Strachey, and Alan Tyson, 24 vols. (London: Hogarth P, 1953–1974) 8 (1960): 78, 110–111.

12. Lawrance Thompson, *Robert Frost: The Early Years, 1874–1915* (New York: Holt, Rinehart and Winston, 1966) 35.

13. *Poetry*, ed. Lathem, 33–34.

14. "Mending Wall" has attracted the attention of many critics, but given the very large body of Frost criticism, I can only hope the list that follows includes them all. I have found many of them helpful and drawn on them both consciously and unconsciously.

Joseph W. Beach, "Robert Frost," *Yale Review* 43 (1953): 210–211; John C. Broderick, "Frost's 'Mending Wall,'" *Explicator* 14 (1955–56): item 24; Babette Deutsch, *This Modern Poetry* (New York: Norton, 1935) 42; Peter B. Clarke, "Frost's MENDING WALL," *Explicator* 43 (1984): 48–50; John R. Doyle, *The Poetry of Robert Frost* (New York: Hafner, 1962) 72–73; Northrop Frye, "Literary Criticism," *The Aims and Methods of Scholarship in Modern Languages and Literatures*, ed. James Thorpe (New York: Modern Language Association, 1963) 65; Carson Gibb, "Frost's 'Mending Wall,'" *Explicator* 20 (1961–62): item 48; F. L. Gwynn, R. W. Condee, and A. O. Lewis, Jr., *The Case for Poetry: A New Anthology, Poems, Cases, Critiques* (Englewood Cliffs NJ: Prentice-Hall, 1954) 147 and *Teacher's Manual*; Edward Jayne, "Up Against the 'Mending Wall': The Psychoanalysis of a Poem by Frost," *College English* 34 (1973): 934–951; Frank Lentricchia, "Experience as Meaning: Robert Frost's 'Mending Wall,'" *CEA Critic* 34.4 (1972): 8–12; Mordecai Marcus, "Psychoanalytic Approaches to 'Mending Wall,'" *Robert Frost: Studies of the Poetry*, ed. Kathryn Gibbs Harris (Boston: G.K. Hall, 1979) 179; John McGiffert, "Something in Robert Frost," *English Journal* 34 (1945): 469–471; George Monteiro, "Unlinked Myth in Frost's 'Mending Wall,'" *Concerning Poetry* 7.1 (1974): 10–11; Marion Montgomery, "Robert Frost and His Use of Barriers: Man vs. Nature Toward God," *South Atlantic Quarterly* 57 (1958): 349–351; George W. Nitchie, *Human Values in the Poetry of Robert Frost* (Durham, N.C.: Duke UP, 1960) 7, 8,

92; M. L. Rosenthal and A. J. M. Smith, *Exploring Poetry* (New York: Macmillan, 1955) 3–6; Barton Levi St. Armand, "Frost's MENDING WALL," *Explicator* 41.1 (1982): 47–48; Dennis Vail, "Tree Imagery in Frost's 'Mending Wall,'" *Notes on Contemporary Literature* 3.2 (1973): 9–11; Patricia Wallace, "Separateness and Solitude in Frost," *Kenyon Review* 6 n.s. (1984):1–12. As with "Once by the Pacific," I have written on this poem, too: "The 'Unconscious' of Literature: The Psychoanalytic Approach," *Contemporary Criticism*, ed. Malcolm Bradbury and David Palmer, Stratford-Upon-Avon Studies 12 (London: Edward Arnold, 1970) 130–153.

15. Richard Poirier, *Robert Frost: The Work of Knowing* (New York: Oxford UP, 1977) 7, 104–106, 259, 281.

16. *Interviews with Robert Frost*, ed. Edward Connery Lathem (New York: Holt, Rinehart and Winston, 1966) 257.

17. Reginald L. Cook, *Robert Frost: A Living Voice* (Amherst MA: U of Massachusetts P, 1974) 82–83.

18. Daniel Stern, *The Interpersonal World of the Infant: A View from Psychoanalysis and Developmental Psychology* (New York: Basic Books, 1985). Stern's book is the latest in the important vein of psychoanalytic thought that runs back through Margaret Mahler's work and René Spitz's, connecting (and, in Stern's case, correcting) psychoanalytic theory about early infancy with systematic, scientific observations of infants. Margaret Mahler, Fred Pine, and Anni Bergman,*The Psychological Birth of the Human Infant: Symbiosis and Individuation* (New York: Basic Books, 1975). René Spitz, *The First Year of Life: A Psychoanalytic Study of Normal and Deviant Development of Object Relations* (New York: International Universities P, 1965). A good account of these developments, related to English object-relations theory, is Nancy Chodorow's *The Reproduction of Mothering: Psychoanalysis and the Sociology of Gender* (Berkeley: U of California P, 1978). Unfortunately, she writes before Stern.

This strain of psychoanalytic thought seems to me to open up major avenues not only for literary theory but for all kinds of political and social issues. I have written about its importance for literature since *The Dynamics of Literary Response* (New York: Oxford UP, 1968) and more generally and recently in *The I* (New Haven and London: Yale UP, 1985).

19. Sigmund Freud, *Civilization and its Discontents* (1930a), *Std. Ed.* 21:59–145, 64–73 (ch. 1). Erik Erikson, *Childhood and Society*, 2d ed. (New York: Norton, 1963). Donald W. Winnicott, *Playing and Reality* (London: Tavistock, 1971). Margaret Mahler, Fred Pine, and Anni Bergman, *The Psychological Birth of the Human Infant: Symbiosis and Individuation* (New York: Basic Books, 1975).

20. Erikson, *Childhood and Society*, 247.

21. Erikson, *Childhood and Society*, 248.

22. Richard Poirier, "Robert Frost" (interview), *Paris Review* No. 24 (1959): 109.

23. *Robert Frost on Writing*, ed. Elaine Barry (New Brunswick NJ: Rutgers UP, 1973) 126–127.

24. *Poetry*, ed. Lathem, 225.

25. *Triumph*, 421. In the quotations from Frost that follow, I am drawing on Lawrance Thompson's encyclopaedic biography, completed at Thompson's death by R. H. Winnick: Thompson, *Robert Frost: The Early Years, 1874–1915* (New York: Holt, Rinehart and Winston, 1966); Thompson, *Robert Frost: The Years of Triumph, 1915–1938* (New York: Holt, Rinehart and Winston, 1970); Thompson and Winnick, *Robert Frost: The Later Years, 1938–1963* (New York: Holt, Rinehart and Winston, 1976). I shall refer to these three volumes simply as *Early*, *Triumph*, and *Later*, followed by a page number.

26. *Frost on Writing*, ed. Barry, 78.

27. *Family Letters of Robert and Elinor Frost*, ed. Arnold Grade (Albany, NY: State U of New York P, 1972), 210. *Later*, 40. William W. E. Slights develops much the same point that I am making here in "The Sense of Frost's Humor," *Concerning Poetry* 16 (1983): 29–42.

28. *Later*, 265.

29. *Triumph*, 649.

30. *Triumph*, 649.

31. *Triumph*, 364, 694.

32. *Early*, 70–71, referring to Emerson's essay "The Poet."

33. *Early*, 55.

34. *Triumph*, 693.

35. *Triumph*, 693.

36. George Bagby, "Frost's Synechdochism," *American Literature* 58 (1986): 379–392.

37. *Later*, 393; *Triumph*, 413.

38. Cook, *Robert Frost*, 215.

39. Quoted by R. W. Flint, "'Not Confused, Just Wild,'" review of Stanley Burnshaw, *Robert Frost Himself*, *New York Times Book Review* (30 November 1986): 24. Lionel Trilling, "A Speech on Robert Frost: A Cultural Episode," *Partisan Review* 26 (1959): 445–452.

40. *Later*, 278.

41. *Later*, 53.

42. Cook, *Robert Frost*, 307, quoting *Early*, 427.

43. *Later*, 338.

44. *Later*, 99.

45. Cook, *Robert Frost*, 41.

46. "The Figure a Poem Makes," *Frost on Writing*, ed. Barry, 128.

47. "The Constant Symbol," *Frost on Writing*, ed. Barry, 130.

48. *Frost on Writing*, ed. Barry, 113.

49. P. Flor-Henry, "On Certain Aspects of the Localization of the Cerebral Systems Regulating and Determining Emotion," *Biological Psychiatry* 4 (1979): 677–694.

50. Aleksandr Romanovich Luria, *Higher Cortical Functions in Man*, 2d. ed., trans. Basil Haigh (New York: Basic Books, 1980) 248.

51. Heinz Lichtenstein, *The Dilemma of Human Identity* (New York: Jason Aronson, 1977).

52. *Frost on Writing*, ed. Barry, 136.

53. "The Constant Symbol," *Frost on Writing*, ed. Barry, 130.

54. "The Constant Symbol," *Frost on Writing*, ed. Barry, 131.

55. Jean-Paul Sartre, *Being and Nothingness: A Phenomenological Essay on Ontology*, trans. Hazel E. Barnes (1956; rpt. New York: Washington Square P, 1966).

56. Paul Diesing, *Patterns of Discovery in the Social Sciences* (Chicago: Aldine-Atherton, 1971) 5–6.

3   Frost Reading

1. *Robert Frost on Writing*, ed. Elaine Barry (New Brunswick NJ: Rutgers UP, 1973) 121–122.

2. *Frost on Writing*, ed. Barry, 123–124.

3. *Frost on Writing*, ed. Barry, 123.

4. Lawrance Thompson, *Robert Frost: The Early Years, 1874–1915* (New York: Holt, Rinehart and Winston, 1966) 549.

5. *Frost on Writing*, ed. Barry, 76.

6. *Frost on Writing*, ed. Barry, 129.

7. *Frost on Writing*, ed. Barry, 60.

8. *Selected Letters of Robert Frost*, ed. Lawrance Thompson (New York: Holt, Rinehart and Winston, 1964) 128.

9. *Frost on Writing*, ed. Barry, 156.

10. *Frost on Writing*, ed. Barry, 159.

11. *Frost on Writing*, ed. Barry, 119.
12. *Frost on Writing*, ed. Barry, 126.
13. *Frost on Writing*, ed. Barry, 126.
14. *Frost on Writing*, ed. Barry, 64.
15. *Frost on Writing*, ed. Barry, 119.
16. *Frost on Writing*, ed. Barry, 118.
17. *Frost on Writing*, ed. Barry, 125.
18. *Selected Letters*, ed. Thompson, 344.
19. "The Constant Symbol," *Frost on Writing*, ed. Barry, 130.
20. "The Figure a Poem Makes," *Frost on Writing*, ed. Barry, 126.
21. "The Figure a Poem Makes," *Frost on Writing*, ed. Barry, 128.
22. E. D. Hirsch, Jr., *The Aims of Interpretation* (Chicago: U of Chicago P, 1976).
23. Stanley Fish, *Is There a Text in This Class? The Authority of Interpretive Communities* (Cambridge MA: Harvard UP, 1980). This is the title of chapter 11.

4   The Miller's Wife and the Six Professors

1. Stanley Fish, *Is There a Text in This Class? The Authority of Interpretive Communities* (Cambridge MA: Harvard UP, 1980) 357, 338, 366, and passim.
2. David Bleich, *Readings and Feelings: An Introduction to Subjective Criticism* (Urbana IL: National Council of Teachers of English, 1975) 49.
3. Wolfgang Iser, *The Act of Reading: A Theory of Aesthetic Response* (Baltimore: Johns Hopkins UP, 1978).
4. Jonathan Culler, "Prolegomena to a Theory of Reading," *The Reader in the Text: Essays on Audience and Interpretation*, ed. Susan R. Suleiman and Inge Crosman (Princeton: Princeton UP, 1980) 46–66, esp. 53–56.
5. Norman N. Holland, *5 Readers Reading* (New Haven: Yale UP, 1975).
6. Joseph C. Campione, Ann L. Brown, and Nancy R. Bryant, "Individual Differences in Learning and Memory," *Human Abilities: An Information-Processing Approach*, ed. Robert J. Sternberg (New York: W. H. Freeman, 1985) 103–126, 121–122.
7. For example, much recent work in *Rezeptionsästhetik* relies on questionnaires. Robert C. Holub, *Reception Theory: A Critical Introduction*, Methuen New Accents Series (London and New York: Methuen, 1984) 128–146. I think my *caveat* is particularly important for using such valuable survey work as the IEA (International Association for the Evaluation of Educational Achievement) data bank or the 3rd National Assessment of Reading and Literature. See Alan C. Purves, "Using the IEA Data Bank for Research in Reading and Response to Literature," *Research in the Teaching of English* 12 (1978): 289–296, or Anthony R. Petrosky, "The 3rd National Assessment of Reading and Literature Versus Norm- and Criterion-Referenced Testing," Paper presented at the Annual Meeting of the International Reading Association, May 1–5, Houston, 1978, ERIC Document No. 159599.

5   "We Are Round"

1. Norman N. Holland, *Poems in Persons* (New York: Norton, 1973). *5 Readers Reading* (New Haven: Yale UP, 1975). *Laughing: A Psychology of Humor* (Ithaca: Cornell UP, 1982). *The I* (New Haven: Yale UP, 1985). In all these books I have drawn on the theory of identity developed by Heinz Lichtenstein and expounded in *The Dilemma of Human Identity* (New York: Jason Aronson, 1977).
2. James Clerk Maxwell, "On Governors," *Proceedings of the Royal Society* 16 (March 5, 1868): 270–283.

188   Notes to Chapter 5

3. Arturo Rosenblueth, Norbert Wiener, and Julian Bigelow, "Behaviour, Purpose, and Teleology," *Philosophy of Science* 10 (1943): 18–24. There is, however, a still earlier paper biologizing feedback, by W. Ross Ashby, "Adaptiveness and Equilibrium," *Journal of Mental Science* 86 (1940): 478–483.

4. Ernest Jones, *The Life and Work of Sigmund Freud*, 3 vols. (New York: Basic Books, 1953–57) 3: 268.

5. Norbert Wiener, *Cybernetics, or Control and Communication in the Animal and the Machine* (New York: Technology P, John Wiley, 1948) 7–39. Wiener points to a conference in New York in 1942 as origin, the first of a long series of important conferences sponsored by the Josiah Macy Foundation in the 1940s and 1950s. From a more psychological point of view Howard Gardner singles out the Hixon Symposium in September, 1948 at the California Institute of Technology and an address by Karl Lashley challenging the behaviorist orthodoxy of the time. *The Mind's New Science: A History of the Cognitive Revolution* (New York: Basic Books, 1985) 10.

6. Wiener, *Cybernetics*, 36.

7. Edward V. Evarts, Yoshikazu Shinoda, and Steven P. Wise, *Neurophysiological Approaches to Higher Brain Functions* (New York: Wiley, 1984) 4, 5–6, 15–20, 171–175.

8. A recent example of a psychology textbook's two-element explanation of feedback is Henry Gleitman's *Psychology* (New York: Norton, 1981) 56–58.

9. John Z. Young, *Programs of the Brain* (New York: Oxford UP, 1978) 17, 265.

10. I am drawing on cybernetic models for the brain developed by William T. Powers, a computer engineer: *Behavior: The Control of Perception* (Chicago: Aldine, 1973). "Feedback: Beyond Behaviorism," *Science* 179 (1973): 351–356. "Quantitative Analysis of Purposive Systems: Some Spadework at the Foundations of Scientific Psychology," *Psychological Review* 85 (1978): 417–435.

11. Sigmund Freud, *The Interpretation of Dreams* (1900), *Std. Edn.* 5 (London: Hogarth P, 1953): 566.

12. Sigmund Freud, *Beyond the Pleasure Principle* (1920g), *Std. Edn.* 18 (London: Hogarth P, 1955): 42.

13. Ludwig von Bertalanffy, "Theoretical Models in Biology and Psychology," David Krech and George Klein, eds., *Theoretical Models and Personality Theory* (Durham NC: Duke UP 1952; rpt. New York: Greenwood P, 1968) 24–38, 37.

14. Paul D. MacLean, *A Triune Concept of the Brain and Behaviour*, The Clarence M. Hincks Memorial Lectures, 1969 (Toronto and Buffalo: U of Toronto P, 1973) 31.

15. Richard M. Restak, *The Brain* (Toronto and New York: Bantam Books, 1984) 131.

16. John Allman, "Reconstructing the Evolution of the Brain in Primates through the Use of Comparative Neurophysicological and Neuroanatomical Data," *Primate Brain Evolution: Methods and Concepts*, ed. Este Armstrong and Dean Falk (New York and London: Plenum P, 1982) 13–28, 22.

17. MacLean, *Triune Brain*, 38.

18. Este Armstrong, "Mosaic Evolution in the Primate Brain: Differences and Similarities in the Hominid Thalamus," *Primate Brain Evolution: Methods and Concepts*, ed. Este Armstrong and Dean Falk (New York and London: Plenum P, 1982) 131–162, 152–153.

19. Jonathan Winson, *Brain and Psyche: The Biology of the Unconscious* (Garden City NY: Anchor P/Doubleday, 1985) 192. See also Jay E. Harris, *Clinical Neuroscience: From Neuroanatomy to Psychodynamics* (New York: Human Sciences P, 1986) 31–32.

20. Winson, *Brain and Psyche*, 186.

21. V. A. Kral, "The Organic Amnesias," in MacLean, *Triune Brain*, 69–80, 77. See also Restak, *The Brain*, 212–214.

22. Armstrong, "Mosaic Evolution in the Primate Brain," 152–153.

23. Harris, *Clinical Neuroscience*, 42.

24. Winson, *Brain and Psyche*, 29.

25. MacLean, *Triune Brain*, 24.

26. Restak, *The Brain*, 211.

27. MacLean, *Triune Brain*, 16–19, 24. Paul D. MacLean, "On the Origin and Progressive Evolution of the Triune Brain," *Primate Brain Evolution: Methods and Concepts*, ed. Este Armstrong and Dean Falk (New York and London: Plenum P, 1982) 291–316, 307.

28. Sigmund Freud, *Three Essays on the Theory of Sexuality* (1905d), *Std. Edn.* 7 (London: Hogarth P, 1953): 203, cited in MacLean, *Triune Brain*, 16–19.

29. MacLean, "Origin and Evolution of the Triune Brain," 295.

30. Armstrong, "Mosaic Evolution in the Primate Brain," 152–153.

31. Winson, *Brain and Psyche*, 217–218.

32. Morton F. Reiser, *Mind, Brain, Body: Toward a Convergence of Psychoanalysis and Neurobiology* (New York: Basic Books, 1984) ch. 6.

33. D. E. Rumelhart, "Schemata: The Building Blocks of Cognition," *Theoretical Issues in Reading Comprehension: Perspectives from Cognitive Psychology, Linguistics, Artificial Intelligence, and Education*, eds. Rand J. Spiro, Bertram C. Bruce, and William F. Brewer (Hillsdale NJ: Erlbaum, 1980) 38.

34. Aleksandr Romanovich Luria, *Higher Cortical Functions in Man*, 2d ed., trans. Basil Haigh (New York: Basic Books, 1980) 532.

35. Luria, *Higher Cortical Functions*, 114, 115, 116.

36. Peter D. Eimas, "Speech Perception in Early Infancy," *Infant Perception: From Sensation to Cognition*, ed. Leslie B. Cohen and Philip Salapatek, Vol I: Basic Visual Processes; Vol. II: Perception of Space, Speech, and Sound (New York: Academic P, 1975) II: 193–231.

37. John D. Bransford and Marcia K. Johnson, "Considerations of Some Problems of Comprehension," *Visual Information Processing*, ed. William G. Chase (New York: Academic P, 1973) 383–438. Richard C. Anderson et al., "Frameworks for Comprehending Discourse," *American Educational Research Journal* 14(1977): 367–381.

38. Luria, *Higher Cortical Functions*, 381–382.

39. Luria, *Higher Cortical Functions*, 381, 543, 531, 379.

40. David Bordwell in his monumental *Narration in the Fiction Film* (Madison: U of Wisconsin P, 1985) makes exactly this move—a vigorous counter to other film theories in which the film governs its viewers.

41. Luria, *Higher Cortical Functions*, 40.

42. Luria, *Higher Cortical Functions*, 21, 248.

43. Luria, *Higher Cortical Functions*, 31–33 and 192–193.

44. Duilio Giannitrapani, *The Electrophysiology of Intellectual Functions* (Basel and New York: S. Karger, 1985).

45. George Miller, Eugene Galanter, and Karl Pribram, *Plans and the Structure of Behavior* (New York: Holt, Rinehart and Winston, 1960). Howard Gardner says this book "had a tremendous impact on psychology and allied fields." *The Mind's New Science*, 32.

46. George A. Kelly, *The Psychology of Personal Constructs*, 2 v. (New York: Norton, 1955). The first three chapters of this larger work were published as *A Theory of Personality: The Psychology of Personal Constructs* (New York: Norton, 1963).

47. Freud, *Pleasure Principle*, *Std. Edn.* 18:42.

48. Roger Sperry, "Some Effects of Disconnecting the Cerebral Hemispheres," *Science* 217 (24 Sept. 1982): 1223–1226.

6   *Reading and Writing, Codes and Canons*

1. Mark Johnson, *The Body in the Mind: The Bodily Basis of Meaning, Imagination, and Reason* (Chicago and London: U of Chicago P, 1987) 196.

2. William E. Cain, *The Crisis in Criticism: Theory, Literature, and Reform in English Studies* (Baltimore: Johns Hopkins UP, 1985).

3. My sample of the literature in this field would include: Robert G. Crowder, *The Psychology of Reading: An Introduction* (New York: Oxford UP, 1982); George L. Dillon, *Language Processing and the Reading of Literature: Toward a Model of Comprehension* (Bloomington IN: Indiana UP, 1978); Audrey N. Grant, *Young Readers Reading* (Melbourne: Routledge and Kegan Paul, 1987); Eugene R. Kintgen, *The Perception of Poetry* (Bloomington IN: Indiana UP, 1983); Paul A. Kolers, "Experiments in Reading," *Scientific American* (July 1972): 84–91; David Laberge and S. Jay Samuels, eds., *Basic Processes in Reading: Perception and Comprehension* (New York: Lawrence Erlbaum, 1977); Margaret Meek, *Learning to Read* (London: Bodley Head, 1982); Margaret Meek, *Achieving Literacy: Longitudinal Studies of Adolescents Learning To Read* (London and Boston: Routledge and Kegan Paul, 1983); Frank Smith, *Understanding Reading: A Psycholinguistic Analysis of Reading and Learning to Read*, 3d ed. (New York: Holt, Rinehart and Winston, 1982); Rand J. Spiro, Bertram C. Bruce, and William F. Brewer, eds., *Theoretical Issues in Reading Comprehension: Perspectives from Cognitive Psychology, Linguistics, Artificial Intelligence, and Education* (Hillsdale NJ: Erlbaum, 1980); Insup Taylor and M. Martin Taylor, *The Psychology of Reading* (New York: Academic P, 1983). The literature on the psychology of reading is very large, and, so far as I can see, based in recent years wholly on the concept of feedback or even more precisely defined processes applied by an active reader.

4. Mihaly Csikszentmihalyi, "Society, Culture, and Person: A Systems View of Creativity," September 1986, unpub. ms., Department of Psychology, U of Chicago. Howard Gardner, "Freud in Three Frames: A Cognitive-Scientific Approach to Creativity," *Daedalus* (Summer 1986): 105–134. Robert J. Sternberg, "Toward a Triarchic Theory of Human Intelligence," *Behavioral and Brain Sciences* 7.2 (1984): 269–316.

5. I have discussed this principle at greater length in *The I* (New Haven and London: Yale UP, 1985) 131–155.

6. N. P. Bechtevera, *The Neuropsychological Aspects of Human Mental Activity* (New York: Oxford UP, 1978) 135.

7. Jeff Rosen, foreword, *Clinical Neuroscience: From Neuroanatomy to Psychodynamics*, by Jay E. Harris (New York: Human Sciences P, 1986) 11–13.

8. Sir Charles Sherrington, *Man on His Nature*, The Gifford Lectures, Edinburgh University, 1937–38, 2d ed. (Cambridge: Cambridge UP, 1963) 182–183.

9. Herbert A. Simon, *The Sciences of the Artificial* (Cambridge MA: MIT P, 1969) 106.

10. Ragnar Granit, *The Purposive Brain* (Cambridge MA: MIT P, 1977) 85.

11. Nigel Calder, *The Mind of Man: An Investigation into Current Research on the Brain and Human Nature* (New York: Viking, 1970) 260, citing Roger Sperry.

12. Edward V. Evarts, "Brain Mechanisms of Movement," *Scientific American* (September 1979): 164–179.

13. William T. Powers, *Behavior: The Control of Perception* (Chicago: Aldine, 1973) 273–282; "The Nature of Robots, Part 1: Defining Behavior," *Byte* (June 1979): 132–144; "Part 2: Simulated Control System," *Byte* (July 1979): 134–152; "Part 3: A Closer Look at Human Behavior," *Byte* (August 1979): 94–116; "Part 4: Looking for Controlled Variables," *Byte* (September 1979): 96–112.

14. Earl Hunt, "Verbal Ability," *Human Abilities: An Information-Processing Approach*, ed. Robert J. Sternberg (New York: W. H. Freeman, 1985) 31–58, 55.

15. Roger Sperry, "Some Effects of Disconnecting the Cerebral Hemispheres," *Science*, 217 (24 Sept. 1982): 1223–1226. For some examples of modern feedback theories of the brain, see John Zachary Young, *Programs of the Brain* (Oxford: Oxford UP, 1978); Ragnar Granit, *The Purposive Brain* (Cambridge and London: MIT P, 1977); or John C. Eccles, *The Human Psyche*, The Gifford Lectures, Edinburgh University, 1978–1979 (New York and Berlin: Springer International, 1980).

16. John Eccles, *The Human Psyche*. Karl Popper and John C. Eccles, *The Self and Its Brain* (Berlin and New York: Springer Verlag, 1977).

17. In *Behavior: The Control of Perception*, chs. 6–13, Powers works out a nine-level model of the brain. In *The I* 131–139, I have summarized his picture.

18. I believe the following feedback model accords with and usefully amplifies Hans-Georg Gadamer's reworking of Heidegger's theory of interpretation in *Truth and Method* (New York: Seabury P, 1975) 235–240, 258–267, and 333–341. I am grateful to Martin and Gabriele Schwab for calling these passages to my attention.

19. Frank Smith and D. L. Holmes, "The Independence of Letter, Word, and Meaning Identification in Reading," *Reading Research Quarterly* 6 (1971): 394–415. Cp. Aleksandr Romanovich Luria, *Higher Cortical Functions in Man*, 2d ed., trans. Basil Haigh (New York: Basic Books, 1980) 382.

20. Meek, *Learning to Read*, 20–21.

21. Charles A. Perfetti, "Reading Ability," *Human Abilities: An Information-Processing Approach*, ed. Robert J. Sternberg (New York: W. H. Freeman, 1985) 59–82. Eric H. Lenneberg, "Problems in the Comparative Study of Language," *Evolution, Brain, and Behavior: Persistent Problems*, ed. Bruce Masterton, William Hodos, and Harry Jerison (Hillsdale NJ: Lawrence Erlbaum, 1976) 199–213.

22. Barbara Leondar, "Hatching Plots: Genesis of Storymaking," *The Arts and Cognition*, ed. David Perkins and Barbara Leondar (Baltimore: Johns Hopkins UP, 1977) 172–191.

23. Z. W. Pylyshyn, *Computation and Cognition: Toward a Foundation for Cognitive Science* (Cambridge MA: MIT P, 1984). The distinction is also related to one of the modularities proposed by Jerry A. Fodor in *The Modularity of Mind* (Cambridge MA: MIT P/Bradford, 1983).

24. Mary Crawford and Roger Chaffin, "The Reader's Construction of Meaning: Cognitive Research on Gender and Comprehension," *Gender and Reading: Essays on Readers, Texts, and Contexts*, ed. Elizabeth A. Flynn and Patrocinio P. Schweickart (Baltimore and London: Johns Hopkins UP, 1986) 3–30, 11–13.

25. Ferdinand de Saussure, *Cours de Linguistique Générale*, ed. Charles Bally, Albert Sechehaye, and Albert Riedlinger (Paris: Payot, 1955) 157. *Course in General Linguistics*, ed. Charles Bally, Albert Sechehaye, and Albert Reidlinger (sic), trans. Wade Baskin (New York: Philosophical Library, 1959) 113.

26. Lenneberg, "Comparative Study of Language," 202–203.

27. Jonathan Culler, "Literary Competence," *Reader Response Criticism: From Formalism to Post-Structuralism*, ed. Jane P. Tompkins (Baltimore: Johns Hopkins UP, 1980) 101–117, esp. 108–115.

Mary Louise Pratt likewise points out that Culler's "literary competence" is an un-Chomskyan use of "competence." It serves, she writes, to shore up the *status quo*, that is, the interpretive authority of the professoriat. "Interpretive Strategies/Strategic Interpretations: On Anglo-American Reader Response Criticism," *Boundary 2* 11.1–2 (1982–83): 201–231, 215–218.

28. George Dillon, "Styles of Reading," *Poetics Today*, 3 (1982): 77–88, 87n.

29. Murray M. Schwartz, "27th Annual Meeting: Keynote Speaker," *Academy Forum* 27.2 (1983): 13.

7   A Digression on Metaphors

1. George Lakoff and Mark Johnson, *Metaphors We Live By* (Chicago: U of Chicago P, 1980).

2. George Lakoff, *Women, Fire, and Dangerous Things: What Categories Reveal About the Mind* (Chicago and London: U of Chicago P, 1987). Mark Johnson, *The Body in the Mind:*

The Bodily Basis of Meaning, Imagination, and Reason (Chicago and London: U of Chicago P, 1987).

3. Lakoff, *Women, Fire, and Dangerous Things*, 271–284. Johnson, *The Body in the Mind*, 101–138.

4. Lakoff, *Women, Fire, and Dangerous Things*, 274.

5. Robert C. Holub, *Reception Theory: A Critical Introduction* (London and New York: Methuen, 1984).

6. Wolfgang Iser, "Interaction between Text and Reader," *The Reader in the Text: Essays on Audience and Interpretation*, ed. Susan R. Suleiman and Inge Crosman (Princeton: Princeton UP, 1980) 106–119, 110.

7. Michael J. Reddy, "The Conduit Metaphor—A Case of Frame Conflict in Our Language about Language," *Metaphor and Thought*, ed. Andrew Ortony (Cambridge: Cambridge UP, 1979) 284–324.

8. Flint Schier, "Speaking Through Our Clothes," Review of Roland Barthes, *The Fashion System*, *The New York Times Book Review* (24 July 1983): 7 and 18.

9. Roland Barthes, "Myth Today" (1957), *Mythologies*, ed. and trans. Annette Lavers (New York: Hill and Wang, 1972) 117.

10. Henry Gleitman, *Psychology* (New York: Norton, 1981) 609, 617, 618, 623.

11. Clyde Kluckhohn and Henry A. Murray, "Personality Formation: The Determinants" (1948), *Personality: In Nature, Society, and Culture*, ed. Clyde Kluckhohn and Henry A. Murray (New York: Knopf, 1961) 53.

12. Herbert Spiegelberg, *The Phenomenological Movement: A Historical Introduction*, 2d ed. (1960; rpt. The Hague, Martinus Nijhoff, 1976) 688.

13. James Kearns and Ken Newton, "An Interview with Jacques Derrida," *The Literary Review* 14 (18 April–1 May 1980): 21–22.

14. Ferdinand de Saussure, *Cours de Linguistique Générale*, ed. Charles Bally, Albert Sechehaye, and Albert Riedlinger, 3d ed. (Paris: Payot, 1955) ch. 3. *Course in General Linguistics*, ed. Charles Bally, Albert Sechehaye, and Albert Reidlinger (sic), trans. Wade Baskin (New York: Philosophical Library, 1959) ch. 3.

15. Saussure, French text, 29–31; English text, 12–14.

16. Saussure, French text, 38; English text, 19.

17. Saussure, French text, 157; English text, 113.

18. Robert Rosenthal, *Experimenter Effects on Behavioral Research* (New York: Appleton-Century-Crofts, 1966).

19. *Technology Review* (July 1986): sect. MIT, 31.

20. Kenneth J. Gergen, "Social Constructionist Inquiry: Context and Implications," *The Social Construction of the Person*, ed. Kenneth J. Gergen and Keith E. Davis (New York and Berlin: Springer-Verlag, 1985) 3–18, 5, 6.

21. Jan Smedslund, "Necessarily True Cultural Psychologies," *The Social Construction of the Person*, ed. Kenneth J. Gergen and Keith E. Davis (New York and Berlin: Springer-Verlag, 1985) 73–87, 73. See also Peter G. Ossorio, "Notes on Behavior Description," *Advances in Descriptive Psychology* (Greenwich CT: JAI, 1981) 13–36.

22. N. E. Weatherick, "Why Not Psychological Psychology?," *Models of Man*, ed. Antony J. Chapman and Dylan M. Jones (Leicester: British Psychological Society, 1980) 348–353, 350.

23. J. Hillis Miller, "Stevens' Rock and Criticism as Cure," *Georgia Review* 30 (Spring 1976): 31.

24. See my *The I* (New Haven: Yale UP, 1985) ch. 6.

25. See, for example, Richard F. Thompson, *The Brain: An Introduction to Neuroscience* (New York: W. H. Freeman, 1985); or Bryan Kolb and Ian Q. Whishaw, *Fundamentals of Human Neuropsychology*, 2d ed. (New York: W. H. Freeman, 1985); or Walle J. H. Nauta and Michael Feirtag, *Fundamental Neuroanatomy* (New York: W. H. Freeman, 1986).

26. Mary Crawford and Roger Chaffin, "The Reader's Construction of Meaning: Cognitive Research on Gender and Comprehension," *Gender and Reading: Essays on Readers, Texts, and Contexts*, ed. Elizabeth A. Flynn and Patrocinio P. Schweickart (Baltimore and London: Johns Hopkins UP, 1986) 3–30, 24.

27. Stanley Fish, "Pragmatism and Literary Theory: Consequences," *Critical Inquiry* 11 (March 1985): 433–458, 450–451.

8 Literary Process and the Personal Brain

1. *Robert Frost on Writing*, ed. Elaine Barry (New Brunswick NJ: Rutgers UP, 1973) 94.

2. *Frost on Writing*, ed. Barry, 59.

3. *Frost on Writing*, ed. Barry, 60.

4. Jonathan Culler, "Prolegomena to a Theory of Reading," *The Reader in the Text: Essays on Audience and Interpretation*, ed. Susan R. Suleiman and Inge Crosman (Princeton: Princeton UP, 1980) 46–66, 56.

5. Sigmund Freud, "Moral Responsibility for the Content of Dreams," "Some Additional Notes on Dream-Interpretation as a Whole" (1925i), sect. (B), *Std. Edn.* 19 (London: Hogarth P, 1961): 133.

6. Sherry Turkle, "Women and Computer Programming: A Different Approach," *Technology Review* (November/December 1984): 47–50. See also her *The Second Self: Computers and the Human Spirit* (New York: Simon and Schuster, 1984).

7. See Sandra Harding and Merrill B. Hintikka, eds., *Discovering Reality: Feminist Perspectives on Epistemology, Metaphysics, Methodology, and Philosophy of Science* (Dordrecht: D. Reidel, 1983); Evelyn Fox Keller, *Reflections on Gender and Science* (New Haven CT: Yale UP, 1985).

8. For "Delphi" teaching, see Norman N. Holland and Murray Schwartz, "The Delphi Seminar," *College English* 36 (1975): 789–800; Holland, "Transactive Teaching: Cordelia's Death," *College English* 39 (1977): 276–285; and Holland (with the members of English 692: Colloquium in Psychoanalytic Criticism), "Poem Opening: An Invitation to Transactive Criticism," *College English* 40 (1978): 2–16.

9. Reader-response teaching thus accords with the urgings of Hans-Georg Gadamer in *Truth and Method* (New York: Seabury P, 1975) 235–240, that we read best by making explicit the biases and prejudices we bring to bear.

10. Aleksandr Romanovich Luria, *Higher Cortical Functions in Man*, 2d ed., trans. Basil Haigh (New York: Basic Books, 1980) 113–116.

11. See my "Not So Little Hans: Identity and Aging," *Memory and Desire: Aging — Literature — Psychoanalysis*, ed. Kathleen Woodward and Murray M. Schwartz (Bloomington: Indiana UP, 1986) 51–75.

12. Murray M. Schwartz, "27th Annual Meeting: Keynote Speaker," *Academy Forum* 27.2 (1983): 13 referred to in note 29, chapter 6.

13. Jonathan Culler, *The Pursuit of Signs: Semiotics, Literature, Deconstruction* (Ithaca NY: Cornell UP, 1981) 32–33.

14. Ambrose Bierce, *The Enlarged Devil's Dictionary* (New York: Doubleday, 1967) s.v. mind.

15. Jürgen Habermas, "Wahrheitstheorien," *Wirklichkeit und Reflexion: Walter Schulz zum 60. Geburtstag* (Pfullingen: Nesge, 1973) 211–265.

16. Marilyn Jager Adams, "Failures to Comprehend and Levels of Processing in Reading," *Theoretical Issues in Reading Comprehension: Perspectives from Cognitive Psychology, Linguistics, Artificial Intelligence, and Education*, ed. Rand J. Spiro, Bertram C. Bruce, and William F. Brewer (Hillsdale NJ: Erlbaum, 1980) 11–32, 23.

9   Hearing Ourselves Think

1. Jonathan Miller, *The Body in Question* (New York: Random House, 1978) 10.

2. Wolfgang Iser, *The Act of Reading: A Theory of Aesthetic Response* (Baltimore and London: Johns Hopkins UP, 1978) 27.

3. Iser, *Act of Reading*, 53.

4. Herbert Simon, "The Architecture of Complexity" (1962), *The Science of the Artificial* (Cambridge MA: MIT P, 1969) 84–118, 117.

5. W. John Harker, "The New Imperative in Literary Criticism," *Visible Language* 19 (1985): 356–372, 356.

6. Mark Johnson, *The Body in the Mind: The Bodily Basis of Meaning, Imagination, and Reason* (Chicago and London: U of Chicago P, 1987) 196.

7. Marilyn Jager Adams, "Failures to Comprehend and Levels of Processing in Reading," *Theoretical Issues in Reading Comprehension: Perspectives from Cognitive Psychology, Linguistics, Artificial Intelligence, and Education*, ed. Rand J. Spiro, Bertram C. Bruce, and William F. Brewer (Hillsdale NJ: Erlbaum, 1980) 11–32, 23. See above, cited ch. 8, n. 16.

8. "The Trial by Existence" (1906), *The Poetry of Robert Frost: The Collected Poems, Complete and Unabridged*, ed. Edward Connery Lathem (New York: Holt, Rinehart and Winston, 1979) 19.

9. "The White-Tailed Hornet" (1936), *Poetry*, ed. Lathem, 277.

10. David Quint, Introduction, *Literary Theory/Renaissance Texts*, ed. Patricia Parker and David Quint (Baltimore: Johns Hopkins UP, 1986) 1–19, 7, 16.

11. Geoffrey H. Hartman, "Preface," Harold Bloom, Paul de Man, Jacques Derrida, Geoffrey H. Hartman, and J. Hillis Miller, *Deconstruction and Criticism*, A Continuum Book (New York: Seabury Press, 1979) vii-ix, vii-viii.

12. Hilary Putnam, *Reason, Truth, and History* (Cambridge: Cambridge UP, 1981) 55.

13. George Lakoff, *Women, Fire, and Dangerous Things: What Categories Reveal About the Mind* (Chicago and London: U of Chicago P, 1987) 260–261, 301.

14. Mark Johnson, *The Body in the Mind: The Bodily Basis of Meaning, Imagination, and Reason* (Chicago and London: U of Chicago P, 1987) 177.

15. Patrocinio P. Schweickart, "Toward a Feminist Theory of Reading," *Gender and Reading: Essays on Readers, Texts, and Contexts*, ed. Elizabeth A. Flynn and Patrocinio P. Schweickart (Baltimore and London: Johns Hopkins UP, 1986), 31–62.

16. Daniel N. Stern, *The Interpersonal World of the Infant: A View from Psychoanalysis and Developmental Psychology* (New York: Basic Books, 1985) 124.

Index